Sartorial Fandom

T0384197

Sartorial Fandom

Fashion, Beauty Culture, Identity

Elizabeth Affuso

and

Suzanne Scott

EDITORS

University of Michigan Press
Ann Arbor

Published in the United States of America by the
University of Michigan Press
Manufactured in the United States of America
Printed on acid-free paper
First published April 2023

A CIP catalog record for this book is available from the British Library.

Library of Congress Cataloging-in-Publication data has been applied for.

ISBN 978-0-472-07604-8 (hardcover : alk. paper)
ISBN 978-0-472-05604-0 (paper : alk. paper)
ISBN 978-0-472-90338-2 (OA)

https://doi.org/10.3998/mpub.12315327

To all who express their fandom through fashion, or are fans of fashion. We like your style.

Contents

Digital materials related to this title can be found on the Fulcrum platform via the following citable URL: https://doi.org/10.3998/mpub.12315327

Illustrations

Acknowledgments

Bringing together an edited collection is always a challenging exercise, and attempting to do so during a global pandemic even more so. First and foremost, we would like to express our deepest gratitude to each and every one of our incredible contributors, who have weathered this long process with equal parts intellectual rigor and understanding. We are so excited to finally be able to share their wonderful work with all of you.

Our home institutions, Pitzer College and the University of Texas at Austin, have been essential support systems for us throughout this process. In particular, we would like to express thanks to our colleagues, who are always available to talk through ideas and offer advice.

We feel incredibly fortunate to have partnered with the University of Michigan Press for this project, and in particular we could not have asked for a better editor or advocate than Sara Jo Cohen. Sara has championed this project from its inception, and has been a guiding light throughout the process. Wrangling images is often thankless work, yet essential for a project such as this one, and accordingly we also offer our sincerest appreciation to Anna Pohlod for her attentiveness to this component of the manuscript's production. We would also like to thank Jessica Hinds-Bond for being a truly exemplary copyeditor, as well as Melissa Scholke and Marcia LaBrenz for facilitating such a smooth copyediting process. We would also like to acknowledge our cover artist, Jett Allen, who was both a font of creativity and an excellent collaborator throughout the design process.

This collection would not have been possible without our dear friends Kate Fortmueller, Kristen Fuhs, and Dave Lerner, who kept us sane and entertained for the duration of this process. You are the only people we still get excited to zoom with. Finally, we offer our deepest appreciation to our partners, Geoff Harris and Luke Pebler, who were forced to eavesdrop on hundreds of hours of calls and strategy sessions. Your love and support, particularly over the past few years, means everything to us.

Introduction

Fandom, But Make It Fashion

Elizabeth Affuso and Suzanne Scott

Our tastes as consumers and fans are reflected back to us whenever we open our closets. We immediately see our go-to clothing labels, often representing years of fannish brand loyalty. We rifle through leaning towers of folded T-shirts featuring an eclectic mix of fan-designed and licensed imagery referencing beloved media objects. As we move through the world, these forms of fannish self-presentation create community, ranging from a knowing head nod between two people wearing an obscure band's T-shirt to full conversations about how to procure a limited-edition Coach Basquiat handbag. These connections, however ephemeral, are significant exercises in mutual recognition of shared fan objects, but also in self-recognition of how our fan identities and lived identities intersect. Vitally, this remains the case when we consider the forms of sartorial expression that, by design, do not visibly self-identify us as fans: a pair of Super Mario Bros. socks, MAC Cosmetics *Star Trek* nail polish in "Skin of Evil," Wonder Woman underwear.

Broadly grouped as style, fashion and beauty cultures are a key element of the self-presentation of taste, knowledge, and identity in modern culture. Working from Pierre Bourdieu's notion of taste, fashion scholar Minh-Ha T. Pham (2015, 5) notes, "our tastes locate us in a particular social context that is itself structured by a system of sensibilities, dispositions, and values (what Bourdieu terms 'habitus')." Fashion and beauty become a key mode of expressing these structures, especially in our everyday lives. As defined by Joanne Bubolz Eicher (1995, 1), "dress is a coded sensory system of non-verbal communication that aids human interaction in space and time." In Eicher's definition, dress encompasses the visual, the sensory, the cognitive, and the affective to cover the complete appearance. This collection takes up that same model for the sartorial, but uses the term *style* in lieu of *dress* because of the link to the phrase "personal style" and the connection to individual expression that it evokes.

As theorized by Dick Hebdige (1979, 94) in his foundational work *Subculture: The Meaning of Style*, fashion and beauty cultures provide opportunities to both reflect cultural norms and push against them. Like Hebdige, scholars in this collection are concerned with "the conversion of subcultural signs (dress, music, etc.) into mass-produced objects (i.e. the commodity form)" in their consideration of the boom in fan-oriented fashion and beauty products, but they are equally invested in how mass-produced fashion objects, like sneakers or bachelorette party sashes, can function as subcultural signs. Media cultures have long been seen as arbiters of fashion trends, able to create, circulate, and reinforce style cues within culture writ large. Digital culture has created new spaces for fashion expression and commoditization, enabling style cultures to expand beyond officially sanctioned venues and to be widely disseminated across blogs, e-commerce sites, social media platforms, and grassroots crafting communities. This collection is invested both in the subcultural and mainstream expression of style and in the spaces where the two intersect.

Fan culture is, in many respects, an optimal space to situate a study of style because of the unique ways it echoes these tensions. Fan culture, much as fashion as a mode of expression, often exists in a liminal space between the subcultural and the mainstream. It has also been widely debated as a space where hegemonic culture might be either resisted or reinforced. As a mode of personal expression or fannish performance, it occupies both digital domains and physical spaces, from the everyday and banal, such as walking down the street in your favorite band's T-shirt, to the highly specific and situational, such as attending a football match or fan convention. Fan culture has moved from the margins to the mainstream over the past several decades (Jenkins 2006; Scott 2019), and a primary indicator of this shift is the parallel proliferation of—and increased access to—fashion and beauty objects aimed squarely at media fans. Unlike early accounts of fashion as a form of fan expression, such as John Fiske's (1991, 95–114) framing of Madonna fans' mimicking the star's iconic style as a form of bricolage or self-empowerment, much of the contemporary literature on fan fashion focuses on its capacity to reinforce postfeminist and neoliberal logics (Johnson 2015; Affuso 2018; Scott 2019). Just as Hebdige noted that subcultural style is invariably incorporated via either ideological or commercial means (potentially losing its potency as a mode of sociopolitical commentary in the process), the proliferation of fan fashion and beauty products since the 2010s has been, for some, emblematic of not only the mainstreaming of fan culture, but also the "the reconstitution of fandom as a lifestyle category rather than a communal experience" (Santo 2018, 329).

Part of this anxiety is rooted in fan studies' propensity to celebrate fans as critical makers of content while downplaying the more overtly consumerist facets of fan participation. Accordingly, despite being one of the most enduring and essential modes of both fannish consumption and expression, fan fashion and beauty culture remains comparatively undertheorized within the rapidly growing field of fan studies, something that this collection aims to rectify. Sartorial means, broadly, "of or relating to clothes," but in speech it generally refers to distinctive style, often with a hint of class (with all that term implies), as in phrases such as sartorial flair or sartorial elegance (*Merriam-Webster*, n.d.). Because of the propensity to infantilize fan fashion, our use of the term *sartorial fandom* is deliberate, to encourage us think more expansively about the interconnectedness of fandom and style. We are also interested in moving the study of fans and fashion beyond the cosplay and merchandise studies that are so often at the core of these analyses, while still acknowledging how much more theoretical work needs to be done in these arenas.

FANDOM, NOW IN FASHION

Building from the recent special issue of *Film Criticism* on "Films and Merchandise," which attempted to expand the range of objects considered as merchandise by fan and media industry studies (Affuso and Santo 2018), this collection reflects the breadth of sartorial objects related to fandom and the myriad ways fans utilize fashion and beauty culture as a mode of self-expression. It is increasingly vital to theorize how fandom of media objects connects with fandom of fashion objects as part of a broader expressive culture, as the fashion and beauty industries have taken notice of fandom being on trend and have responded with a wide variety of collaborations at a range of price points. If we take *Star Wars* as an example, recent years have brought high-end collaborations with luxury fashion brands, such as Vetements and Rag & Bone; midrange collaborations with Levi's, Uniqlo, and Toms; and mass-market ones with Target. Makeup collaborations include the higher-end *Rise of Skywalker* collection with Pat McGrath Labs and the drugstore-range collaboration with CoverGirl. These collaborations provide opportunities for fans to combine their fandom of *Star Wars* with their fandom of particular fashion brands, never more obvious than in the frequent Adidas collaborations that include *Star Wars*–branded Ultraboosts and Stan Smiths appealing to sneaker collectors and *Star Wars* fans alike. Fashion cultures have not been historically thought of as fandoms, but this collection reimagines them as such by linking fandom of media objects and associated behaviors (collecting, community, subcultural knowledge) to fashion brands. The rise of fast fashion has shifted how consumers shop for clothes toward a nonstop conspicuous consumption model creating even greater demand for sartorial fan objects.

Sartorial fandom also provides a place where structures of production and consumption come together, where the producer and consumer merge. Examining this intersection provides a disruption to fashion discourse, which historically seeks to make a spectacle of consumption while hiding production, especially within global late capitalism, where structures of production are deliberately obscured from consumption and the spectacle is predicated on this separation. Fan studies, with its central focus on labor, provides a methodology for linking production and consumption within fashion cultures. As Angela McRobbie (1997, 87) has noted, "if consumers were to be thoroughly alerted to the inhumane activities which eventually bring clothes to the rails of many of the department stores in the way that the politics of food production has made some impact on food consumption then pressure might also be brought to bear by consumer organizations for changes in the fashion industry." These issues have come to the surface in fashion cultures in recent years, with the rising focus on labor, transparency, and the environment. Sartorial fandom, with its dual emphasis on the mass market and the homemade, brings these labor issues to the fore, often personalizing the production labor for consumers through emphasis on the DIY.

Using sartorial fandom as a frame, this collection thus seeks to link fashion and fandom to larger trends. Many essays in this book reflect sartorial fan practices that circulate via social media sites like Instagram and YouTube, reflecting a culture of neoliberal entrepreneurship. Though late capitalism encourages people to be brands and to imagine all hobbies and interests as potentially gigable, these spaces where the fan-producer and the fan-consumer merge also importantly afford opportunities for more inclusive representation. Sartorial fandom tends to move away from the historically theorized gift economy of fans (Hellekson 2009), linking fan production with the larger sectors of the consumer industry. While monetization tends to complicate issues of authenticity within fan studies, we don't want to negate the pleasures of fashion for consumers. Many fan fashion businesses are part of larger sharing economies operating on the idea that the worker can work when it's convenient for them, not the other way around. This logic makes such businesses especially appealing to women who may be looking for economic opportunities that can be performed in concert with the domestic, thereby connecting these practices to older theorizations of fan labor as "women's work." Of course, this convenience comes at the expense of job security, benefits, and opportunities for professional advancement. While this collection is not solely focused on female-identifying fans, much of the writing in it focuses on the ways that fandom can be used as part of larger tools of stylistic expression broadly coded as feminine within culture. We are interested in centralizing how sartorial fandom infuses fans' everyday lives and becomes part of lived experience, particularly as fashion and beauty products have become a core industrial strategy to hail fans and convey their demographic desirability.

IN THIS (CAPSULE) COLLECTION

Much as fashion shows are thoughtfully organized affairs, carefully designed to most effectively present a designer's collection and narrativize its core themes, influences, and interventions, academic collections such as this one are inevitably exercises in "performative presentation to help put across the intellectual message" (Odabaşi 2019, 547). Like a capsule collection, this volume reflects the structural limitations of the fashion industry, with its fetishization of binary gender categories, whiteness, and straight-size and able-bodied consumers. As in the fashion industry, there is work to be done in fan studies to think more expansively and inclusively with regard to gender, race, sexuality, and ability. It is our hope that this collection lays the groundwork for more consideration of these issues in sartorial fandom studies moving forward. As the first book-length exploration of sartorial fandom, this collection is organized to exhibit the breadth of emergent work on this topic.

   Much like a capsule collection in the fashion world, which stresses both accessibility (the ability to immediately purchase items) and interchangeability (a selection of pieces designed to be mixed and matched), this book is organized both to introduce readers to some core theoretical concerns and topical approaches to the study of sartorial fandom across media forms and also to acknowledge that many entries might occupy several categories simultaneously. If the ultimate purpose of the capsule collection is to provide "the least number of pieces to create the greatest number of looks," then the sections explicated below constitute what we consider to be four essential "pieces" to the study of sartorial fandom that any scholar should have in their conceptual closet (Baumgartner 2012, 187). Building an academic field, like building one's wardrobe, is a lifelong pursuit. Styles will change, topics will fall out of fashion, but we look forward to seeing how future work on sartorial fandom will accessorize, appliqué, and embroider new works from the foundational topics explored in this collection.

PART I: HISTORIES OF SARTORIAL FANDOM

Within film and media studies, much of the work about fans and fashion has been rendered through analysis of merchandise and fashion tie-up lines that link these products to larger synergistic strategies of the media industries. Historical studies of merchandise such as those of Charles Eckert (1991) and Jane Gaines (1989) connect fashion tie-up lines to larger histories of consumer culture, retail spectacle, and branding in modernity. Sartorial fandom in relationship to fashion objects is often linked to celebrity and to fans' seeking to emulate stars' looks, such as in Marsha Orgeron's (2003) work on Clara Bow, which notes that henna hair dye sold out in the 1920s because fans wanted to mimic Bow's look. The anthology *Fabrications: Costume and the Female Body* (Gaines and Herzog 1990) situates Hollywood's representation of fashion alongside larger structures of feminized commodity culture, particularly within the Hollywood studio system. More recent studies such as Pamela Church Gibson's *Fashion and Celebrity Culture* (2012) and Alyxandra Vesey's "Putting Her on the Shelf" (2015) build on these historical studies to think about how celebrity is utilized within the fashion and beauty industries to sell commodity products.

The chapters in this section build on this robust body of scholarship in order to survey historical examples of sartorial fandom, engage the sociopolitical contexts of particular sartorial fan expressions, and explore alternate histories that manifest through sartorial fandom. Kate Fortmueller's "'Hollywood Fashions for Everygirl's Wardrobe!': Stealth Cosplay and 1930s *Photoplay*" uses archival materials to examine how female fandom was positioned by the fan magazine *Photoplay* and the fashion retailer Marshall Field's. Taken together, these materials provide a case study of how female fans were imagined in the 1930s and how fandom was mobilized as a tool in the fashion business by both ready-to-wear retailers and purveyors of DIY copies. While Fortmueller examines mainstream fashion history, Elodie A. Roy's "'Anorak City': Indie Pop's Resistance through Regression" explores anorak subculture, which emerged around indie music fans in Margaret Thatcher's Britain. These fans reappropriated the anorak—a fashion item most associated with children—to resist the models of productivity espoused by Thatcher's administration. Continuing in this subcultural vein, Samantha Close's "Five Little

Victorian Londons" creates a style topography of steampunk fashion rooted in British Victoriana. Close identifies five modes (revolutionary, historical, aesthetic, dandy, and imperial) and positions these style types within larger histories of colonialism, gender, and sexuality to think about how fashion objects link to larger national histories.

PART II: SARTORIAL FANDOM AS BUSINESS, LIFESTYLE, AND BRAND

The business of sartorial fandom is rooted in two main sectors of the retail industry: the mainstream, branded, retail marketplace, as seen in the historical tie-ups and merchandise tie-ins discussed in the previous section; and the online retail and e-commerce marketplace. This section seeks to bridge the gig economies of DIY sartorial fandom with those of the mainstream fashion industry to think about how these two industries provide a bottom-up/top-down model for sartorial fandom. This model emerges out of a larger shift in the fashion industry, articulated in the early twentieth century by designer Coco Chanel in her declaration that "fashion must come up from the streets." Mary E. Davis (2006, 153) has noted that this statement articulated "a philosophy that would revolutionize style and change women's dress forever." As with the up-from-the-streets rearticulation of style influence, mass fan fashion cultures often borrow from indie sellers and vice versa, creating a symbiotic relationship where fandom becomes a branding opportunity to drive visitors to storefronts. Accordingly, fan scholars have begun to theorize fantrepreneurial practices that have exploded alongside digital commerce sites (Scott 2019). These practices can be linked to historical notions of fans' bringing existing skills into their fan practices and also to the emergence of gig economies in the aftermath of the 2008 recession. Much of the drive toward products in this area is centered on fashion and beauty objects made by female-identifying fans for other female-identifying fans. This links sartorial fan entrepreneurialism to larger histories of women's work, particularly around homemade objects that utilize traditionally feminine skills, such as embroidery, sewing, knitting, and crafting (Cherry 2016). Fantrepreneurial interventions often seek to widen the merchandise model by making fan fashions that are more size-inclusive or featuring characters that are not part of official merchandise lines.

Fandom has historically been thought of as a gift economy, but digital culture provides new spaces and new opportunities for fans to mobilize their skills into products for sale. Within fandom, Etsy and related e-commerce spaces ideologically bridge market economies and gift economies, with the handmade, exclusive nature of the objects for sale. This structure creates an affective link between consumer and entrepreneur, especially given the custom work so often done by Etsy sellers, which Avi Santo (2018) has noted. Of this market, Arun Sundararajan (2016, 35) has written: "there may be deeper reasons why the term 'sharing economy' is so popular: It captures some of the thinking and idealism of the early proponents of economy-wide sharing approaches. It hints at the shift away from faceless, impersonal 20th-century capitalism and toward exchange that is somehow more connected, more embedded in community, more reflective of shared purpose." These alternative forms of capital are especially appealing in fannish spaces because they are predicated on the idea of community.

The chapters in this section consider the symbiotic relationship between the conventional retail sector and fan-produced fashion to explore how the fashion industry borrows from fantrepreneurial spaces, continuing a long history of subcultural appropriation. Avi Santo's "Fanning the Flames of Fan Lifestyles at Hot Topic" provides a history of the mall retailer to theorize fandom as a curated lifestyle brand within the structures of consumer capitalism. While the piece is Hot Topic specific, Santo's argument provides a history of how fans have been deployed by retailers in the fashion market in the postmillennium. Whereas Santo focuses on the officially licensed retail sector of the lifestyle fan fashion industry, Lauren Boumaroun's "Flying under the Radar: Culture and Community in the Unlicensed Geek Fashion Industry" addresses the unlicensed sector with her exploration of independent geek fashion designers. Boumaroun links these designers to larger histories of women's work, using interviews with designers to examine how this sector disrupts notions of fandom as a gift economy through their alternative fashion economy. Finally, in "Droids on the Runway: Fandom, Business, and Transmedia in *Star Wars* Luxury Fashion," Nicolle Lamerichs examines the relationship between fashion and the source text to think about the transmedia positionality of *Star Wars* fashion objects. Focused especially on luxury fan fashion from brands such as Rodarte, Rag & Bone, and Preen, Lamerichs explores how fabric, color, texture, and editorial images evoke story worlds for consumers. The range of price points in this section, from Hot Topic to indie designers to luxury brands, facilitates an exploration of the wide range of fashion fans in the contemporary economy and the diversity of fashion content for fan bodies.

Beyond these retail collaborations, the rearticulation of style, as coming up from the streets, has seen its deepest impacts in the twentieth and twenty-first centuries within the popular music realm. From bobby soxers to punk to hip-hop, grunge, and beyond, popular music fans have developed styles that permeate mainstream culture (Miller 2011; Luvaas 2012; McRobbie 1988). Pop musicians crucially appropriate subcultural styles into the mainstream, and fashion brands and fans alike reinterpret these looks back into street style. Paxton C. Haven's "'I Am Not in a Cult': Poppy and the Gendered Implications of Ironic Beauty Fan Cult(ure)" considers how pop star Poppy satirizes feminized beauty influencer models to engage fans and build communities. Haven's piece explores the ways in which Poppy's beauty influence is positioned in relationship to historical notions of pop divas, the concept of the industry plant, and the branding of hyperfeminine style. Alyxandra Vesey's "In the Navy: Savage X Fenty's Fandorsement Work" explores the role of celebrity endorsement of other celebrity brands within the music industry. Vesey positions these dynamics within the specifics of Black entrepreneurship in popular music cultures, wider neoliberal feminist discourses, and internet influencer culture. Taken together, these two chapters consider the particular obstacles that female celebrities face in the branding and dissemination of style due to the ways women's bodies are contested sites.

PART III: FANS OF FASHION + FASHION AS FAN EXPRESSION

John Fiske's (1992, 38) oft-cited taxonomy of fan participation lumps forms of stylistic expression under the broader category of "enunciative productivity," which includes varying forms of "fan talk" that circulate "certain meanings of the object of fandom within a local community." Moving beyond the abundance of critical discursive work on forms of fan talk on digital platforms, this section centers sartorial fandom as a distinct and decidedly more complex form of fan expression. Sartorial fan expressions may still convey localized meanings about a particular fan object, but they can also speak loudly about individual fan identities as well as larger structural systems of power. We needn't look further than aggressively gendered sports fan merchandise, which often eradicates team colors in lieu of pink and bedazzled team T-shirts and jerseys when hailing female fans, to witness how hegemonic power is rearticulated through a androcentric conception of fan identity (Johnson 2016; Sveinson, Hoeber, and Toffoletti 2019). Likewise, the expressive function of sartorial fan objects is often highly dependent on contextual factors, such as the distinction between a fan purchasing at auction an item of clothing worn on their favorite television program (Stenger 2006; Williams 2018), and another buying a replica of that clothing item through a licensed and mass-produced fashion tie-in line. The aura of authenticity of the auctioned item may increase both its economic and sentimental value for the fan; however, sizing or other factors may prohibit or severely limit the embodied pleasures or performance of fan identity that replicas can afford.

Not only is fashion a key, albeit often overlooked, component of more conventional forms of fan discourse or fan talk (Andò 2015)—particularly for programs like *Sex and the City, Gossip Girl,* or *Scandal,* which actively convey character through clothing—it also reveals the frequent slippage between fan attachment to a given media text and to fashion more generally. Consider the proliferation of shopping sites such as Worn on TV that help fans identify and purchase ready-to-wear pieces worn by their favorite characters, or the way that fashion retailers capitalize on fan trends such as 2009's vampire craze (spurred by the popularity of *Twilight* and *True Blood*) to sell an array of unaffiliated but aesthetically "Goth" fashion (Chau 2011). Importantly, then, in addition to exploring the relationship between fashion and fan identity, this section addresses how fashion can operate as a fan object in its own right.

In "Drop Culture: Masculinity, Fashion Performance, and Collecting in Hypebeast Brand Communities," Elizabeth Affuso explores fans of fashion, specifically the masculinized subcultural shopping community that thrives on tracking, collecting, and selling exclusive merchandise. Through textual analysis of hypebeast influencer feeds and related hashtags such as #WDYWT (What Did You Wear Today?), online forums, and retail merchandise events, Affuso situates hypebeast culture within larger discourses around race and masculinity in fashion cultures and the transnational positioning of subcultures in a globally connected commodity marketplace. In their chapter "This Is My (Floral) Design: Flower Crowns, Fannibals, and Fan/Producer Permeability," EJ Nielsen and Lori Morimoto trace the history of the flower crown as a sartorial fan trend from One Direction boy band fandom on Tumblr to fans of the NBC horror series *Hannibal.* Through their analysis of the flower crown's semiotic significance and the way that *Hannibal*'s creators and stars embraced and legitimated it, Nielsen and Morimoto show how instances of sartorial fan expression offer a site to build intimacies between producers and fans. Jacqueline E. Johnson's contribution, "From Muggle to Mrs.: The *Harry Potter* Bachelorette Party and 'Crafting' Femininity on Etsy," examines the cottage industry of bachelorette party merchandise such as shirts and sashes aimed at aging fans of the franchise. Johnson's chapter offers a powerful case study of how sartorial fan objects can ultimately reinforce hegemonic conceptions of white female fan identity. Finally, A. Luxx Mishou's "Retcon: Revisiting Cosplay Studies" challenges a core premise of our understanding of cosplay as a fan practice, namely the assumption that cosplayers are fans of the characters they choose to embody. Cosplay, a term broadly used to describe the practice of "fans donning costumes and performing as characters from popular media texts" (Mountfort, Peirson-Smith, and Geczy 2019, 3), is an increasingly flexible and multifaceted form of fan expression. Drawing on interviews with cosplayers, Mishou's chapter grapples with this complexity and interrogates both the common methodological frameworks for studying cosplayers and the presumptions that tend to be made about their motivations, ultimately arguing for the need to study the act of playing in costumes as a fandom in and of itself.

PART IV: FASHIONING FAN BODIES

The final section of this collection explores sartorial fandom through fan bodies and embodiment. While there has been an abundance of literature within fashion and marketing studies on the relationship between fashion and the body, the chapters in this section develop emergent lines of inquiry on embodied fan practices and the body as a canvas for fannish expression (Williams 2020; Lamerichs 2018; Jones 2014). Even within current design and marketing trends in fashion and beauty culture that tout inclusivity, body positivity, and affirmation and move beyond straight sizing practices and white models, rigid understandings of gender identity as well as ageism, racism, colorism, sizeism, and ableism persist. These biases often begin at the sketching stage of design (Ahmed 2021) and are codified in both fashion illustration textbooks (Reddy-Best, Choi, and Park 2018) and the eventual marketing of clothing and beauty products (Parekh and Schmidt 2003; Lewis, Medvedev, and Seponski 2010; Jha 2016). This is even the case in some emergent examples of "genderless" fashion that ultimately reinforce the binary conceptions of gender they seek to disrupt (Luna and Barros 2019).

Fan culture and fan studies, despite the fact that they are often painted as progressive spaces, face similar issues around the reproduction of "normative" bodies and the alienating effects this has on fans of color, queer or genderqueer fans, and disabled or neurodiverse fans. For example, fan scholars are increasingly pointing out that cultural as well as academic understandings of fan identity too often presuppose a fan body that is white (Pande 2018, 2020; Woo 2018; Stanfill 2018; Martin 2019). While the chapters in this section do not seek to tackle these structural issues within the field directly, their attentiveness to racial and national contexts, as well as gender identity, opens up important new lines of inquiry within fan studies of how fan bodies are fashioned, surveilled, remediated, and transformed.

The first two chapters in this section complicate existing theorizations of cosplay, which has thus far been one of the primary sites of scholarly work on fan bodies and embodied fan practices. In "Disneybounding and Beyond: Fandom, Cosplay, and Embodiment in Themed Spaces," Rebecca Williams builds on her foundational work on theme parks and fan tourist spaces by drawing on extensive participant observation at theme parks around the globe, notably focusing on *kawaii* (or "cute") fan fashion at Universal Studios Japan. Williams contemplates how theme park rules and regulations surrounding guest costuming, when coupled with a growing corporate awareness of and desire to capitalize on grassroots fan fashion practices, structure more or less subversive performances of embodied sartorial fan expression. Minka Stoyanova's "Wigs, Corsets, Cosmetics, and Instagram: The Prosthetics of Crossplay" also addresses cosplay as an embodied practice, albeit a cyborg one that spans both physical and digital contexts. As a form of sartorial fan labor, cosplay is an inherently liminal practice that exists between affirmational and transformative modes of fan production (Hills 2014), real-world and digital fan spaces (Booth 2015), and embodied and performed fan identities. Stoyanova's chapter explores this liminality—both through the physical prostheses (such as binders) that female cosplayers might use to "crossplay" or portray male characters, and through digital extensions (platforms like Instagram)—to consider the cosplayer's body as a site of remediation.

The final two chapters in this section turn their attention to a spectrum of more or less visible efforts to (re)fashion the fan body as a site of transformation. Anthony Tran's "'Model Tries Crazy IU KPop Diet': Embodied K-Pop Fandoms and Fashionable Diets on YouTube" explores the diet phenomenon inspired by K-pop superstar IU to examine how fans are inspired not just by celebrity fashion, but also by celebrity bodies. These conditions are compounded by the rise of digital lifestyle and influencer culture, creating even more opportunities for the dissemination of pop music and subcultural fan style to the masses. Utilizing K-pop diet reaction vlogs on YouTube, Tran explores how this content allows fans to embody the experience of being a K-pop star through the mental experience of performing their diet. On the other end of this spectrum, Suzanne Scott's chapter, "Underwear That's Fun to Wear: Theorizing Fan Lingerie," explores forms of fan expression via fashion that are, quite literally, intimate. Fan underwear and lingerie, precisely because they are comparatively invisible as a form of fan performance, a site of inconspicuous consumption, open up a unique space to consider the "expressive" properties of sartorial fan objects.

CONCLUSION

Collectively, the chapters across these four sections explore how various axes of lived identity interact with a growing movement to consider fandom as a lifestyle category, ultimately contending that sartorial practices are central to fan expression but also indicative of the primacy of fandom in contemporary taste cultures. Using fashion and beauty culture as a framework allows us to better understand both the hegemonic and the subversive potentiality of individual expressions of fandom and fashion, but it also affords a larger consideration of consumer citizenship in late capitalism. Crossing identities and national contexts, this collection provides new points of connection to developing fields within fashion studies, especially those around transnationalism, entrepreneurship, and digital culture. Even as we seek to actively thread together fan studies and fashion studies, this collection's focus on sartorial fandom also strives to nuance long-standing interstices between fan studies, media industry studies, and studies of identity.

REFERENCES

Affuso, Elizabeth. 2018. "Everyday Costume: Feminized Fandom, Retail, and Beauty Culture." In *The Routledge Companion to Media Fandom*, edited by Melissa Click and Suzanne Scott, 184–94. New York: Routledge.

Affuso, Elizabeth, and Avi Santo, eds. 2018. "Film and Merchandise." Special issue, *Film Criticism* 42 (2).

Ahmed, Tanveer. 2021. "Are Fashion Sketchbooks Racist?" *Fashion, Style & Popular Culture*. https://doi.org/10.1386/fspc_00055_1

Andò, Romana. 2015. "Fashion and Fandom on TV and Social Media: Claire Underwood's Power Dressing." *Critical Studies in Fashion & Beauty* 6 (2): 207–31.

Baumgartner, Jennifer J. 2012. *You Are What You Wear: What Your Clothes Reveal About You*. Boston: Da Capo Press.

Booth, Paul. 2015. *Playing Fans: Negotiating Fandom and Media in the Digital Age*. Iowa City: University of Iowa Press.

Chau, Angie. 2011. "Fashion Sucks . . . Blood: Clothes and Covens in *Twilight* and Hollywood Culture." In *Bringing Light to Twilight: Perspectives on a Pop Culture Phenomenon*, edited by Giselle Lisa Anatol, 179–89. New York: Palgrave MacMillan.

Cherry, Brigid. 2016. *Cult Media, Fandom, and Textiles: Handicrafting as Fan Art*. New York: Bloomsbury Academic.

Davis, Mary E. 2006. *Classic Chic: Music, Fashion, and Modernism*. Berkeley: University of California Press.

Eckert, Charles. 1991. "The Carole Lombard in the Macy's Window." In *Stardom: Industry of Desire*, edited by Christine Gledhill, 30–39. London: Routledge.

Eicher, Joanne Bubolz. 1995. *Dress and Ethnicity: Change Across Space and Time*. Oxford: Berg.

Fiske, John. 1991. *Reading the Popular*. New York: Routledge.

Fiske, John. 1992. "The Cultural Economy of Fandom." In *The Adoring Audience: Fan Culture and Popular Media*, edited by Lisa A. Lewis, 30–49. New York: Routledge.

Gaines, Jane. 1989. "The Queen Christina Tie-Ups: Convergence of Show Window and Screen." *Quarterly Review of Film and Video* 11:35–60.

Gaines, Jane, and Charlotte Herzog. 1990. *Fabrications: Costume and the Female Body*. New York: Routledge.

Gibson, Pamela Church. 2012. *Fashion and Celebrity Culture*. London: Berg.

Hebdige, Dick. 1979. *Subculture: The Meaning of Style*. New York: Routledge.

Hellekson, Karen. 2009. "A Fannish Field of Value: Online Fan Gift Culture." *Cinema Journal* 48 (4): 113–18.

Hills, Matt. 2014. "From Dalek Half Balls to Daft Punk Helmets: Mimetic Fandom and the Crafting of Replicas." *Transformative Works and Cultures* 16. https://doi.org/10.3983/twc.2014.0531

Jenkins, Henry. 2006. *Convergence Culture: Where Old and New Media Collide*. New York: New York University Press.

Jha, Meeta Rani. 2016. *The Global Beauty Industry: Colorism, Racism, and the National Body*. New York: Routledge.

Johnson, Derek. 2015. "May the Force Be with Katie: Pink Media Franchising and the Postfeminist Politics of Her Universe." *Feminist Media Studies* 14 (6): 895–911.

Johnson, Victoria E. 2016. "'Together, We Make Football': The NFL's 'Feminine' Discourses." *Popular Communication* 14 (1): 12–20.

Jones, Bethan. 2014. "Written on the Body: Experiencing Affect and Identity in My Fannish Tattoos." *Transformative Works and Cultures* 16. https://doi.org/10.3983/twc.2014.0527

Lamerichs, Nicolle. 2018. *Productive Fandom: Intermediality and Affective Reception in Fan Cultures*. Amsterdam: Amsterdam University Press.

Lewis, Denise C., Katalin Medvedev, and Desiree M. Seponski. 2010. "Awakening to the Desires of Older Women: Deconstructing Ageism within Fashion Magazines." *Journal of Aging Studies* 25 (2): 101–9.

Luna, Camilla Pinto, and Denise Franca Barros. 2019. "Genderless Fashion: A (Still) Binary Market." *Latin American Business Review* 20 (3): 269–94.

Luvaas, Brent Adam. 2012. *DIY Style: Fashion, Music and Global Digital Cultures*. London: Berg.

Martin, Alfred L. 2019. "Fandom while Black: Misty Copeland, Black Panther, Tyler Perry and the Contours of US Black Fandoms." *International Journal of Cultural Studies* 22 (6): 737–53.

McRobbie, Angela. 1988. *Zoot Suits and Second-Hand Dresses: An Anthology of Fashion and Music*. Boston: Unwin Hyman.

McRobbie, Angela. 1997. "Bridging the Gap: Feminism, Fashion and Consumption." *Feminist Review* 55 (1): 73–89.

Merriam-Webster. n.d. "Sartorial." Accessed June 2, 2021. https://www.merriam-webster.com/dictionary/sartorial

Miller, Janice. 2011. *Fashion and Music*. Oxford: Berg.

Mountfort, Paul, Anne Peirson-Smith, and Adam Geczy. 2019. *Planet Cosplay: Costume Play, Identity and Global Fandom*. Bristol, UK: Intellect.

Odabaşi, Sanem. 2019. "Narratives of a Designer's Collection: Fashion Shows and Artistic Applications." *Turkish Online Journal of Design Art and Communication* 9 (4): 546–54. http://www.tojdac.org/tojdac/VOLUME9-ISSUE4.html

Orgeron, Marsha. 2003. "Making It in Hollywood: Clara Bow, Fandom, and Consumer Culture." *Cinema Journal* 42 (4): 76–97.

Pande, Rukmini. 2018. *Squee from the Margins: Fandom and Race*. Iowa City: University of Iowa Press.

Pande, Rukmini, ed. 2020. *Fandom, Now in Color*. Iowa City: University of Iowa Press.

Parekh, Fatima S., and Ruth A. Schmidt. 2003. "In Pursuit of an Identity—Fashion Marketing and the Development of Eating Disorders." *British Food Journal* 105 (4/5): 220–38.

Pham, Minh-Ha T. 2015. *Asians Wear Clothes on the Internet: Race, Gender, and the Work of Personal Style Blogging*. Durham, NC: Duke University Press.

Reddy-Best, Kelly L., Eunji Choi, and Hangael Park. 2018. "Race, Colorism, Body Size, Body Position, and Sexiness: Critically Analyzing Women in Fashion Illustration Textbooks." *Clothing and Textiles Research Journal* 36 (4): 281–95.

Santo, Avi. 2018. "Fans and Merchandise." In *The Routledge Companion to Media Fandom*, edited by Melissa Click and Suzanne Scott, 329–36. New York: Routledge.

Scott, Suzanne. 2019. *Fake Geek Girls: Fandom, Gender, and the Convergence Culture Industry*. New York: New York University Press.

Stanfill, Mel. 2018. "The Unbearable Whiteness of Fandom and Fan Studies." In *A Companion to Media Fandom and Fan Studies*, edited by Paul Booth, 305–17. Hoboken, NJ: Wiley-Blackwell.

Stenger, Josh. 2006. "The Clothes Make the Fan: Fashion and Online Fandom When 'Buffy the Vampire Slayer' Goes to eBay." *Cinema Journal* 45 (4): 26–44.

Sundararajan, Arun. 2016. *The Sharing Economy: The End of Employment and the Rise of Crowd-Based Capitalism*. Cambridge: MIT Press.

Sveinson, Katherine, Larena Hoeber, and Kim Toffoletti. 2019. "'If People Are Wearing Pink Stuff They're Probably Not Real Fans': Exploring Women's Perceptions of Sport Fan Clothing." *Sport Management Review* 22 (5): 736–47.

Vesey, Alyxandra. 2015. "Putting Her on the Shelf." *Feminist Media Studies* 15 (6): 992–1008.

Williams, Rebecca. 2018. "'Fate Has a Habit of Not Letting Us Choose Our Own Endings': Post-Object Fandom, Social Media and Material Culture at the End of *Hannibal*." In *A Companion to Media Fandom and Fan Studies*, edited by Paul Booth, 447–60. Hoboken, NJ: Wiley Blackwell.

Williams, Rebecca. 2020. *Theme Park Fandom: Spatial Transmedia, Materiality and Participatory Cultures*. Amsterdam: Amsterdam University Press.

Woo, Benjamin. 2018. "The Invisible Bag of Holding: Whiteness and Media Fandom." In *The Routledge Companion to Media Fandom*, edited by Melissa A. Click and Suzanne Scott, 245–52. New York: Routledge.

PART I

Histories of Sartorial Fandom

1

"Hollywood Fashions for Everygirl's Wardrobe!"

Stealth Cosplay and 1930s *Photoplay*

Kate Fortmueller

"Now!" an advertisement screams from *Photoplay*'s back pages, "You, Too, May Wear the *Fashions of the Films!*" (*Photoplay* 1932, 90). A row of stars float along an invisible staircase, alongside text announcing a new clothing line based on the latest character fashions. These designs, introduced several pages earlier as *Photoplay*'s Hollywood Fashions, developed as a partnership between the magazine and "many of the country's leading department and ready-to-wear stores," were one of several tie-in lines that offered women the ability to dress like they just stepped out of the screen (figure 1.1). Fan magazines such as *Photoplay* fanned the flames of consumer investment in Hollywood through making-of stories and details of star lives, but advice on how to mimic star fashion added an extra way for readers to relate to Hollywood. The fashion columns of 1930s *Photoplay* taught readers how to integrate the glamour of Hollywood into their closets and out on the streets. Ready-to-wear film fashions not only indicate a market for deeper engagement with Hollywood films and cultures, they also demonstrate an attempt to assimilate fan desires into acceptable consumer behaviors and the everyday domestic lives of modern women.

Beyond simply offering women on-screen fantasies, Hollywood provided an image of strong professional women working in a highly visible and modern industry. It was this vision of Hollywood as a potential employer that led women to Hollywood in the 1910s and 1920s. As Samantha Barbas (2001), Hilary A. Hallett (2013), Shelley Stamp (2004), and others have demonstrated, moving to Hollywood to break into the business was characterized in the popular press and by Hollywood leadership alike as a culturally suspect and potentially dangerous way for women to demonstrate their love of the movies. In order to redirect these women, fan magazines such as *Photoplay* and *Modern Screen* tried to contain female fan impulses through cautionary tales warning aspirants of lecherous directors who would proposition young

Figure 1.1. From the screen to the pages of *Photoplay*, to your very own closet: *Photoplay* advertises the fashions of Hollywood in the back pages of the magazine. "Now! You, Too, May Wear the Fashions of the Films!" *Photoplay*, October 1932, 90.

actresses and by hosting screenwriting competitions that might help keep them safe at home (*Modern Screen* 1935, 30; Barbas 2001, 69–73). Beauty and fashion, on the other hand, offered an outlet for women to engage with Hollywood by participating in the distinctly modern (and domestic) beauty cultures rather than the modern *business* of Hollywood. By poring over the pages of magazines and looking like a star, readers could remotely engage with their favorite Hollywood films all from the comfort of their hometowns.

This chapter offers a look at how female fandom was imagined by magazines and clothing retailers in the formative years of industrialized Hollywood film production. Drawing on primary documents from the National Museum of American History as well as the Media History Digital Library, I bring together *Photoplay* and Marshall Field's department store catalogs and advertisements as a case study of early fan merchandising. Films, fan magazines, and department stores all offered fantasies of glamour, but each had a different barrier to access. Like Suzanne Scott (2019) and Avi Santo (2018), I am interested in how fan merchandise both provides and limits access to fandom and how fandom fit in with other consumer fantasies and goals of mass culture purveyors in the 1930s. Commercially available apparel, including Hollywood Fashions and other similar lines, was pitched toward white middle-class female consumers. Amid the Depression, these styles offered a financially accessible version of glamour in contrast to the pricey furs and designer apparel of the Marshall Field's catalog. Dresses from Hollywood Fashions ranged from approximately seventeen dollars to almost thirty dollars, which meant they were priced well above Depression-era "street dresses," which cost under five dollars in the early 1930s (USTNEC 1940, 245). Despite this higher price point, catalogs, advertisements, and lists of where these dresses were available for purchase show that these film fashions were intended for a broader consumer audience than the designer fashions featured in high-end department stores. Taken together, the dresses, articles in *Photoplay*, and advertisements demonstrate strategies for integrating Hollywood style and mass culture into regional department stores and women's closets.

This moment of fan magazine marketing offers one possible starting point for a history of female fans and an early iteration of cosplay. In the period covered in this chapter, the merchandising of the clothing that appeared in *Photoplay* affirms the dominant understanding of fandom as a gendered female practice. Although there were certainly male movie fans, as Samantha Barbas (2001) points out, the film industry in the early twentieth century actively courted women—oftentimes drawing women to films for fashions. The history of fan fashion involves consumption, but it is also about the process of actively constructing and creating outfits and embodying characters through clothing. A lineage of consumer products targeting fans and consumption practices is different than the one proposed by Francesca Coppa (2006), which begins with histories of active engagement, art, and writings of male sci-fi fans in the 1920s. This chapter looks at a top-down model of fandom in which women were being conditioned to channel their desires in acceptable ways. One of the challenges of looking at merchandise and consumer offerings is that one might not have access to a range of archival materials, such as letters from customers writing about their feelings about the clothing, or archived versions of the garments. Thus, this approach provides less context about the individual fans who wore these items, or about the material objects themselves, than we can glean from fan creations such as art or writings. Fan merchandise is only one aspect of fan history in the 1930s, but it allows for an approach in which fandom is not positioned as male dominated. As such, fan merchandising offers a compelling starting point for a history of fans and fandom that situates women at the center and that might hopefully inspire more consideration of the social and material histories of fan practices.

The dresses in *Photoplay* came from a variety of filmic sources, but frequently the designs were duplicates of dresses from B films and serials. In discussions of film fashions, the popularity of the frilly reproductions of Joan Crawford's white gown in *Letty Lynton* (dir. Clarence Brown, 1932) is often cited as an example of film's power to drive consumerism (Barbas 2001; Berry 2000, Eckert 1990; Herzog and Gaines 1991). The Lynton dress is always noted for its layers of fabric and ruffles; in contrast, many of the dresses *Photoplay* copied and sold in department stores were the simple dresses and hats of B-film molls and serial heroines. Fan apparel offered audiences of the 1930s the ability to enact on-screen identities, and rather than presenting women with fantasies of domesticity, it offered fantasies of action, adventure, and danger.

While the language of *Photoplay* figures film fans as a mass audience rather than a niche group of devoted viewers, Hollywood Fashions and its position within the beauty and fashion features in *Photoplay* resonate with late twentieth- and early twenty-first-century fan discourse and everyday cosplay. Fan costumes, as Nicolle Lamerichs (2001, 1.2) explains, have four elements: "a narrative, a set of clothing, a play or performance before spectators, and a subject." Hollywood Fashions and lines like it were examples of mass-produced outfits or patterns of character apparel, and they provided women with the ability to imagine themselves as these characters. To be clear, *Photoplay* and others were not selling character engagement; instead, the availability of these dresses promised a different kind of connection with

Hollywood and the culture of the screen. In the case of *Photoplay*, the magazine often tried both to associate the dresses with Hollywood (in general) and to distance those same dresses from the content of the films, creating a kind of stealth cosplay that differs from Suzanne Scott's (2019, 201) characterization of "covert cosplay," or clothing *inspired by* character apparel. Despite the fact that the dresses were duplicates of character costumes, they were not positioned as costumes or recognizable character outfits. Although concepts of fans and fandom differed in the 1930s, Hollywood studios, fan magazines, and department stores provided women with the opportunity to dress like the characters on screen, and in doing so allowed wearers to inhabit rebellious and adventurous subject positions from female screen characters, all under the guise of apparel that conformed to conventional standards of femininity.

FASHIONING FANS

Magazines such as *Photoplay* are commonly referred to as fan magazines, but in this context the use of the word *fan* is dramatically different than we have come to understand the term in the late twentieth and early twenty-first centuries. As Anthony Slide (2010, 11) explains, the clearest antecedents to fan magazines are 1880s and 1890s "popular general magazines promoting consumer culture and social issues." Fan magazines like *Photoplay* (launched in 1911) were part of the growing mass culture, and they ushered in cultures of mass production while helping shape the language and expansion of film and stars in popular discourse. Further revealing fan magazines' mass culture aims was the language, which was heavily laced with commercialism, such that "advertising and text supported each other" (Barbas 2001, 80). *Photoplay* grew and expanded its scope, and by the 1930s it had expanded columns not just about movie news and star gossip, but about film fashion and makeup.

When *Photoplay* eventually started to market its Hollywood Fashions in 1932, the structure of advertisements intertwined with advice columns provided a venue to insert film-inspired apparel for purchase. Initially the fashion columns were penned by the single-named Seymour, but this role was later taken over by Kathleen Howard, followed by Gwenn Walters. Despite turnover in the byline, the structure of the fashion section remained relatively consistent in this period: five to ten pages focused on fashion, with a combination of photographs and sketches highlighting the latest on-screen looks. The language explicitly invites readers to engage in the fantasy of owning and wearing the various outfits. Speaking of Karen Morley's dress in RKO's

The Phantom of Crestwood (dir. J. Walter Ruben, 1932), Seymour (1932d, 64) explains, "Imagine being able to have this stunning costume. . . . She wears it in 'The Phantom of Crestwood' but you may wear it all winter either with or without its fur trimmed cape that buttons so snugly about the throat. Karen's dress is gray woolen (all the stars are wearing gray)." This description, which offers no detail about how the dress fits into its narrative context or whether it is available for purchase as part of Hollywood Fashions, is typical of Seymour's explanations. By remaining purely descriptive, this brief paragraph focuses attention on the dress rather than the character, film, or even the details about how to purchase the dress. *Photoplay* traded in fantasy, and the magazine did not directly hawk its own merchandise. In the early 1930s the *Photoplay* discussions of fashion withheld details about price and simply instructed readers to find "firm names" in the back pages of the magazine, which was home to other advertisements.

Seymour's columns included discussion of dresses replicated for the Hollywood Fashions line alongside those that were not available for purchase. This could have simply been a strategy to create an illusion of a more substantial fashion line, but the effect of this writing and structure was to mask the fact that many of the designs for Hollywood Fashions came from B films and serials. In the early twentieth century these films were important for modern working women. Nan Enstad (1999, 187) explains how B films and genre films offered women in the audience opportunities to identify with heroines who "desired and received dramatic social recognition as a worker and a woman." These modern women required practical and fitted fashions for the workplace. Keeping in line with these demands, and keeping manufacturing costs down, the fashionable dresses and coats of *Photoplay* featured smaller furs (capes or shawls) and sleek modern lines, rather than the yards of fabric that characterized Hollywood gowns. The prose in these articles also pitched the dresses to a broadly construed modern woman. As is evident in the description of Karen Morley's dress, the descriptions did not belie their source material. The lack of detail likely speaks to an effort to pitch the look to a wide consumer audience. Those familiar with *The Phantom of Crestwood* might know that Morley's character (Jenny Wren) extorts money from ex-lovers in this murder mystery, but other readers might simply like the lines of the dress paired with the fur cape. In other cases, the use of a sketch (rather than a photograph), paired with Seymour's descriptions, distanced a dress even further from its character. The description of Myrna Loy's dress in *Thirteen Women* (dir. George Archainbaud, 1932) reads: "Sleeves, as you know, are the pet child of fashion this season. They do all sorts of gay things as on this wool frock"

(Seymour 1932c, 63). This jaunty description of voluminous sleeves seems intentionally anachronistic and aimed to avoid the issue that Loy's character in *Thirteen Women* attempts to kill twelve women. The decision to replicate dresses from B films and serials appears to be aimed at the filmgoer interested in these pre-Code genre films, but the treatment of these dresses in the magazine indicates that *Photoplay* wanted these dresses to appeal to a wide audience of moviegoers.

Making Hollywood fashion part of mass culture meant that *Photoplay* had to acknowledge women's sewing, crafting, and cost-saving strategies in the construction of outfits. Nan Enstad (1999, 179) explains that the growing fan culture in the 1900s and 1910s emerged in relation to mass-produced consumer products, especially items handed out in theaters. "Fan paraphernalia," Enstad writes, "certainly was not working women's own cultural creation, but the product of producers' promotional efforts." By the 1930s some of these promotional strategies changed, and the emphasis was not solely on selling mass-produced items, but also on selling cheap patterns for Hollywood styles. The emphasis on making and remaking clothing, and the expansion of the pattern market into Hollywood fashion, reflects a time-worn response to economic depressions and recessions. As Jane Farrell-Beck and Joyce Starr Johnson (1992, 39) explain, "In every year between 1870 and 1933, writers in the sampled [women's and household] periodicals offered women readers advice about how to remake or refresh their clothes." Trading on Hollywood's cachet gave the struggling high-end pattern manufacturers a way to promote glamour at a reasonable price point, with patterns that could be sold in chain stores to consumers struggling during the Depression. DIY fan practices of the late twentieth and twenty-first century are typically associated with an aesthetic of remix or bespoke crafted items that do not exist for mass market purchase. These fan creations are often bound up in debates around whether these practices represent forms of copyright infringement or fair use and transformative engagement with texts. Pattern sales, however, were simply one way that character apparel was sold, and it was done with no regard to how women might alter these dresses. Patterns offered a way for a wider audience of women to engage with Hollywood and help spread its aesthetic influence.

Dressing like a star, as *Photoplay* would occasionally point out, was not solely about purchasing the correct mass-produced items: it was about understanding the rules of style. *Photoplay* typically balanced low- and no-cost DIY strategies, including makeup tips, accessorizing ideas, and advice on how to make minor alterations to refresh old outfits. It was common for

Seymour to point out how even the stars styled clothing to vary the appearance with accessories. Seymour (1932a, 121) touted "an inexpensive way of padding out the sports wardrobe," by explaining how Joan Bennett swapped ascot scarves to change the appearance of a white dress. In another issue Seymour praised Joan Crawford's "grand evening gown gag," in which she paired a plain straight evening gown with different blouses tied around her waist. According to Seymour (1932b, 104), "each blouse is a little different in design and color so that one evening gown looks like several!" Although there is no way to verify whether these anecdotes are true, they make glamorous stars more relatable. These points also underscore the creativity inherent in assembling an outfit. Dressing like a star was not simply about buying a dress, but about consistently reinventing and refashioning outfits to always appear glamorous.

Photoplay stopped marketing film fashions at the end of the 1930s and developed a new relationship between films and department stores. By 1940 *Photoplay* still featured fashions for sale but had moved away from prominently advertising its own brand and instead described fashions, listed prices for items available in urban department stores, and encouraged those interested in the designs to write to their fashion secretary. Further, the featured fashions were no longer limited to screen costumes. In March 1940, the magazine contained a spread on Patricia Morison's travel apparel and luggage and only briefly mentioned her appearance in Paramount's adventure film *Untamed* (dir. George Archainbaud, 1940) (Walters 1940, 52–53). *Photoplay* would again change its approach to marketing fashions later in the 1940s, when it began to sell dress patterns for on-screen dresses (Emery 2001, 97). *Photoplay*'s line of character fashions receded from the magazine, but the magazine continued to advertise and offer attire to keep its readers buying screen fashions and aspiring to Hollywood styles.

Although the dress designs were often somewhat staid, they provided women with the opportunity to embody an array of different characters, from femme fatales to adventurers. Hollywood Fashions offered a version of everyday cosplay most similar to what Suzanne Scott (2019, 201) describes as "authenticated everyday cosplay," in which fan consumers can buy clothing that resembles what they see on screen. Twenty-first-century women are often linked to expensive designer versions of on-screen clothing or authentic on-screen costumes on eBay, which Scott acknowledges can raise questions about economic access to this kind of participatory culture. In the 1930s this form of cosplay attempted to be more financially accessible than the designer gowns of A pictures and red-carpet appearances. These dresses also offered modern women the ability to embody characters who lived not only glamou-rous lives, but dangerous and exciting ones. Yet the chance to dress as a char-acter was not the focus of these columns. Fandom and the desire to dress like on-screen characters were envisioned as an experience that would appeal to a mass audience, rather than an experience that catered to group devoted to a particular film.

FILM FASHIONS AND THE MODERN DEPARTMENT STORE

The commercialization of film fashion was a marriage of two growing and thriving industries of the 1930s: film and retail. By the 1930s studio indus-trial structures, labor systems, and publicity machines like *Photoplay* were well established. Retail in the United States had also undergone significant transformations in the latter half of the nineteenth century with the arrival of chain stores, which were able to reduce consumer costs of mass-produced goods (Strasser 2015, 45–46). Department stores such as Marshall Field's in Chicago, which offered over half a million square feet of a retail experience accompanied by restaurants, a children's theater, and the famous Tiffany dome, were also expanding (Hull 1993, 40–41). Well-appointed department stores and movie palaces both housed a number of services within their lav-ish spaces that created glamorous consumer experiences. The spatial simi-larities reflected a desire within both industries to elevate their cultural sta-tus. Their audiences differed in subtle ways: in the case of film, Hollywood had to court a national audience; in contrast, Marshall Field's had to focus more narrowly on the elite and middle-class consumers of Chicago.

The relationship between the film industry and urban retail has been noted by scholars of film and consumer culture. In the foundational essay "The Carole Lombard in Macy's Window," Charles Eckert (1990, 103) simulta-neously marvels at and critiques "the almost incestuous hegemony that char-acterized Hollywood's relations with vast reaches of the American economy by the mid-1930s." One power of film was to model style and consumption habits for a broad audience, and, through fashion, there was presumed to be a direct line of influence from the screen to consumers. Thus, from the earli-est decades of Hollywood, the studios offered ways for film fans to costume themselves in the film fashions of the day. Historical studies such as Sarah Berry's *Screen Style* demonstrate the many ways screen fashions were mer-chandised. According to Berry (2000, xv), in the 1930s, "the film industries gave rise to a culture of cross-promotion that would now be called 'synergy':

a boom in star endorsements, the merchandising of film costumes through Hollywood 'tie-in' labels, product placement in movies, and the extensive use of fashion publicity for upcoming films." By the 1930s, advertisements indicate that manufacturers of this apparel and retailers took for granted that women watched Hollywood films with a consumer's eye. As one Marshall Field's ad says: "Is it possible to have that adorable dress the star wore in the picture I saw last night? Photoplay Magazine has thousands of such inquiries . . . and from now on the answer is FIELD'S" (*Chicago Daily Tribune* 1932, 9).

Although there was a presumption of a direct line between films and consumers, department stores complicated this chain of access through their regional advertising. Despite the many similarities between the retail and film industries, they were cultivating different types of consumers. Hollywood's desire to reach a broad range of consumers across the nation was in conflict with Marshall Field's aim to reach high-end regional consumers. Marshall Field's advertised its latest apparel both in the newspaper and in *Fashions of the Hour*, a catalog for the latest fashions (but more importantly a larger advertisement for the cosmopolitanism of the Marshall Field's department store and Chicago). *Fashions of the Hour* features lengthy descriptions, stories about exotic travel, and occasionally photographs and stories about famous actors visiting Chicago and shopping at Marshall Field's. For example, a 1923 issue devoted a full page to Irene Fenwick and Lionel Barrymore's shopping trip in a feature titled "Mr. and Mrs. Lionel Barrymore's visit to Marshall Field's." Accompanying photographs of the couple, the copy explains: "They came to the Custom Apparel Section of Marshall Field & Co to have a new costume designed and made, during the run of the play in Chicago, in anticipation of their New York Opening" (Marshall Field 1923, 5). In addition to showcasing famous guests to the department store, these kinds of stories supported Marshall Field's high-end image of a department store that was good enough for famous actors, better than the costume department at one of the local theaters, and perhaps even fashionable enough for New York. Marshall Field's *Fashions of the Hour* not only presented the latest fashions, but carefully depicted Chicago as a modern and cosmopolitan city worthy of high-end apparel.

Advertisements for film fashions played a more significant role in film magazines like *Photoplay* than they did in the catalogs of the department stores that sold these dresses. Although Hollywood connoted glamour, the Hollywood Fashions knockoffs were cheaper alternatives to many of the offerings in Marshall Field's. As Joy Emery (2001, 93) points out, in order to retain the status of Vogue Patterns, Condé Nast produced the brand Hollywood

Patterns as a cheap Depression-era alternative. Hollywood Patterns, unlike Hollywood Fashions, provides an example of what Suzanne Scott (2019, 201) terms "covert everyday cosplay," because its patterns were *inspired by* (rather than licensed from) character costumes. Despite this difference between Hollywood Patterns and Hollywood Fashions, neither's designs catered to a high-end clientele. Since Hollywood Fashions catered to a mass and lower-end clientele, its dresses were marketed differently than the Schiaparelli, furs, and European designers that were often highlighted in *Fashions of the Hour*. Instead, Marshall Field's opted to advertise Hollywood Fashions to a broader audience, by placing ads in the *Chicago Tribune*.

Advertisements that showcased Hollywood's presence in Chicago created connections to the city, but further distanced the advertised dresses from the specifics of the film. In *Photoplay* discussions of dresses tended to be peppy and descriptive, noting trends and leaving out details about character and plot. Marshall Field's took these general descriptions and often shaped them for its regional audience. For example, a 1933 advertisement points out that Helen Vinson's tunic in *Midnight Club* (dir. Alexander Hall and George Somnes, 1933) was featured both on screen and in Marshall Field's department store (*Chicago Tribune* 1933, 15). What is noteworthy in this advertisement is that it is selling this tunic to readers who likely have not yet seen the film. For Marshall Field's it was not sufficient to simply draw from an audience of filmgoers for these fashions; the apparel had to meet the lofty standards of the Marshall Field's customer. Part of how Marshall Field's was able to maintain this standard was to copy these designs in house. The ads in the *Tribune* promise a quick turnaround in production, which meant buyers could have Hollywood Fashions available on the same day the magazine hit the newsstands. Moreover, items such as serial star Evalyn Knapp's felt and straw hat could be reproduced in any color (*Chicago Daily Tribune* 1932, 9). Thus, even as Hollywood Fashions was presented as mass-produced apparel, its production relied on the infrastructure of the department store, which offered patrons the ability to customize purchases. Efforts to showcase the local—featuring photos of actors in the store or highlighting where films were playing—indicate that retail outlets also helped establish regional audience connections to Hollywood.

Although Marshall Field's sold Hollywood Fashions, the department store did not use these dresses in its prestige advertising. Rather than providing a means for audience members to connect with film fans around the country, Marshall Field's advertisements for Hollywood Fashions seem to hedge, showing the connection to Hollywood while highlighting how Hollywood was also integrated into Chicago. The development and marketing of film fashions demonstrate not only how film functioned as a mass cultural force, but also how regional department stores reconciled or deepened tensions between local and mass cultures. Hollywood and *Photoplay* may have been committed to promoting film fashions, but Marshall Field's was more ambivalent in its promotions of Hollywood styles.

CONCLUSION

Photoplay and its Hollywood Fashions provide an example of proto-cosplay for a mainstream audience. This apparel was marketed not as costume, but as clothing that should fit in a woman's everyday life. Hollywood Fashions was advertised in mainstream newspapers and positioned as one retail choice among Marshall Field's many offerings. These dresses, hats, and coats were made in-house with options for customization. Historically, many women challenged the limits imposed by commercial fashion, and several excellent scholarly works demonstrate how women customized rather than copied star styles to suit their bodies, tastes, and personal desires (Herzog and Gaines 1991; Moseley 2001; Stacey 1994). However, because Hollywood Fashions lines were aimed at a mass audience, the dresses themselves lack some aspects of the subcultural participation and cultural resistance that characterize late twentieth- and early twenty-first-century cosplay.

The dresses reproduced for Hollywood Fashions offered wearers a way to stealthily engage in fantasies of on-screen adventures and the dangerous worlds of gangsters. Although this apparel offered an alternative to ruffles and domestic femininity, acknowledgment of different types of desires and femininity was a poor substitute for actual participation in the film business. As women's roles in the Hollywood industry were dwindling, *Photoplay* created fashions that would help women cultivate a fantasy life filled with excitement, adventure, and romance, but failed to offer ways to share these ideas and worlds with a broader public.

REFERENCES

Barbas, Samantha. 2001. *Movie Crazy*. New York: Palgrave.
Berry, Sarah. 2000. *Screen Style: Fashion and Femininity in 1930s Hollywood*. Minneapolis: University of Minnesota Press.

Chicago Daily Tribune. 1932. "Out Today! Photoplay Fashions." February 15, 1932, 9.

Chicago Tribune. 1933. "Advertisement." August 11, 1933, 15.

Coppa, Francesca. 2006. "A Brief History of Media Fandom." In *Fan Fiction and Fan Communities in the Age of the Internet*. Edited by Karen Hellekson and Kristina Busse, 225–44. Jefferson, NC: McFarland.

Eckert, Charles. 1990. "The Carole Lombard in Macy's Window." In *Fabrications: Costume and the Female Body*. Edited by Jane Gaines and Charlotte Herzog, 100–121. London: Routledge.

Emery, Joy. 2001. "Dress Like a Star: Hollywood and the Pattern Industry." *Dress* 28 (1): 92–99.

Enstad, Nan. 1999. *Ladies of Labor, Girls of Adventure*. New York: Columbia University Press.

Farrell-Beck, Jane, and Joyce Starr Johnson. 1992. "Remodeling and Renovating Clothes, 1870–1933." *Dress* 19 (1): 37–46.

Hallett, Hilary A. 2013. *Go West, Young Women! The Rise of Early Hollywood*. Berkeley: University of California Press.

Herzog, Charlotte, and Jane Gaines. 1991. "'Puffed Sleeves before Tea-Time': Joan Crawford, Adrian and Women Audiences." In *Stardom: Industry of Desire*, edited by Christine Gledhill, 74–91. London: Routledge.

Hull, Hamilton. 1993. *Our Trip through Field's*. Chicago: Marshall Field. American History Museum Library, Smithsonian Library, Washington, DC.

Lamerichs, Nicolle. 2011. "Stranger than Fiction: Fan Identity in Cosplay." *Transformative Works and Cultures* 7, https://doi.org/10.3983/twc.2011.0246

Marshall Field. 1923. *Fashions of the Hour*. Chicago: Marshall Field. American History Museum Library, Smithsonian Library, Washington, DC.

Modern Screen. 1935. "Confessions of an Extra Girl, Part I." August 1935, 30–31, 87.

Moseley, Rachel. 2001. "Respectability Sewn Up: Dressmaking and Film Star Style in the Fifties and Sixties." *European Journal of Cultural Studies* 4 (4): 473–90.

Photoplay. 1932. "Now! You, Too, May Wear the Fashions of the Films!" October 1932, 90. Media History Digital Library. https://mediahistoryproject.org

Santo, Avi. 2018. "Fans and Merchandise." In *The Routledge Companion to Media Fandom*, edited by Melissa A. Click and Suzanne Scott, 329–36. New York: Routledge.

Scott, Suzanne. 2019. *Fake Geek Girls: Fandom, Gender, and the Convergence Culture Industry*. New York: New York University Press.

Seymour. 1932a. "Hollywood on Dress Parade." *Photoplay*, July 1932, 121. Media History Digital Library. https://mediahistoryproject.org

Seymour. 1932b. "Little Tricks Make Hollywood Fashions Individual." *Photoplay*, September 1932, 104. Media History Digital Library. https://mediahistoryproject.org

Seymour. 1932c. "Starring the New Trends." *Photoplay*, October 1932, 61–64. Media History Digital Library. https://mediahistoryproject.org

Seymour, 1932d. "Photoplay's Style Authority." *Photoplay*, November 1932, 62–68. Media History Digital Library. https://mediahistoryproject.org

Slide, Anthony. 2010. *Inside the Hollywood Fan Magazine: A History of Star Makers, Fabricators, and Gossip Mongers.* Oxford: University of Mississippi Press.

Stacey, Jackie. 1994. *Star Gazing: Hollywood Cinema and Female Spectatorship.* London: Routledge.

Stamp, Shelley. 2004. "'It's a Long Way to Filmland': Starlets, Screen Hopefuls and Extras in Early Hollywood." In *American Cinema's Transitional Era: Audiences, Institutions, Practices,* edited by Charlie Keil and Shelley Stamp, 322–52. Berkeley: University of California Press.

Strasser, Susan. 2015. "Woolworth to Walmart: Mass Merchandising and the Changing Culture of Consumption." In *Shopping,* edited by Deborah C. Andrews, 33–56. Newark: University of Delaware Press.

USTNEC (US Temporary National Economic Committee). 1940. *Investigation of Concentration of Economic Power.* Washington: US Government Printing Office.

Walters, Gwenn. 1940. "Photoplay Fashions." *Photoplay,* March 1940, 50–58. Media History Digital Library. https://mediahistoryproject.org

2

"Anorak City"

Indie Pop's Resistance through Regression

Elodie A. Roy

> The country of our childhood survives, if only in our minds, and retains our
> loyalty even when casting us into exile; we carry its image from city to city as our
> most essential baggage.
>
> —Malcolm Cowley, *Exile's Return: A Literary Odyssey of the 1920s*

Toward the end of her long mandate (1979–90), British prime minister
Margaret Thatcher would bluntly state that "fashion is important because
it raises the quality of life when people take the trouble to dress well and it
also provides employment for many, many people" (quoted in Stanfill 2013,
10), explicitly connecting the realm of (power) dressing to that of respect-
able employment and conservatism at a time when, ironically, much of the
British textile industry was being brutally dismantled and delocalized. The
Thatcherite 1980s are routinely remembered as a decade of excess and flam-
boyance. The sartorial culture of the period—often reduced to a handful of
glittering vignettes—seems to exude a larger-than-life, spectacular quality.[1]
Its superficial shimmer, however, is not enough to conceal a much darker yet
equally intense counterpoint, in the form of mass unemployment, ruthless
privatization schemes, repeated attacks on the welfare state, and the spread
of HIV.

While the mainstream ideology celebrated power, careers, and mon-
eyed maturity, myriad alternative discourses and gestures of resistance also
consolidated across the decade. This chapter uncovers one of the less visible (fashion) stories of the period by engaging with the British indie pop
or anorak subculture of the mid- to late 1980s. Anorak fashion was adopted
by young fans of indie pop music, who readily dressed in a regressive, "gen-

---

1. Typical style items of the period include exaggerated shoulder pads, fluorescent
man-made fabrics (Lycra and latex), sequins, stilettos, and bright makeup.

tle" way, metonymically embracing the weak, powerless, and economically unproductive qualities associated with children. Their style, nodding to the colorful, androgynous imagery of the 1960s, incorporated items of children's clothing, infantile haircuts (such as bowl cuts), and children's accessories (such as barrettes and toys; see Cavanagh 2001, 190–91). A staple item of the style was the anorak, often purchased secondhand, and worn by both sexes.

This chapter examines and contextualizes a subcultural style that was deliberately unspectacular or antifashionable, largely existing within the elusive space of the everyday. Accordingly, I am interested in invisibility, regression, and smallness as possible strategies of cultural transgression and resistance—a theme running from the Situationists' celebration of the "lost children" right through to Michel de Certeau's (1988) quietly provocative advocating of in-between dwelling, poaching, and borrowing. If in previous decades subcultural groups embraced anger, provocation, and "perversity" as a means of cultural resistance (Mekas [1958] 2015, 14), what are the disruptive potentials of nonspectacular and apparently innocuous, more passive behaviors? Early subcultural analyses—those of Phil Cohen (1972) or Dick Hebdige (1979), for instance—focused on clear moments of sartorial disruption and extremism in postwar British youth movements. But how does one understand, as Gary Clarke (1982) bemusedly wondered, the more subdued but possibly radical statements offered by "ski-jumpers"? How does one write about benign, unobvious components of style—or about their everyday recurrence? While recent readings of subcultures recognize their fluid and mobile nature (Muggleton 2000), these are still often framed in terms of deviance, sensational subversion, and exclusive or fixed meanings. Part of the challenge is thus to retrace or recover what largely existed and circulated beyond the threshold of mainstream visibility. My primary sources were principally derived from underground publications (fanzines) as well as formal and informal conversations with members of the independent scene carried out over a decade.

SARTORIAL TOTEMS

The anorak style evolved from the more restrained indie look of the first half of the 1980s. In the 1994 *Streetstyle* exhibition, held at the Victoria and Albert Museum in London, the earlier style was illustrated by a pair of faded Levi's blue jeans with cuffs, black Doc Martens shoes, and a brown suede and wool cardigan worn over a baggy Smiths T-shirt (De la Haye and Dingwall 1996;

see also Polhemus 1994).[2] While the muted, unisex clothes of the indie look suggested a form of subcultural camouflage, the anorak style—frequently incorporating colorful items and too-tight or too-big clothes—was more overtly incongruous (Cook 2004, 100). Up until its subcultural appropriation in the mid-1980s, the anorak had remained an inconspicuous style item mainly associated with the "soft" realm of childhood and girlhood. Prior to the 1950s, quilted or fur-lined anoraks had been worn by European children and women for winter sports; it became an everyday, urban garment in the middle of the century. In the 1960s, anoraks (which had traditionally been plain) were enlivened with bright-colored patterns (Guppy 1978, 244; Reynolds 1989, 251). Though they were increasingly imported from the British colonies including Hong Kong (Guppy 1978, 224), and available for purchase in town, many mothers continued to sew them at home for their children, using an attractive range of new, inexpensive "ready quilted materials padded with Terylene or Fortred wadding" (Mordle-Barnes 1977, 121).

Indie pop can be seen as the first grown-up, nationwide subcultural scene to emulate childhood in a seemingly unironic way.[3] It was associated with the emergence of bands such as Orange Juice, Television Personalities, Talulah Gosh, the Fat Tulips, and the Pastels, as well as countless amateur, unsigned groups who visually and sonically embraced a more primitive, untutored—but also sensitive—style of songwriting often influenced by 1960s psychedelia and folk-rock (the Byrds, Love, Donovan). Their short, sketchy pop songs were frequently home recorded on four-track tape machines and inexpensively pressed on flexi discs, which were commonly distributed with fanzines (bearing the mark of the DIY approach of punk). These musical artifacts were circulated nationally and internationally through the postal network and informal hand-to-hand exchanges (for instance at gigs). Though it existed throughout the United Kingdom, the anorak subculture is most strongly linked to a number of underground record labels and fanzines, springing from British university towns such as Glasgow, Edinburgh, Bristol, Newcastle, and Manchester.

A reinterpretation of the "fun worshippers" of the early 1960s (Cook 2004, 136), the self-appointed pop kids—who averaged in ages between fifteen

---

2. For a full discussion of the indie look and its historical evolution in the United Kingdom, see Lifter 2020.

3. A precursor of the anorak style was the regressive, posthippie "babytime" look identified in 1984 by Peter York (1985, 64). The style was popular from approximately 1968 to 1980 among the baby boomers, "the first generation ever to deny the life-cycle: marriage, commitment, baby-making."

and twenty-five—were animated with the paradoxical desire for lightheart-
edness in a time of economic drabness. *Under My Hat*, a fanzine from 1990,
humorously (and self-knowingly) lists seventeen rules for becoming a pop
kid. The second "commandment" reads "own an anorak" (Rachel 1990, 4).
In this context, the anorak can be understood as a totemic "shortcut" that,
much like rockers' leather jackets, "[came] to symbolize ideas and ideals,
taking on almost magical properties in [its] changed, subcultural meanings"
(Miller 2011, 96). In addition to donning an anorak, *Under My Hat* listed pop
kids tended to "be poor, idealistic and/or a student," "write [one's] own fanzine and be generally silly," "listen to John Peel," and "disagree with the NME"
(Rachel 1990, 4)[4]

The leading fashion and music monthlies of the time, the *Face* and *i-D*
(both founded in 1980), were deeply rooted in London and mostly overlooked
the unsophisticated, regionally scattered, and uncommercial, self-proclaimed
pop kids.[5] One of the only in-depth nationwide exposures came from *Melody
Maker* writer Simon Reynolds in 1986.[6] Reynolds (1989, 251), an early chroni-
cler, theorist, and dedicated participant of the scene, eloquently inventoried
his peers' "overtly childish things—dufflecoats, birthday-boy shirts with the
top button done up, outsize pullovers; for girls—bows and ribbons and pony-
tails, plimsolls and dainty white ankle socks, floral or polka-dot frocks, hardly
any make-up and no high heels."[7]

As evidenced by Reynolds's list, the indie pop style was rooted in the
material culture of the everyday. Rather than embracing the typical trajectory of childhood "from dependence to independence" (Cook 2004, 13), its
participants seemed to seek, at least symbolically, a form of dependence
in the self-enclosed safety of the house. The latter existed as a prime location for music-making, creating, and performing identities. This emphasis
on domestic spaces marked a rupture with mainstream culture as well as a

---

4. The *NME* (*New Musical Express*), founded in 1952, was the most widely read music
publication in the United Kingdom in the 1980s. See Long 2012.

5. The *Face* was founded by *New Musical Express* editor Nick Logan, and *i-D* was founded by Terry Jones, who had served as *Vogue* art director (Stanfill 2013, 19).

6. The year 1986 was when indie pop consolidated as a "scene," notably with the *New
Musical Express*'s release of the *C86* tape, which compiled tracks by many anorak bands.
"C86" subsequently became used as a synonym for anorak and indie pop.

7. There are transatlantic sartorial resonances between the anorak style and grunge
and riot grrrls. K Records in Olympia, Washington, which licensed some of British indie
pop bands such as Talulah Gosh and Heavenly, was instrumental in visually and musically
disseminating the indie pop style in the United States, while also contributing to shaping a
more US-specific interpretation of the indie look.

distancing from the traditional geography of popular music, which glorified more exposed public spaces (including the street, the road, the club, and the stage). It follows that the movement significantly differed from the musical subcultures of the early 1980s, most notably the New Romantics and their bold, extraverted dressing up. The New Romantic subculture was closely bound with a handful of Birmingham and London nightclubs (most notably Billy's in Soho and Blitz in Covent Garden) and the sleekly produced songs of David Bowie, Duran Duran, Roxy Music, and Boy George (Rimmer 2003). In the wake of Bowie, fans made a point of dressing up and outdressing one another, embracing a restless search for new forms, new genres, and new styles. Their systematic commitment to dressing up (and cross-dressing) seemed to playfully mirror the acceleration and instant obsolescence of style in late capitalism—at a time when fashion was construed as "something to be *used up*" (Ewen 1988, 52). The New Romantics can be approached as a perfect enactment of the postmodern style, where identity was consolidated and immediately dissolved in a quick succession of looks, all of them disposable and interchangeable at will. In contrast with this speed and emphasis on dressing up as a self-conscious practice—and celebration—of consumerist excess, pop kids used clothes as a visual means to control, or even slow down and revert, the flow of time.

OUT OF TIME

The consumption of residual commodities, often anonymously designed, can be understood as a refusal to engage with the quick and capricious turnovers of the 1980s fashion market and its culture of brands. A participant of the scene recalls: "there was a part of me that wanted to look like I didn't belong to a particular country or place or year" (quoted in Knee 2014, 38). On a superficial level, the indie pop look can therefore be conceived of as a wider retro mode or, in the words of cultural theorist Elizabeth Wilson (1985, 172), a "fantasy culture of the 1980s" where "there is no real history, no real past" but "an instant, magical nostalgia, a strangely *unmotivated* appropriation of the past." Themes of pastiche, appropriation, and playful imitation are frequently discussed in relation to the ever-changing kaleidoscope of 1980s fashions. However, I would suggest that the indie pop style was clearly motivated, delimited, and carefully constructed from the outset. Its participants ultimately sought to create a legible canon, coherently linking music, image, and text, an ambition that seems inconsistent with David Muggleton's (2000) reading of 1980s and 1990s subcultural styles as simultaneously enacting and producing the fractured aesthetics of postmodernism. Muggleton insisted on the mobility, reversibility, and inconsistence of subcultural styles, while anthropologist Ted Polhemus (1994, 130–35) discussed the merging of sub-cultural styles as they irresistibly converged toward the ultimate postmodern "supermarket of style." The indie subculture in this regard does not fit easily within these readings. It can be suggested that what indie pop participants achieved—weaving together visual, material, and sonic threads—was a form of closely knit narrative unity, a "perfect pop story" largely at odds with the open-ended eclecticism of postmodern cultural forms (Roy 2014). With its holistic, totalizing impulse, indie pop therefore exposed a more overtly mod-ern rather than postmodern sensibility.

Such a totalizing impulse was encapsulated, for instance, in the 1988 song "Anorak City" (by Plymouth one-man band Another Sunny Day), in which the singer-narrator invited his beloved to join him and stay "till the end of time" in the permanently enchanted—and therefore curiously frozen—Anorak City, a town where nobody ever aged and lovers never parted.[8] The song betrays the ingrained anachronism of indie pop, often characterized by its participants' will to create a legible world within—or outside—the world. The paradoxi-cal desire for reification (or arrested time) and permanence may express the refusal to grow up in a country largely perceived to be without a (desirable or acceptable) future. In this case, the choice to adopt the aesthetics of child-hood is also an attempt to reclaim the real or perceived territory of childhood as an autonomous realm of innocence, stability, and possibility. To a large extent, the feeling lyrically conveyed by "Anorak City"—most notably the desire for eternal youth—traverses the entire continuum of popular music (with pop stars' meticulously designed stage costumes reinforcing illusions of timelessness and otherworldliness). Yet it is also generally understood that a stage persona only ever exists in the limited—and exceptional—time and space of the performance. In the indie pop movement, childishness becomes a common practice and routine: a way of inhabiting the world while paradox-ically keeping it at a distance.[9] It may be noted that the aesthetics and vocab-ulary of childhood, far from being limited to clothing, infiltrated the larger

8. There are resonances between Anorak City and the arrested paradise of Shangri-la as imagined by US director Frank Capra in *Lost Horizon* (1937).

9. The anorak style may have also partially recaptured a more classic image of the child, which was becoming obsolete in 1980s pop culture, a period marked by the success of teen pop stars groomed like grown-ups.

aesthetics of the indie pop scene.[10] Because many albums were originally recorded at home, indie pop became familiarly known as "bedroom pop."

"THE VITAL LINK": BUILDING THE FANZINE NATION

The indie pop subculture consolidated as a structured or organized culture, mediated through a distribution network (the Cartel), established fanzines, and independent record labels. The richness and diversity of indie fanzines, produced in all regions of the United Kingdom, may be seen as cementing the scene together; fanzines were further responsible for the movement's diffusion in France, Germany, and Japan. The independent network relied on national and international postal communication, letter-writing, and one-to-one exchanges, rather than the actual copresence of a group. Furthermore, the independent distribution network of the Cartel (whose moto was "the Vital Link"), initially founded in 1978 to distribute records and tapes, was also used to circulate fanzines across music shops in the United Kingdom. The Rough Trade shop in London was the first link of a network that included regional record shops such as Fast Forward (Edinburgh), Red Rhino (York), Probe (Liverpool), Nine Mile (Leamington Spa), Backs (Norwich), and Revolver (Bristol). It is important to underline the role of the written and printed word in the visual mediation and homogenization of the indie pop style. It may be argued that fanzines, cheaper to produce and purchase than records, were a primary means of circulating the indie identity—notably making it accessible to geographically, economically, or socially isolated members unable to regularly attend live shows. The relationship between fashion and its visual and written representation in subcultures is crucial; in the case of the indie pop scene, this relationship was obsessive, becoming hyperbolized through acts of naming, writing, marking, and labeling. Fanzines contained low-resolution photocopies of bands' photographs but also countless approximate drawings of the anorak look, thus keeping it open to interpretation. In a 2015 interview, Krischan, an indie pop fan and musician from the German town of Friedberg, remembered developing his own look through British indie pop fanzines. He began wearing sailor suits and anoraks with "black 501s, striped T-shirts,

---

10. This aesthetic appeared across artworks, song titles, band names (Orange Juice, BMX Bandits, the Pastels, Talulah Gosh), record label names (Sarah Records, Tea Time, Teddy Bear, Kitchenware), and even names of recording studios (Picnic, the Chocolate Factory).

Figure 2.1. German indie pop fans Krischan and Matn in Paris, September 1987. Krischan's personal collection.

rubber-soled shoes" out of affective solidarity with British pop kids, and he listed his sartorial influences as "the DIY ethos and Xerox aesthetics of punk fanzines . . '50s and '60s picture books for children, American pop culture just before the British Invasion swept over it, psychedelic without the drugs" (pers. comm., 2015; see figure 2.1).[11]

Various theorists have emphasized the homogenizing and transnational force of media in the formation of subcultural scenes, an approach that was inspired by French sociologist Gabriel Tarde's (1890) early suggestion that emulation—or "imitation"—represented the primary force behind the formation of social groups. Lawrence Grossberg (1984, 227), for instance, describes

---

11. Krischan eventually penned, in German, a song called "Babyanorak."

flexible networks of communication as "affective alliances," a notion that further relates to music as that which produces "its own affective and aggrega-
tive identity effects, its own modes of 'imitation' or contagion" (Born 2011,
382). More broadly, it may be that any scene that relies on written communication inevitably becomes homogenized, not the least because language, as
philosopher Agnes Heller (1984, 159) argues, constitutes "the homogeneous
medium of everyday life." Fanzines are most strikingly language as print: language that can be inexpensively and easily photocopied, quoted, reprinted,
and circulated. In this sense, the written trace retrospectively constitutes the
indie group, ensuring its continuity through the reproduction and survival of
a text. It may therefore be suggested that the indie pop movement was partially disseminated through imitation. In a context of geographical distance,
objects, names, images, and songs all converged toward the written word,
so that clothes existed simultaneously as objects, symbols, and images. The
term *anorak* was used to describe fans in affectionate, rather than derogative,
ways: Glasgow-based bands were portrayed as "Glasgow anoraks."[12] The noun
anorak also gained increased popularity as an adjective. For instance, Aki,
a Japanese exchange student from the Glasgow School of Art, founded the
Anorak Club once back in Tokyo and penned a bilingual fanzine called *Far
from George Square* that she would send back to her British friends. In France,
Fabien Garcia (of indie pop band Caramel) founded Anorak Records, a label
that used as its emblem the characteristic zip of the jacket. The term *anorak*
can therefore be understood as a generic and dispersed password for indie
pop fans, identifying a broad, cross-national lifestyle.

It must be noted that one of the most crucial terms of the indie lexicon
remains that of the *label*, where label is always a shortcut for "independent
record label." Interestingly, indie pop's obsession with record labels is not
matched by an obsession for designers, so that the history of indie fashion
remains mostly without names, authors, or designers. Such anonymity—and
wider reliance on found, borrowed, and homemade garments—contributes
to differentiating it from earlier fashions associated with music subcultures.
Subcultural groups of the 1960s and 1970s (including the mods, the skinheads,

---

12. Today, rather than simply referring to the indie pop community, the substantive
anorak is informally and derogatively used in British English to describe "a person who is
extremely enthusiastic about and interested in something that other people find boring"
(*Merriam-Webster*, n.d.)—and in some instances a "perverted" or "deviant" personality. The
term is typically linked with the figure of the (male) "geek," and can further be related to the
Japanese term *otaku*. Anoraks have also been considered, in a clichéd way, as the dress of
the radical Left in Britain at the turn of the 1970s (Sandbrook 2019).

and the punks), despite their DIY ethos and resistance to mass culture, came to follow highly regimented sartorial codes, soon becoming dependent on specialized brands, dedicated fashion retailers, and approved designers (the mods, in particular, developed fashion consciousness to its extreme). In the 1990s, rap and hip-hop subcultures would similarly form close alliances with the fashion realm, while the grunge and riot grrrl movements (partly influenced by the anorak style) retained a largely anticonsumerist stance.

SECONDHAND CHILDHOODS

All through the 1980s, secondhand clothes were widely and inexpensively available through charity shops, army surplus stores, and retro retailers such as Flip (in Glasgow, Edinburgh, and Newcastle) and Afflecks (in Manchester), which contributed to the popularization of retro consumption among younger people and expressed the decade's reconsideration of secondhand clothes as acceptable and desirable.[13] The revaluation—and social destigmatization—of secondhand clothing was perhaps best exemplified by the commercial success of *More Dash Than Cash*, a 1982 Vogue-sponsored lifestyle guide encouraging young women to develop an "individual style" through secondhand clothes purchased in "jumble sales, fêtes, bazaars, auctions or markets." In addition to being purchased "for twenty pence," secondhand garments were also frequently acquired through older relatives, and often had to be altered at home (Hogg [1982] 1984, 89; see also Gregson and Crewe 2003; Jenss 2005, 179). As one of my interviewees recalled, "My first anorak was a green one, which my mother wore on her honeymoon in 1966. Of course the sleeves were too short. So I asked my grandmother to sew in some black stripes" (Krischan, pers. comm., 2015). The link of indie pop to the previous generation is ambiguous. Wearing one's parents' clothes may suggest a sense of intergenerational bondage, where clothes sensorially materialize links between individuals (one of my interviewees, for instance, remembers wearing his father's corduroy trousers). Yet, despite its explicit acknowledgment of the 1960s, the indie pop subculture may also be seen as trivializing earlier youth movements by avoiding frontal engagement with contemporary issues. In the words of Holly Kruse (1993, 40), it failed to politically embrace

---

13. Afflecks sold the postwar parkas and raincoats so coveted by the northern post-punk bands of the early 1980s. The original Flip shop opened in Glasgow's Merchant City in 1980; it sold army surplus as well as American stock from the 1950s.

a "'cause' deemed acceptable by ex-members of the 'authentic' youth culture of the 1960s." In contrast with the overt anti-Thatcherite activism of collectives such as Red Wedge (led by left-wing songwriter Billy Bragg), indie pop fans' strategy often appeared to be one of withdrawal, playfulness, and passive resistance. The provocative optimism of indie pop fanzines contrasted deeply with the glossy and often gloomy pages of style magazines such as the *Face*, with its columns on drug culture and sarcastic wittiness. The main music monthlies, when they acknowledged indie pop, tended to dismiss it as incomprehensibly "cutie" and "wimpy"—bearing no connection to "real" pop music, let alone real life.

As they dressed like children, college or university students arguably enacted a soft and historically recognizable form of rebellion, possibly inspired by previous sartorial subcultures. On US campuses, for example, ill-fitting clothes—most emblematically the oversize "sloppy joe" sweaters sported by college girls—were worn as a mark of dissent from the late 1930s through the 1960s (Guppy 1978, 291; Clemente 2014, 35). The reclamation of ill-fitting clothes as fashion items arguably expresses a conspicuous form of consumption as such items would have been dismissed as unpractical or unsuitable by those who relied on charity shops out of necessity. It follows that ill-fitting garments tended to be purchased by individuals for whom there existed no strict—or immediate—obligation to conform and who were authorized to look different as they still benefited from the (relative) shelter of educational institutions. Yet being a pop kid could also yield concrete consequences beyond the enclosed safety of the home or the classroom. The example of Pete Dale (cofounder of Newcastle's Slampt Records) suggests that walking down the streets of Sunderland in unisex clothes required courage: in his fanzine *Vertical Orange Car Crash*, he recalled being openly criticized and abused in his working-class hometown for looking androgynous (Dale 1990, n.p.).[14] Regressive style is provocative because it does not clearly map onto a set, stereotypical identity. As it disrupts conventionally gendered modes of self-presentation, it also muddies "normal" patterns of interpretation and social interaction. In his oral history of unemployment, Jeremy Seabrook (1982, 127) documented his encounters in Sunderland with young punks, another demography that subverted expected dress codes and was heavily stigmatized for its nonconformist image.

---

14. While the indie pop subculture was not primarily a working-class or street subculture, numerous participants lived in more deprived areas, including Scotland and the North East of England, where many micro record labels and bands originated.

The childish style had antecedents in British fashion culture: it has been noted, for instance, that the androgynous men and women of the Swinging Sixties resembled children (Wilson 1985, 176–77). At the time, London-based new young designers were busy designing grown-ups' as well as children's clothes, deliberately blurring the boundaries between genders and age groups as the same patterns, cuts, and materials were used for women, men, and children (Guppy 1978, 248). It may be noted that unisex and infantile clothing, rather than completely effacing the gender of the adult wearer, may anticipate an ambiguous reappropriation of the body and its sexual attributes: too-small clothes, for instance, may simultaneously reveal and heighten a mature body (Wright 1993, 55).[15] Dress historian Jo B. Paoletti (2015, 120), charting the development of unisex fashion in the United States in the 1960s and 1970s, insists that unisex garments eventually "called attention to the male or female body," contributing in many ways to ironically "highlighting" rather than "blur[ring] the differences between men and women."[16] While Simon Reynolds (1989, 250) identified the anorak style as expressing a strict refusal of the body and of sexuality, it is perhaps best understood as articulating a questioning of gender boundaries, conventions, and stereotypes. In Glasgow, for instance, a specific subtrend emerged among male indie pop fans, who provocatively combined children's jackets such as duffle coats with leather trousers, typically associated with rock 'n' roll, hypermasculinity, and aggressiveness.[17] Also in Scotland, gendered "cowboy outfits" gained prominence among Orange Juice fans.

It is worth remarking that children's clothes were the last category of clothes to be mass produced (Cook 2004, 101). Their rapid ascent into the realm of fashion initially caused distress amid a number of social commentators and journalists who lamented the appropriation of childhood by the industry (Guppy 1978, 235). To resist the mainstream fashion of the 1980s by

---

15. As Judith Williamson (1985, 53) notes in relation to Boy George and the New Romantics, asexual or presexual styles are akin to a form of irresponsibility and withdrawal: "If you present yourself as pre-sexual, you may arouse desire in others, but you can also absolve yourself of the responsibility for it."

16. Paoletti (2015, 121) also draws attention to the problematic implications of children's fashions emulating adult trends.

17. The sartorial trajectory of duffle coats is particularly interesting. Initially worn by the Royal Navy, duffle coats became a subcultural style item in the 1950s and 1960s. They were worn by antiwar and antinuclear protesters in the 1950s and 1960s, as well as by children in the United Kingdom. Their adoption by pop kids in the 1980s denotes a further deactivation—and effacement—of their military origins.

engaging with the mainstream fashion of another decade is to use the (commercial) past against the present. It is not so much a choice to resist capitalism as it is to replace capitalism with its leftovers and lingering commodities. Though offering a different form of cultural consumption, the indie pop subculture cannot be strictly divorced from consumption and ownership—despondently described as "the *only* form of control legitimised in our culture" (Williamson 1985, 231).

CONCLUSION: "LIKE LOST CHILDREN"

The motif of childhood played a central part in twentieth-century countercultural thought, most particularly in the interwar and postwar periods—from the bohemia of Greenwich Village in the 1920s to the Situationism of the 1950s (see Cowley [1951] 1976, 60). In his autobiographical writings and film scripts, Guy Debord developed a substantial romance of the "lost children," exploring the revolutionary or subversive potential of childhood (the theme was particularly present in his 1952 film *Howls for Sade*). For Debord, childhood was not materially or visually palpable: it existed as an invisible and immaterial, innermost quality of the soul, and referred to a state of heightened perception and of openness (akin, perhaps, to a cosmic, prerational understanding of the world). His theory relied on a romantic perception of children as uncorrupted and closer to "truth" than grown-ups were. Indeed, in a hopeful reversion of roles, children are seen as those who can redeem and redress a corrupted adult world, for they symbolize the future; time that has not been spent; events that are yet to happen. It must be underlined that Debord's prescient lost children defiantly lie outside history and remain unmarked by consumer culture—as they exist outside capitalism, they may be able to eventually overthrow it. The idea of childhood as intrinsic innocence first gained credence in the sixteenth and seventeenth centuries (Cook 2004, 27). For historian Carolyn Steedman, modernity is haunted by the phantasm of its lost, or sacrificed, children (cited in Jenks [1996] 2005, 66), while Elizabeth Wilson (1985, 61) insists that children were first thought of as autonomous beings when "the Romantics asserted the superior value of the natural and spontaneous against the mechanical and cerebral, the truth of feeling against reason and the scientific spirit. . . . Childhood was idealized as a period of spontaneity and innocence; and children came to be seen as closer to nature and to the quick of experience." It follows that the idea of childhood as a realm of innocence was historically produced, stemming from industrial capitalism. Accordingly, to "revolt into childhood" (Reynolds 1989)—or into the calculated *image* of childhood—may simply indicate another form of conformity, or an alienated form of protest. By the end of the 1980s, "outgrown clothes for grown-up people" had become a mainstream element of style—and the anorak now existed as an indifferent (or deactivated) sartorial totem, part of the larger cultural aesthetic of twee (Wright 1993, 49; Spitz 2014).

REFERENCES

Born, Georgina. 2011. "Music and the Materialization of Identities." *Journal of Material Culture* 16 (4): 376–88.

Cavanagh, David. 2001. *The Creation Records Story: My Magpie Eyes Are Hungry for the Prize.* London: Virgin Books.

Certeau, Michel de. 1988. *The Practice of Everyday Life.* Berkeley: University of California Press.

Clarke, Gary. 1982. "Defending Ski-Jumpers: A Critique of Theories of Youth Sub-Cultures." Centre for Contemporary Cultural Studies Stencilled Occasional Paper, no. 71.

Clemente, Deirdre. 2014. *Dress Casual: How College Students Redefined American Style.* Chapel Hill: University of North Carolina Press.

Cohen, Phil. 1972. "Sub-Cultural Conflict and Working Class Community." Centre for Contemporary Cultural Studies Working Paper in Cultural Studies, no. 2.

Cook, Daniel Thomas. 2004. *The Commodification of Childhood: The Children's Clothing Industry and the Rise of the Child Consumer.* Durham, NC: Duke University Press.

Cowley, Malcolm. (1951) 1976. *Exile's Return: A Literary Odyssey of the 1920s.* Middlesex: Penguin Books.

Dale, Pete. 1990. *Vertical Orange Car Crash.* Sunderland: self-published.

De la Haye, Amy, and Cathy Dingwall, eds. 1996. *Surfers, Soulies, Skinheads and Skaters: Subcultural Style from the Forties to the Nineties.* London: Victoria and Albert Museum.

Ewen, Stuart. 1988. *All Consuming Images: The Politics of Style in Contemporary Culture.* New York: Basic Books.

Gregson, Nicky, and Louise Crewe. 2003. *Second-Hand Cultures.* Oxford: Berg.

Grossberg, Lawrence. 1984. "Another Boring Day in Paradise: Rock and Roll and the Empowerment of Everyday Life." *Popular Music* 4:225–58.

Guppy, Alice. 1978. *Children's Clothes, 1939–1970: The Advent of Fashion.* Poole, Dorset, UK: Blandford Press.

Hebdige, Dick. 1979. *Subculture: The Meaning of Style.* London: Methuen.

Heller, Agnes. 1984. *Everyday Life*. London: Routledge.

Hogg, Kate. (1982) 1984. *More Dash Than Cash*. London: Hutchinson.

Jenks, Chris. (1996) 2005. *Childhood*. 2nd ed. Abingdon: Routledge.

Jenss, Heike. 2005. "Sixties Dress Only! The Consumption of the Past in a Retro Scene." In *Old Clothes, New Looks: Second-Hand Fashion*, edited by Alexandra Palmer and Hazel Clark, 177–96. Oxford: Berg.

Knee, Sam. 2014. *A Scene in Between: Tripping through the Fashions of UK Indie Music, 1980–1988*. London: Circada.

Kruse, Holly. 1993. "Subcultural Identity in Alternative Music Culture." *Popular Music* 12 (1): 33–41.

Lifter, Rachel. 2020. *Fashioning Indie: Popular Fashion, Music and Gender*. London: Bloomsbury.

Long, Pat. 2012. *The History of the NME: High Times and Low Lives at the World's Most Famous Music Magazine*. London: Portico.

Mekas, Jonas. (1958) 2015. "In Defense of Perversity." In *Scrapbook of the Sixties: Writings, 1954–2010*, by Jonas Mekas, 13–15. Leipzig: Spector Books.

Merriam-Webster. n.d. "Anorak." Accessed July 1, 2022. https://www.merriam-webster.com/dictionary/anorak

Miller, Janice. 2011. *Fashion and Music*. Oxford: Berg.

Mordle-Barnes, Mollie. 1977. *Making Children's Clothes*. London: Book Club.

Muggleton, David. 2000. *Inside Subculture: The Postmodern Meaning of Style*. London: Berg.

Paoletti, Jo B. 2015. *Sex and Unisex: Fashion, Feminism, and the Sexual Revolution*. Bloomington: Indiana University Press.

Polhemus, Ted. 1994. *Streetstyle*. London: Thames and Hudson.

Rachel. 1990. *Under my Hat*. Issue 2. Ashford, Kent: self-published.

Reynolds, Simon. 1989. "Against Health and Efficiency: Independent Music in the 1980s." In *Zoot Suits and Second-Hand Dresses: An Anthology of Fashion and Music*, edited by Angela McRobbie, 245–55. London: Macmillan.

Rimmer, Dave. 2003. *New Romantics: The Look*. London: Omnibus Press.

Roy, Elodie A. 2014. "Perfect Pop Story: Sarah Records (1987–1995)." In *LitPop: Writing and Popular Music*, edited by Rachel Carroll and Adam Hansen, 63–75. Farnham, Burlington: Ashgate.

Sandbrook, Dominic. 2019. *Who Dares Wins: Britain, 1979–1982*. London: Penguin.

Seabrook, Jeremy. 1982. *Unemployment*. London: Quartet Books.

Spitz, Marc. 2014. *Twee: The Gentle Revolution in Music, Books, Television, Fashion, and Film*. New York: It Books.

Stanfill, Sonnet. 2013. Introduction to *80s Fashion: From Club to Catwalk*, edited by Sonnet Stanfill, 8–19. London: V&A.

Tarde, Gabriel. 1890. *Les lois de l'imitation*. Paris: Félix Alcan.

Williamson, Judith. 1985. *Consuming Passions: The Dynamics of Popular Culture*. London: Marion Boyars.

Wilson, Elizabeth. 1985. *Adorned in Dreams: Fashion and Modernity*. London: Virago.

Wright, Lee. 1993. "Outgrown Clothes for Grown-Up People." In *Chic Thrills: A Fashion Reader*, edited by Juliet Ash and Elizabeth Wilson, 49–57. Berkeley: University of California Press.

York, Peter. 1985. *Modern Times*. London: Futura.

3
Five Little Victorian Londons

Samantha Close

In 1973, Umberto Eco (1990, 65) identified the resurgence of interest in the Middle Ages as a way to deal with then-present troubles, as "the Middle Ages are the root of all our contemporary 'hot' problems . . . we go back to that period every time we ask ourselves about our origin." Now a decade or two into the new millennium and catching our breath as the cyberdust of the Digital Revolution starts to settle, we have unsurprisingly found ourselves looking back to the Industrial one. The Victorian era is, likewise, the origin of many contemporary "hot" problems, beginning quite literally with greenhouse gas emissions from industrial factories, overheating the planet and changing the earth's climate. Consider the obscene concentration of wealth in railroads and search engines: monopolistic technology-driven industries with robber barons at their heads. Or the invention and popularization of the telegraph and telephone, the "Victorian Internet," allowing information to move faster than previously thought possible (Standage 2014). Or the lingering toxic funk of colonialism, white supremacy, and conservative ethnic nationalism. Trying to imagine our way forward some decades after cultural critics declared the end of history, we are dreaming of Victorian London.

But where Eco is consistently dismissive of popular culture and despondent that people dream of fantasies, rather than the sober, scholarly Middle Ages, I see meaning precisely in subcultural aesthetic fantasies and the participatory culture that animates them. Today this means a dream not of the Middle Ages but of the Victorian age: steampunk. At an analytic level, steampunk is an aesthetic animated by participatory culture that coalesces around a mix of technofantasy, neo-Victorianism, and retrofuturism (Perschon 2010, 2011). Arguments about steampunk's politics (or lack thereof) have raged both within and without fannish spaces for years, perhaps best indexed by a flourishing "steampunk obituary" metadiscourse. As Sara Goodwin (2015) wrote for the *Mary Sue*, "apparently, steampunk was 'over' before I even discovered that it existed, and it seems that since I've been a fan it's died a few more times."

Steampunk fashion, however, flourishes. Cosplayers commonly deploy the aesthetic, either on its own or remixed with other canons. Goodwin (2015) described "be[ing] informed that steampunk is over and outdated (while selling steampunk items to customers) at my table." To me, this is a clear paradox. But some disagree. Eric Renderking Fisk (2017) wrote that steampunk died precisely by becoming "'Steam-powered Fantasy Dress-up'...not 'punk' anything anymore." In other words, steampunk fashion's ascendancy marks "true" steampunk's obliteration. Clearly, steampunk cannot be approached as an ideological monolith. Equally, it exceeds meaningless postmodern play (Ferguson 2011). Rather, just as with Eco's overdetermined Middle Ages, different fans dream of very different Victorian Londons. In this chapter, I analyze the steampunk aesthetic with a metonymic logic, looking at individual artifacts that materialize the "desire of part for whole which animates narrative and, in fact, creates the illusion of the real" (Stewart 1993, xii). These souvenirs of a world that never was narrate multiple Victorian Londons past and, through them, present desires (figure 3.1).

STEAMPUNK: AESTHETIC SUBCULTURE, SUBCULTURAL AESTHETIC

Before I focus on the particular artifacts, some background on steampunk is in order. Mike Rugnetta (2016) argues that the heart of aesthetic experience is that "while not everything *is* art, anything can be appreciated *as* art." Steampunk takes up this position in regard to history; the fandom appreciates the Victorian era as art, ripe for both adulation and remix. Steampunk heavily focuses on London, but fans have also congregated around other settings like the American westward expansion, and created new portmanteaus to steampunk these different eras.

Steampunk's origins are conventionally traced back to sci-fi literature and fandoms. The term *steampunk* was first used in print in a 1987 letter from American author K. W. Jeter to *Locus*, a magazine and trade journal for sci-fi and fantasy writing. Jeter was punning off of cyberpunk's popularity in describing his and others' work that looked to the past, rather than a dystopian future, for inspiration. The term stuck. As is perhaps appropriate for a retrofuturist aesthetic, fans have applied it backward as well as forward. In an influential fannish history of the genre, Cory Gross (2007) argues that

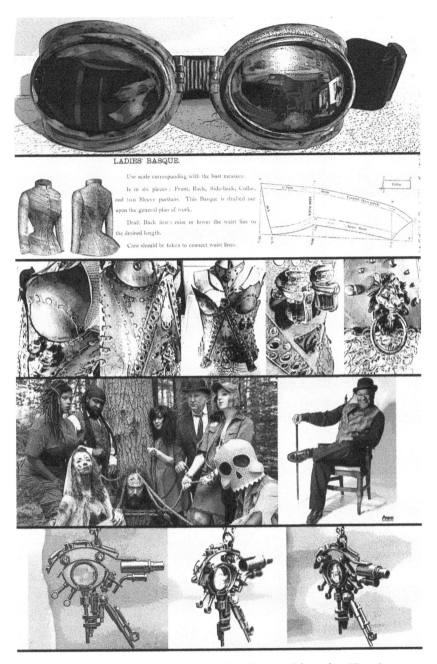

Figure 3.1. *Top to bottom:* DIY steampunk goggles, photograph by author; Victorian-era dress pattern from *The National Garment Cutter Book of Diagrams* (1888), scan by Etsy shop How to Books; steampunk corset crafted and photographed by Deadlance Steamworks, posted on Deviant Art; *The Army of Broken Toys* album cover, posted on Instagram by @armyoftoys (*left*), photo of Maurice Broaddus by Ankh Photography (*right*); "Eye of Horus" steampunk brass pendant by Denki Endorphin and A Story Tokyo.

steampunk began in the Victorian era itself, with the writings of H. G. Wells and Jules Verne.

In terms of the subculture, however, more fans arguably came to steampunk through maker culture (Perschon 2010). It is also difficult to account for the vibrant steampunk fandoms outside Anglophone spheres if we insist on tracing its origins back to English-language science fiction, whether Victorian or relatively modern. Antonija Primorac (2015) demonstrates that *translations* of canonical Victorian works—such as the Sherlock Holmes stories—are a much more appropriate origin for steampunk in Russia and Croatia than are the English-language works themselves. The rough span of years defined by the Victorian era is, in Japanese history, referred to as the Meiji era, which is itself a source for much historical, fictional, and material remixing. Beyond this, many Japanese writers and manga creators set original stories in their own fantasies of Victorian England (Jones 2015).

Theorized as a fandom, steampunk is unique in lacking a definitive canon. Even as fans may remix, critique, affirm, ignore, or transform their central canon into an alternate universe, its simple existence exerts a structuring force. For steampunk, some fashion designers argue that the relationship is reversed, such that steampunk "borrows steampunk fashion, not the reverse" (Rauch and Bolton 2010, 181). Steampunk provides further evidence that fannish crafting "is a medium for the artistic and transformative work of fans on a par with other forms of fan production," such as the oft-studied fan fiction or vid (Cherry 2016, 131).

Studying an aesthetic animated by participatory culture like this presents difficulties at the analytic and methodological levels. Although not quite as diffuse as aesthetic categories like zany, interesting, and cute, steampunk is less a style (and certainly less a genre) than it is "discursive judgments—culturally formalized ways of publicly sharing our pleasures and displeasures" (Ngai 2010, 954). It is the same kind of cultural phenomenon as the shōjo, a "family of forms" instantly recognizable but devilishly difficult to pin down (Lunning 2011). In the sections that follow, I approach this problem metonymically by closely considering individual articles of clothing and musical lyrics, then extrapolating the whole fantasy of Victorian London that these parts narrate. There are five such wholes: Revolutionary London, Historical London, Aesthetic London, Dandy London, and Imperial London.

REVOLUTIONARY LONDON

> *I made my own machine.*
> *Yes, we're building steam.*
> *I hate the same routine.*
> —Abney Park, "Building Steam"

Consider perhaps the most ubiquitous signifier of the steampunk aesthetic: brass goggles. In terms of physical function and design, brass goggles may be aviation goggles, welding goggles, lab goggles, and so on. Brass signifies effortful, physical work. The ability to artfully patinate and scuff it distinguishes brass from the plastics and stainless steels of modern technology; its character as an industrial, working metal distinguishes it from the merely precious gold or silver. This association with function means that "even the most elegant of steampunk outfits can obtain the grungy, punk feel of the subculture with the inclusion of goggles" (Steampunk Wiki 2022).

Brass goggles index the participatory, DIY element of the aesthetic. Consider my goggles in figure 3.1. They're instantly recognizable and yet simple to make—they started life as an inexpensive pair of swim googles that I painted to give the sense of aged metal. Many simple brass goggle tutorials exist, some requiring only toilet paper rolls, masking tape, and brads (Tinkergirl 2006). Although the goggles are ostensibly eyewear, steampunk fans rarely wear brass goggles over their eyes. They function much more commonly as necklaces, hair pieces, hat bands, and the like. This practice means there is no shame in having goggles you can't actually see through—further lowering the necessary skill, time, and expense involved. On the other hand, there is almost no limit to how elaborate brass goggles can be. Online galleries show jaw-dropping pieces with multiple working lenses, elaborate designs, and high-quality but difficult-to-work materials. This range of examples, from low-bar invitations to try to high-quality exemplars to inspire, is essential for participatory cultures to function (Ito 2010). And this is Revolutionary London's essence, as narrated by Abney Park: participation (I made my own machine) and community effort (we're building steam) against a backdrop of clearly demarcated hierarchy (the same routine). Revolutionary London heavily romanticizes this participation, embodying what Gross (2007, 2019) terms "nostalgic" steampunk.

A story of participatory rebellion against the status quo is politically undefined, as the contemporary upsurge of both progressive and regressive populist movements suggests. World-weary but brilliant (cis, straight, white) men struggling against the confining (artificial, feminine, politically correct) social order can easily inhabit Revolutionary London, propping up the hegemonic neoliberal ideals that plague maker and cyber cultures both. But so too can postcolonial rebellion. As steampunk fan and scholar Diana M. Pho (2009) points out, "steampunk subverts so much, so let's have it subvert our histories too . . . let [steampunk] also be about the Boxer Rebellion and King Chulalongkorn of Siam, and fighting the British Raj."

HISTORICAL LONDON

> The difficulty, however, is one that can easily be overcome by the simple remedy of "knowing how."
>
> —Butterick, *The Dressmaker*, 1911

Historical London is Revolutionary London's antithesis. It is the twin of Eco's favored historical Middle Ages. Fantasies of Historical London are devoid of romanticism, much like the "melancholic" steampunk outlook (Eco 1990, 71). It is constructed largely from research rather than remix. What tales it has are those of a realist who would, for instance, "recognize that women were unfairly restricted by a patriarchal society and that first-wave feminism was tied to repugnant authoritarian ideologies, without making excuses for either" (Gross 2019). So far, so true, and indeed welcome.

But it's telling that Historical London's inhabitants reject fashion. As Gross (2019) sneers, "Melancholic Steampunk is relentlessly un-Romantic and consequently difficult to translate into a fashionable couture." Eco (1990, 70–71) similarly writes: "This philological attitude can be applied either to great historical events or to the imperceptibility of underlying social and technological structures, and to the forms of everyday life. Fortunately in this case no one would speak of 'medieval fashion.'" Only a patriarchal analytic lens could suggest that the "forms of everyday life" do not include clothing. Such a Historical London rejects femininity—fashion, affect, intensive personal participation—through its rejection of romanticism. This rejection is thus not of clothing's existence so much as of its importance.

Ironically, part of the Industrial Revolution's history is the widespread democratization of fashionable clothing. Technologies such as the sewing machine and paper patterns, like the dress pattern in figure 3.1, put metropolitan fashions within reach of both lower-class and more rural home sewers (Fernandez 1994; Dickson 1979). These same technologies also heralded conflict between artisanal tailoring and dressmaking guilds with mass-production factories that employed poor women and children in hideously dangerous work. Contemporary parallels abound in the conflict between fast fashion, made overwhelmingly by Global South workers in sweatshop conditions, and Global North activism seeking to return to handmade or "Made in the USA" clothing.

Here and there are glimpses of a Historical London open to the feminine. E-commerce platform Etsy's dual emphasis on the vintage and the handmade allows shops like How to Books, which restores and digitizes Victorian-period craft manuals, to circulate patterns (like the excerpt in figure 3.1) among fans. History-focused groups on fiber arts platform Ravelry value "what research into the historical record or re-enactment of the crafting methods as a form of living history can tell us about making and the made in the past" (Cherry 2016, 162). Making clothing according to a period pattern, including on a sewing machine, is a historically accurate form of steampunk participation. But perhaps because the loudest Historical Londoners reject femininity and fashion so strongly, these largely female fans rarely see themselves as steampunk at all. They tend to identify instead with historical reenactment societies or others using the same craft techniques.

AESTHETIC LONDON

> (Tea-party face with an airship ruffle) Lady has bustle!
> —Desert Rose Theatre, "Lady Has Bustle" (Baby Got Back parody video)"

In Aesthetic London, it's all about the style. This fantasy of the city lies an easy distance from fashion subcultures such as Goth, Lolita, kink, and the American Wild West. In stark contrast to Historical London, Aesthetic London fans take Victorian clothing design as a creative springboard, not an ideal, and gleefully explore the fantastical possibilities of corsets, hats, pouches, belts, boots, buckles, leather, lace, feathers, brass, brocade, copper, velvet, and even bone. It is the most immediately recognizable of the Victorian Londons and the one most commonly satirized and critiqued. As craft humor website Regretsy put it, to make something steampunk one can "just glue some gears on it (and call it steampunk)."

Consider the corset in figure 3.1. It is custom made and demonstrates how Aesthetic London corsets, unlike historical Victorian ones, are worn as outerwear. Both underbust and overbust corset styles are common. Unlike in the tight-lacing kink corset subcultures, steampunk fans don't pay much attention to the waist measurement—many replace laces with belt buckles (Steele 1996). This opens Aesthetic London and steampunk fashion to many who are ignored by mainstream fashion. As Sheyne Fleischer of the performance art troupe League of S.T.E.A.M. puts it, "I am a woman of a size. And I think— many of us think—that curvy girls can rock steampunk" (Fleischer et al. 2011). The emphasis is on embellishment, not containment. Like Deadlance Steamworks' piece in figure 3.1, corsets often incorporate weapon holsters, tool belts, and all manner of pouches, imagining an active wearer prepared for any situation they might encounter in the field. Leather, brocade, and the suggestion of metal are the most popular materials, transforming the body into a firm, self-possessed, even armored surface that is clearly visible but also not accessible by touch.

Female steampunk fans largely position their fashion practice as one of empowered sexuality and agency, in much the same way as Desert Rose Theatre of Mesa, Arizona, remixes Sir Mix-A-Lot's song "Baby Got Back" with a female point-of-view in its "Lady Has Bustle." Writer and lead Katherine Stewart warns potential suitors to beware of accidentally stepping on her long trailing dress lest she "box your ears." This is a significantly more feminist take than that of the original song, emphatically so when compared to versions that hail from other Victorian Londons. In Danny Birt's "Lady Hath Bustle," for example, he enthuses that "You could teach a camel to hump / with that antithesis of a masculine rump."

It's uncommon, though not unheard of, for men to wear steampunk corsets. Instead, the two defining symbolic elements of the corset persist for men but are signified by two different articles of clothing. The MacGyver corset, with all its pouches and tools, becomes a piratical aeronaut greatcoat full of visible holsters and secret pockets. The armored, defined corset becomes the elegant three-piece suits and military uniforms of the aristocrat, all precise, contained power.

Aesthetic London's inhabitants tend to be utterly blind to race and cultural appropriation, as also demonstrated by "Lady Has Bustle." White steampunk fans seem surprised but inspired by the way that Mix-A-Lot's idealized woman "sounds a lot like a Victorian lady wearing a corset and bustle . . . an 'itty bitty waist and a round thing in your face'" (Megan S. 2012). But this similarity between the natural shape of many Black women's bodies and the corset-and-bustle silhouette is not coincidental. Victorian England saw the rise of world's fairs and other home-country exhibitions of colonized peoples. This notably included the Khoikhoi woman Saartjie "Sara" Baartman, who was exhibited across Europe as the "Hottentot Venus" and likely inspired the Victorian "Hottentot bustle" (Hobson 2005, 61). European male fixation on Baartman as both an erotic and an ethnographic spectacle crystallized into a cultural turning point whereby fatness became "an intrinsically black, and implicitly off-putting, form of feminine embodiment in the European scientific and popular imagination" (Strings 2019, 89). The "hip-hop booty," prominently featured in Sir Mix-A-Lot's original song, represents the same association between Blackness, femininity, fatness, and hypersexuality but is remixed to have a more positive valence (Durham 2012; Hobson 2005).

Steampunk's sense of itself as a cultural outsider further blocks meaningful engagement with cultural appropriation. One fan argues that "Lady Has Bustle" could not be an instance of cultural appropriation because "it's not taking something negatively associated with Black culture and using it to try and be cool (unless the definition of that word has changed since I was a kid)" (Bruin-Molé 2016). If steampunk fannishness cannot be cool, in other words, it cannot be guilty of cultural appropriation. Such an argument misses both the intrafandom workings of cultural capital and the growing impact—largely through white fans—that geek culture has on the mainstream.

A prominent refrain in the "who killed steampunk?" discourse opposes Aesthetic London, "people . . . drawn to steampunk because of the stories and the style," with Revolutionary London, or "an arrogant attempt to politicize [steampunk]" (Ottens 2019). This critique singles out steampunk fans, predominantly of color, who critique steampunk practices like the "Victorientalist" steampunk, which uncritically replicates—or even glorifies—Victorian Britain's colonialism. Aesthetic London here follows the depressing trajectory that Rukmini Pande (2018) outlines whereby white fans demonize fans of color when they point out racism within their fandoms, rhetorically positioning them as outside agitators seeking to politicize pleasure rather than fellow steampunks developing the subculture further.

DANDY LONDON

> Shit—don't you start it. I beg your pardon.
>   —the Harlem James Gang, "My Strut Is Incredible"

Consider the vest. Specifically, the brightly colored and patterned vests worn in figure 3.1 by Walter Sickert, of the Boston-based musical group the Army of Broken Toys, and Maurice Broaddus, author of *Pimp My Airship* among several other books. In giving advice on a shared androgynous wardrobe that would satisfy partners with steampunk and glam punk styles, Sarah Rose (2016) points to the patterned vest as a staple piece that "creates a polished, traditionally masculine of center look that's fun to play with." That play is particularly effective when the vest's fabric incorporates bold, attention-grabbing, colors and patterns. Vests are formal and masculine, a key part of the three-piece suit, and, simultaneously, informal and feminine through their bright colors and intricate patterns. Like corsets, vests also offer an attachment point for steampunk accoutrements like pocket watches, weaponry, and emergency teacups. Musicians and other performers often adopt the vest for how it lets them move on stage while also conveying their inherent fabulousness.

Dandy London is the fantasy of the fabulous, "a unique set of aesthetic properties engaged by people who take the risk of making a spectacle of themselves—when it would be much easier, though no less toxic, to be normative" (Moore 2018, 22). "Dandy" fashion is a predominantly male style that developed in the Black diaspora as well as European queer cultures (Kelley 1996; Miller 2009). Dandy steampunk shares elements with both Revolutionary London and Aesthetic London but is distinct from both in its fusion of marginalized ethnicities, sexualities, and gender identities with performative sartorial spectacle. Both Aesthetic and Revolutionary Londons build on steampunk fashion as a collection of floating signifiers, able to take on a wide variety of specific meanings structured by the general narrative. Dandy Londoners know that despite what any one fan of any ethnicity might want to be true, "much of this fashion—for people of African descent and other People of Color—represents oppression, suppression, theft, rape, murder and enslavement" (Balogun 2012). Dandy London accepts this but insists, nevertheless, on its possible value.

The Harlem James Gang's "My Strut is Incredible" exemplifies Dandy London in its lyrics by mashing up African American Vernacular English construction, "shit—don't you start it," with a steampunk invocation of Victorian manners, "I beg your pardon." "Start shit" first appeared in print as an expression meaning "make trouble" in the urban novel *Street Players* (1973) by Donald Goines. Goines's protagonist, "Earl the Black Pearl," is a dandy whose style perfectly matches his luxurious Cadillac, unlike (as the text puts it) other Black men who have the wealth to own and drive such a car but who persist in wearing work uniforms while doing so. Goine's work has been cited as influential by a number of Black musicians, particularly rappers like Nas and Ludacris. Dandy London reflects the way Black media fans create enclave networked spaces for themselves where they can "engage in a culturally inflected fandom that uses Black culture to interpret and celebrate their beloved media text, often reading Black cultural specificity into a text with a notable absence of Black bodies" (Florini 2019, 1.4). This retrofuturism grasps the fashions of the past to create a utopia in the present for people whom imperial Victorian Britain would have denied a future.

IMPERIAL LONDON

> *A man can lose himself, in a country like this.*
> *Rewrite the story;*
> *Recapture the glory.*
>
> —Rush, in collaboration with Kevin J. Anderson, "Seven Cities of Gold"

Imperial London is the villain in Revolutionary London's tales, and the threat that makes Dandy London's beauty so fragile. It is what happens when Aesthetic London's romanticism collides with Historical London's reminder that London was not only a city nestled amongst the home counties but an imperial capital. Pith-helmeted safari explorers off to adventure in virgin lands, stern military officers with clinking medals on their neat uniforms who shout "For Albion," and majestic royals on whose noble brows sit the crown inhabit Imperial London.

The pith helmet is the most obvious correlate of Imperial London, as commonly mentioned by steampunk fans who decry it as it is by those who excuse it. But this hat, which "embodie[s] adventure into the unknown, discovery, grit, adventure and various other Pulp accoutrements" only to the extent that the fan ignores the sovereignty and perhaps even the existence of non-English Victorians, is too obvious (Morris 2019). It could as well fit into Revolutionary London's rugged individualist tales of adventurous misfits shocking the bourgeoise—this is often how white nationalist steampunk fans seem to see themselves when complaining about political correctness.

Instead, consider the Eye of Horus pendant in figure 3.1. It is created and sold by Japanese shop A Story Tokyo, known for its expensive, handmade steampunk watches and other accessories. The pendant is aesthetically breathtaking: it arranges cast-off screws, bolts, tubes, and wing nuts to depict the ancient Egyptian religious symbol the Eye of Horus. All the mechanical bits and bobs display slightly differing but coordinating shades of brass and copper, lightly patinaed but still shining. A thick glass lens sits at the center of the eye, and the pendant's soldered lines draw both Horus and the viewer's eye toward the mock "telescope" arrangement on the pendant's left.

This pendant is steeped in the logic of Egyptology, the Orientalist study of Egypt by the British and French, which strongly affected Victorian fashion. Egyptology remains today—just consider the eclectic selection in many bookstores' "Egypt section . . . a mismatch of pharaohs' biographies, introductions to ancient Egyptian art, and mummification manuals . . . one may also find speculative treatises on an alien connection to the pyramids." The Eye of Horus, in particular, is so commonly adopted to signify ancient Egypt that it has become "symbolic of the Western predatory gaze on a former European colony which continues to be culturally pillaged" (Mentxaka 2018, 175, 189). The pendant materializes this by having the eye look through a telescope not once but twice. First, a convex lens, the type used in telescopes and binoculars, is placed directly in the eye itself. Then, the left-to-right design mimics the posture of so many pith-helmeted explorers eager to map so-called uncharted lands—and thus, as the Rush lyrics above suggest, re-create themselves as glorious heroes. This reorientation of perspective is not just cultural appropriation of a religious symbol but also part of the process by which "the local European history turned into a narrative of global history," and other local histories were deemphasized or ignored (Langer 2017, 183). This has had such an impact on steampunk that many, particularly white, fans only belatedly (and only through engagement with antiracist steampunk critiques) "realized that the Victorian age covers a world; but Victorian England does not" (Morris 2019).

What makes this pendant particularly illustrative of Imperial London is that it emerges from Japanese steampunk, not from British or even Western fans. Japan did not, historically, colonize Egypt. An Anglocentric Historical London might place Japanese steampunk within Dandy London, noting that the "Victorientalism" within steampunk discriminates against Japanese steampunks. Which, to be clear, it does—particularly for steampunk fans of Japanese heritage living in Western countries. But such a characterization repeats the mistake of Orientalism by not centering the perspective of the

Eastern Other, instead continuing to view Japan from the West but with a different political inflection. When considered independently of its relationship with the West, Japan has a long imperialist history. Its contemporary society remains entangled with structural racism against Indigenous, Korean, and Brazilian Japanese peoples. Colonial tropes resonate through its popular culture, much as they do through England's (Katsuno and Maret 2004). Imperial London's inhabitants are not only the British but all steampunks who enthusiastically adopt imperialist modes.

CONCLUSION: RETROFUTURIST SOUVENIRS

Somehow, it seems that nothing is ever supposed to be about fashion. If you read the cultural theory canon, fashion is either the place where meaning goes to die (Fredric Jameson) or something to be unmasked as simply a sign of wealth and status (Thorstein Veblen). Even an aca-fan (academic fan) very alive to popular material culture's power can fall into the trap of rhetorically discarding fashion, writing "steampunk is no more about the goggles than Cyberpunk was about the mirrorshades: they both simply constitute powerful metaphors" for alternative worldviews (Jenkins 2013). But at the same time, fashion is arguably the "most popular aesthetic practice of all" since just about everyone wears clothes—even men (Wilson 2009, 452). Not everyone, however, wears steampunk clothes.

Steampunk fashion, like shōjo or kink, is the materialization of half-known, half-unknown narratives (Lunning 2011; Steele 1996). Like all souvenirs, it "must be removed from its context in order to serve as a trace of it, but it must also be restored through narrative and/or reverie" (Stewart 1993, 150). Unlike with other souvenirs, its context is an invented history, an imagined place. These fantasies of Victorian London "underwrite our present efforts to imagine possibilities for the future, to enact transformations in the present, and to think critically about time" (Lothian 2018, 4). And we have never needed to think more critically about time than now, as we "live in the future" only to find our present ways of living systematically destroying the conditions for life. This dystopian reality inspires many to want a radical break with the past, a chance to start over and imagine anew. Steampunk fashion argues this is impossible. Our imaginations can never be innocent; they inevitably draw inspiration from our problematic past. What we can do is craft our relationship to that past carefully, accepting its problems but remixing them into a story that leads to a better future.

REFERENCES

Balogun. 2012. "The Mahogany Masquerade: The Politics of Fashion in Steamfunk!" *Chronicles of Harriet* (blog), October 1, 2012. https://chroniclesofharriet.com/2012/09/30/the-mahogany-masquerade-the-politics-of-fashion-in-steamfunk/

Bruin-Molé, Megen de. 2016. "Bustle Envy (Steampunk Meets Sir Mix-a-Lot)." *Frankenfiction* (blog), June 22, 2016. http://frankenfiction.com/bustle-envy/

Cherry, Brigid. 2016. *Cult Media, Fandom, and Textiles: Handicrafting as Fan Art*. London: Bloomsbury Academic.

Dickson, Carol Anne. 1979. "Patterns for Garments: A History of the Paper Garment Pattern Industry in America to 1976." PhD diss., Ohio State University.

Durham, Aisha. 2012. "'Check on It': Beyoncé, Southern Booty, and Black Femininities in Music Video." *Feminist Media Studies* 12 (1): 35–49.

Eco, Umberto. 1990. *Travels in Hyper Reality: Essays*. Translated by William Weaver. San Diego: Harcourt Brace.

Ferguson, Christine. 2011. "Surface Tensions: Steampunk, Subculture, and the Ideology of Style." *Neo-Victorian Studies* 4 (2): 66–90.

Fernandez, Nancy Page. 1994. "Innovations for Home Dressmaking and the Popularization of Stylish Dress." *Journal of American Culture* 17 (3): 23–33.

Fisk, Eric Renderking. 2017. "Requiem for Steampunk." *The Fedora Chronicles* (blog), March 4, 2017. https://thefedorachronicles.com/rants/2017/requiem_for_steampunk.html

Fleischer, Sheyne, Nick Bauman, Robin Blackburn, and Russell Isler. 2011. "The Guild." *S.T.E.A.M.Geeks*, September 15, 2011. Podcast, 1:05:48. http://leagueofsteam.com/steamgeeks/blog/2011/09/steam-geeks-18

Florini, Sarah. 2019. "Enclaving and Cultural Resonance in Black 'Game of Thrones' Fandom." *Transformative Works and Cultures* 29. https://doi.org/10.3983/twc.2019.1498

Goodwin, Sara. 2015. "What Is Steampunk, and Is It 'Over'?" *Mary Sue* (blog), December 23, 2015. https://www.themarysue.com/what-is-steampunk-and-is-it-over/

Gross, Cory. 2007. "Varieties of Steampunk Experience: Nostalgic versus Melancholic." *SteamPunk Magazine*, March 2007.

Gross, Cory. 2019. "Revisiting Nostalgic and Melancholic Steampunk: Correcting the 'Varieties of Steampunk Experience.'" *Never Was Magazine* (blog), September 8, 2019. https://neverwasmag.com/2019/09/revisiting-nostalgic-and-melancholic-steampunk-correcting-the-varieties-of-steampunk-experience/

Hobson, Janell. 2005. *Venus in the Dark: Blackness and Beauty in Popular Culture*. New York: Routledge.

Ito, Mizuko. 2010. "The Rewards of Non-Commercial Production: Distinctions and Status in the Anime Music Video Scene." *First Monday* 15 (5). https://doi.org/10.5210/fm.v15i5.2968

Jenkins, Henry. 2013. "Foreword: Any Questions?" In *Vintage Tomorrows*, edited by James H. Carrott and Brian David Johnson, vii–xvi. Beijing: O'Reilly.

Jones, Anna Maria. 2015. "'Palimpsestuous' Attachments: Framing a Manga Theory of the Global Neo-Victorian." *Neo-Victorian Studies* 8 (1): 17–47.

Katsuno, Hirofumi, and Jeffrey Maret. 2004. "Localizing the Pokémon TV Series for the American Market." In *Pikachu's Global Adventure: The Rise and Fall of Pokémon*, edited by Joseph Jay Tobin, 80–107. Durham, NC: Duke University Press.

Kelley, Robin D. G. 1996. *Race Rebels: Culture, Politics, and the Black Working Class*. New York: Free Press.

Langer, Christian. 2017. "The Informal Colonialism of Egyptology: From the French Expedition to the Security State." In *Critical Epistemologies of Global Politics*, edited by Marc Woons and Sebastian Weier, 182–202. Bristol: E-International Relations.

Lothian, Alexis. 2018. *Old Futures: Speculative Fiction and Queer Possibility*. New York: New York University Press.

Lunning, Frenchy. 2011. "Under the Ruffles: Shojo and the Morphology of Power." *Mechademia* 6, *User Enhanced*, 3–20.

Megan S. 2012. "Baby Got Bustle." *Stellar Four* (blog), March 5, 2012. http://www.stellarfour.com/2012/03/baby-got-bustle.html

Mentxaka, Aintzane Legarreta. 2018. "Egypt in Western Popular Culture: From Bram Stoker to *The Jewel of the Nile*." *Otherness: Essays and Studies* 6 (2): 162–93.

Miller, Monica L. 2009. *Slaves to Fashion: Black Dandyism and the Styling of Black Diasporic Identity*. Durham, NC: Duke University Press.

Moore, Madison. 2018. *Fabulous: The Rise of the Beautiful Eccentric*. New Haven, CT: Yale University Press.

Morris, Colin. 2019. "Steampunk Is Dead, Who Told Steampunk?" *Von Explaino* (blog), April 19, 2019. https://vonexplaino.com/blog/posts/article/2019/04/steampunk-is-dead-who-told-steampunk.html

Ngai, Sianne. 2010. "Our Aesthetic Categories." *PMLA* 125 (4): 948–58.

Ottens, Nick. 2019. "Who Killed Steampunk?" *Never Was Magazine* (blog), April 14, 2019. https://neverwasmag.com/2019/04/who-killed-steampunk/

Pande, Rukmini. 2018. *Squee from the Margins: Fandom and Race*. Iowa City: University of Iowa Press.

Perschon, Mike. 2010. "Steam Wars." *Neo-Victorian Studies* 3 (1): 127–66.

Perschon, Mike. 2011. "Advocating for Aesthetic." *STEAMED!* (blog), July 14, 2011. https://ageofsteam.wordpress.com/2011/07/14/advocating-for-aesthetic/

Pho, Diana M. [dmp]. 2009. "Thoughts about Orientalism, Imperialism & Steampunking Asia." *Tales of the Urban Adventurer* (blog), June 25, 2009. https://dmp.dreamwidth.org/848.html

Primorac, Antonija. 2015. "Other Neo-Victorians: Neo-Victorianism, Translation and Global Literature." *Neo-Victorian Studies* 8 (1): 48–76.

Rauch, Eron, and Christopher Bolton. 2010. "A Cosplay Photography Sampler." *Mechademia* 5, *Fanthropologies*, 176–90.

Rose, Sarah. 2016. "Qweary: Capsule Steampunk Wardrobe?" *Qwear Fashion* (online platform), April 5, 2016. https://www.qwearfashion.com/home/2016/4/5/qweary -capsule-steampunk-wardrobe

Rugnetta, Mike. 2016. "What Is ~A E S T H E T I C~ Experience?" Uploaded by PBS Idea Channel, February 24, 2016. YouTube video, 14:24. https://www.youtube.com/wa tch?v=Q_rQbXlmgHI

Standage, Tom. 2014. *The Victorian Internet: The Remarkable Story of the Telegraph and the Nineteenth Century's Online Pioneers*. New York: Bloomsbury.

Steampunk Wiki. 2022. "Steampunk Fashion." Last modified July 1, 2022. https://stea mpunk.fandom.com/wiki/Steampunk_fashion

Steele, Valerie. 1996. *Fetish: Fashion, Sex, and Power*. New York: Oxford University Press.

Stewart, Susan. 1993. *On Longing: Narratives of the Miniature, the Gigantic, the Souvenir, the Collection*. Durham, NC: Duke University Press.

Strings, Sabrina. *Fearing the Black Body: The Racial Origins of Fat Phobia*. New York: New York University Press, 2019.

Tinkergirl. 2006. "How-To: Costume Goggles." *Brass Goggles: The Lighter Side of Steampunk* (blog), October 30, 2006. http://brassgoggles.co.uk/blog/steampunk-resour ces/how-to-quick-costume-goggles/

Wilson, Elizabeth. 2009. "Fashion and Postmodernism." In *Cultural Theory and Popular Culture: A Reader*, edited by John Storey, 4th ed., 444–53. Harlow, UK: Pearson Longman.

PART II

Sartorial Fandom as Business, Lifestyle, and Brand

4

Fanning the Flames of Fan Lifestyles at Hot Topic

Avi Santo

Scouring Hot Topic's online selection of fandom-themed fashions, I recently came across a white T-shirt with black print that said: "My Fandom > Your Fandom" (figure 4.1). The T-shirt's generic design and lack of reference to any particular fandom implies that at Hot Topic they are largely interchangeable. Moreover, the T-shirt's messaging suggests a competitive dimension to fandom, where individuals must find ways to differentiate themselves from others seeking membership in the same club. Meanwhile, the model who wears the T-shirt bears a disdainful expression as she glares at the camera. Her pink highlights, dark mascara and lipstick, studded leather bracelet, and visible shoulder tattoo are all recognizable signifiers of Hot Topic's version of "alternative," which has repeatedly been critiqued as inauthentic, conformist, and commoditized (Hanks 2011). The version of fandom Hot Topic promotes simultaneously appears to be outside the mainstream but also comfortably uses licensed and branded commodities to express its outsiderness. Perhaps unsurprisingly, the T-shirt was sold out when I encountered it, in late 2019.

In some ways this T-shirt and other fancentric items available for sale at Hot Topic could be seen as epitomizing Dick Hebdige's (1979) classic assertions about the commodification of subcultural styles by market forces as part of a broader hegemonic process of incorporation. Yet, this does not fully capture the value of these items of clothing for Hot Topic's shifting brand identity or consumer engagement practices. Nor does it reflect how some fan identities and practices have adapted to—and, frankly, have always coexisted with and been formed within—consumer capitalism (Carter 2018). In this essay, I am particularly interested in how the category of fandom is now being reconceptualized by retailers like Hot Topic as part of the industrial turn toward lifestyle branding, wherein branded merchandise is an integral resource through which people can assert their uniqueness, style, and worldview and cultivate what Sarah Banet-Weiser (2012) calls their "self-brand." I

Figure 4.1. "My
Fandom > Your
Fandom" T-shirt on
HotTopic.com.

argue that today's brand owners, licensors, and retailers are explicitly court-
ing consumers as fans—or inviting them to see themselves as fans—while
depicting fandom as a desirable assertion of difference and distinction from
societal norms, albeit one rooted in mainstream consumerism and brand
culture. While fan lifestyle brands do not rely exclusively on apparel, clothing
is often a key driver of lifestyle branding.

Through the prism of lifestyle branding, there has been an increased focus
on coordinating self-branding with product promotion as a form of entrepreneurship boosted by brand affiliation. I refer to such emergent practices as
"curatorial mediation," wherein consumers are encouraged to fashion their
identities on social media platforms by promoting their purchases, often by
wearing them. Curatorial mediation is perfectly attuned to industry-friendly
conceptualizations of fandom as emphasizing a relationship to branded consumer products that offer opportunities for self-expression. It is also perfectly

attuned to the contemporary social media environment. Curation is mediated through the affordances of online social media platforms that encourage a conflation of self-expression and self-promotion and the promulgation of networked individualism, wherein belonging to a community seems predicated on standing out within it (Wellman et al. 2003).

Curation has transformational potential to challenge the organizational logics of the scriptural economy, but, filtered through neoliberalism's emphasis on self-promotion, curatorial mediation is typically apolitical and often brand agnostic beyond what a given media property might convey about the curator's self-brand and investment in a fan lifestyle. Curatorial mediation typically exhibits a fascination with fandom's self-transformational potential as expressed through the fan gear one wears and shares.

Curatorial mediation conflates curation of the self with curation of branded merchandise (Marwick 2013). As is often the case in the current neoliberal climate of aspirational work, curatorial mediation is typically performed as a form of unpaid labor with the promise that it might be parlayed into capital (Duffy and Hund 2015). Curatorial mediation is increasingly encouraged by retailers as part of their loyalty programs and efforts to cultivate brand communities, wherein customers get to show off how their purchases exemplify their fandom and how, in turn, their fandom allows them to express themselves.

As such, I argue that the fandom-as-lifestyle category complicates the traditional binary within fan studies between affirmational and transformative forms of fandom. Rather, one's affirmation of industry-sanctioned merchandise is predicated on its transformative potential for that person to harness their self-brand and distinguish themselves among peers (Obsession Inc. 2009; Hills 2014). Complicating the traditional binary is useful for two intersecting purposes: (1) it recognizes how transformative potential is built in to the marketing and merchandising of licensed objects that otherwise seemingly encourage affirmation via their acquisition, which in turn complicates how media industries imagine consumer engagement; and (2) it challenges the notion that affirmational fans are uncritical consumers by placing greater emphasis on their self-interested objectives in acquiring licensed merchandise. For Hot Topic, curatorial mediation involves customers showing off their fan-inspired lifestyle in the service of demonstrating their #HTFandom. Through its #HTFandom efforts, designed to incentivize shoppers to become brand ambassadors, Hot Topic has championed curatorial mediation as acts of both transformation and affirmation via fandom. The hashtag captures both the affection shoppers are expected to have for the retailer if they hope to become its brand ambassadors and the notion that Hot Topic sells access to fandom as self-expression. Hot Topic emerges through these forms of curatorial mediation as a site both for and of fandom.

FANNING THE FANDOM LIFESTYLE AT HOT TOPIC

There can be little doubt that consumer products and licensed merchandise occupy an increasingly central role in how contemporary entertainment conglomerates develop media properties. In 2018, licensed merchandise accounted for US$280.3 billion in global retail sales and earned brand owners US$15 billion in royalties. Character and entertainment licenses were by far the greatest slice of the licensing pie, at 43.8 percent of all licensed products. Apparel was the largest product category for licensing, accounting for 15 percent of all licensed products, eclipsing both toys (12.6 percent) and fashion accessories (11.5 percent) (Licensing International 2019). Hot Topic exemplifies a new stage in the convergence of entertainment and retail, one focused on cultivating fandom as a lifestyle.

Hot Topic's investment in entertainment franchise–themed fashions is a continuation of a long-standing relationship between Hollywood and retailers in selling clothing inspired by films, television, and celebrity styles (Affuso and Santo 2018; Fortmueller in this collection). Of course, the imagined consumers of fashions inspired by *Queen Christina* (dir. Rouben Mamoulian, 1933) weren't necessarily thought of by retailers as "fans" of either the film or its star, Greta Garbo; rather, they were seen as women looking for guidance on emerging fashion trends, for whom the film offered inspiration (Gaines 1989). While there has always been an effort to court fans as consumers, this previously took place along the margins of retail, at memorabilia and comic book stores, through mail order and at conventions (Geraghty 2014). It was only in the late 1980s—commensurate with the arrival of Hot Topic in shopping malls across the United States—that T-shirts and other licensed apparel for films like *Batman* (dir. Tim Burton, 1989) began to be sold in department stores marketed at teen and adult demographics (Meehan 1991). From the mid-1990s onward, efforts to sell merchandise to fans have become increasingly mainstreamed, with a particular focus on so-called geeks as an emerging consumer category (Kohnen 2014). Geeks are overtly identified as fans and are typically envisioned both by the entertainment industry and by fan studies scholars as affirming rather than challenging the scriptural economy claimed by media corporations. Geeks do this through their acquisitional dispositions, which are understood to signify loyalty and filial devotion to texts produced by IP owners (as opposed to created by other fans) (Hills 2014).

Hot Topic explicitly identifies its core consumers as fans of popular culture. As a privately owned company, Hot Topic does not publicly disclose the precise amount of licensed merchandise that it sells, but 75 percent of the retailer's stock is estimated to consist of items inspired by films, TV, video games, and music (Mejia 2019). An exploration of Hot Topic's website (as of December 2019) quickly establishes the retailer as a significant outlet for entertainment-themed merchandise. Running across the top of Hot Topic's homepage are the shopping categories it privileges. The very first tab is "Popular Culture," and the drop-down menu lists nearly two dozen entertainment franchises for consumers to select from: everything from *Avengers* and *Beetlejuice* to *Harry Potter* and *Star Wars*. More traditional consumer categories like "Girls," "Guys," "Jeans," "Tees," and "Accessories" also exist, but under each of these tabs similar entertainment franchise categories are listed as ways to organize one's shopping experience. Virtually all the images used on the website feature licensed and branded merchandise. Even selecting a broad category like "Girls Button Up Tops" calls up a selection of models showcasing merchandise primarily identified with entertainment franchises, including *Stranger Things*, *The Lion King*, and *BeetleJuice*. In total, nine of the first twelve items listed under this category in December 2019 were officially licensed entertainment properties.

Hot Topic's first store opened in 1989 in Montclair, California. Early on, it identified itself as a site specializing in clothing and accessories associated with Goth, punk, and heavy metal subcultures, particularly for twelve-to-eighteen-year-old boys. By February 2008, Hot Topic operated 690 franchises across the United States and Canada (Hot Topic 2008; Mejia 2019). In February 2013, its annual report listed net sales of US$741,745,000 and net profits of US$19,470,000 (Hot Topic 2013). In part this boom contributed to its acquisition by Sycamore Partners in 2013 for an estimated US$600 million (Hsu 2013). It was also during this period that the retailer began retooling its image by downplaying its music associations and ramping up its broader investment in popular culture. The company's 2008 annual report, for example, identifies a business strategy "built on the foundation of pop culture and its relevance to our target teen customer" (Hot Topic 2008).

Beyond its merchandise selection, this refocusing is evident in Hot Topic's hiring practices for retail staff. Where Hot Topic previously looked to hire teens and young adults who had knowledge about underground music and who embraced a punk/Goth/emo aesthetic, job ads—like a sales associate ad from 2019—now emphasize how employees are expected to "use [their] fandom knowledge to drive add-on sales" because "[customers] will be impressed by [their] product knowledge, customer experience skills, and use of the force." The tongue-in-cheek *Star Wars* reference signifies not only a move away from privileging music knowledge as cultural capital, but also the recognition of fan knowledge as a hirable job skill.

This shift can also be seen in the retailer's foray to Comic-Con, where, since 2014, it has cosponsored the Her Universe geek fashion show, for which it also hosts an annual after-party. Hot Topic has explicitly stated that its presence at Comic-Con and sponsorship of Her Universe's geek couture fashion show are intended "to see what everyone was wearing, what they were inspired by and what may be emerging among fans . . . [because] geek fashion has become an integral part of the culture and convention experience, not just in terms of what you can buy, but also in how it's being used by attendees to express themselves and connect with each other" (Granshaw 2015). Hot Topic eventually acquired Her Universe in 2018 (*License Global* 2018).

Hot Topic's rationale for investing in fandom is largely economic. Increasingly, marketers and retailers have stressed fandom as integral to mainstream consumer purchases. A 2016 *YPulse* study berated retailers for their slow embrace of fandom. It found that almost half of thirteen-to-thirty-three-year-olds said they were in a fandom and, moreover, that 58 percent of this subset had purchased something only because it was related to their fandom, averaging US$400 annually on those objects (*YPulse* 2016). Similarly, a study by marketing firm Troika (2017, 8) called *The Power of Fandom*, which sought to explain why brand owners needed to cultivate fandoms for their properties, claimed that 78 percent of surveyed individuals self-identified as "a fan of something," ergo, "almost all of us" are fans. Meanwhile, 17 percent of the millennials *YPulse* (2016) surveyed claimed to shop at Hot Topic. This claim both demonstrates the mainstreaming of shopping one's fandom, which Hot Topic facilitates, and gestures at the emerging fandom for Hot Topic, which the retailer actively cultivates.

While still looking to maintain a nonconformist air, Hot Topic, by embracing fandom, has repositioned itself from a site that attracted customers seeking things that would assist them in establishing their outsider status (and membership in outcast communities) to one that assists shoppers with their efforts to stand out among peers through merchandise that expresses their individual styles and tastes. In this configuration, rather than selling products to "outsiders," Hot Topic now sells the idea that everyone can be an outsider without ever needing to reject mainstream social positions or practices.

Accordingly, it might be argued that fandom has emerged as a marketable identity attainable through branded product acquisition. If "subcultures use material style and social practice to express and attempt to resolve the contradictions of mainstream culture" (Mullins 2013), fandom resolves tensions over consumerism as conformist by positioning the fan as rule breaker—with brand owners and retailers there to ensure that there is merchandise that can be acquired that will allow them to reject social conventions (all the while legitimating those same conventions). Hot Topic accomplishes this by celebrating the arrival of fan-supported franchises and fan-driven practices in the mainstream.

As one cultural commentator notes, Hot Topic is "still 'outsider-y,' . . . but welcoming to a wider range of outsiders" (PYMNTS.com 2016). Or, as a retail clerk explains, "When I shopped at Hot Topic a while ago, only a certain kind of person would shop there: people who were goth or emo. Now there's no specific group I can pinpoint. . . . There's something literally for everyone, no matter your age, gender, sexuality. . . . At Hot Topic, we accept you no matter who you are. You can be yourself here" (Newell-Hanson 2017). This assertion gets at a central tenet of the kind of inclusive fandom Hot Topic traffics in, namely, one comfortably situated within neoliberal constructions of the self: all sorts of different people can find *themselves* (as opposed to finding community) through the retailer's selection of merchandise. In short, shopping at Hot Topic is presented as an access point to fandom as a lifestyle.

According to Kacie Lynn Jung and Matthew Merlin (2002–3), lifestyle branding can be defined as a product or service that provides consumers with an emotional attachment to an identifiable lifestyle—the rugged outdoorsman, the posh executive, or an urban hipster, for example. The consumer then projects this lifestyle to society by purchasing and using particular brands. In making consumer products more central to its brand extension practices, the entertainment industry has not only folded merchandise into the transmedia mix, but also foregrounded the cultivation of franchise-friendly lifestyles as integral to continued consumer engagement with its brands (Santo 2019). Alison Hearn (2008) asserts that brands have gone from guaranteeing product quality to referencing consumer identities and lifestyles. Similarly, Sarah Banet-Weiser (2009, 91) argues, "brand culture functions as a kind of lifestyle politics . . . something someone is, or does, rather than pointing to a particular consumer good one purchases."

Significantly, fandom as lifestyle emphasizes individual forms of self-expression formed through relationships with branded objects over communal practices. The Troika (2017, 16) study specifically claims that "fandom is, first and foremost, a beneficial relationship between the self and an object of fandom," which allows individuals to both better understand and express themselves among people with similar tastes. The focus on fandom is about forming relationships with things rather than with people. This fits well with a lifestyle branding model, wherein objects are essential to crafting an identity that allows individuals to "feel instantly seen and understood" (Troika 2017, 14).

Hot Topic's marketing visually reproduces the logic that fandom is about individuals looking to stand out among their peers through their franchise-inspired attire. Hot Topic's models are often featured standing against an all-white background, typically staring directly into the camera. To the company's credit, it showcases a range of body types for its models, which contributes to the perception of its inclusivity. However, the type of fandom it sells via these models is clearly marked as individualistic and attention grabbing. None of the company's displays of fandom-inspired fashions feature models interacting with one another; they only interact with the would-be shopper. The model's eye contact signifies a desire to be looked at. The white backdrop presents a blank canvas onto which consumers can project their personal backgrounds. Though the fashion remains unchanged, what can be refashioned is the setting in which the clothing will allow its purchaser to stand out. Often, the accompanying product description positions fandom as a means of self-expression rather than textual or communal connection. For example, the description for a *She-Ra* hoodie (sold through the website in December 2019) asks, "Are you the Princess of Power, destined to save Etheria? Of course you are!" This girl-power messaging also dovetails with what Morgan Blue (2013) sees as the marketing of postfeminist celebrations of the self, where self-empowerment via consumption supposedly holds opportunity for self-expression and the overcoming of social inequities.

Hot Topic's shift from catering to would-be Goths and punks to supporting fandom has been billed as a response to a generational shift in the mindsets of teen consumers, who "reject being pigeonholed as just one thing and instead seek to communicate their varied, diverse interests and fandom preferences" (Mejia 2019). While fandom at Hot Topic is marketed as allowing individuals to express aspects of their personality and style through apparel acquisition and, in so doing, stand out among peers, the retailer also advances the notion that fandom does not require deep or filial investments in any one property, but rather is interchangeable depending on trends and personal preferences. This assertion fits with industry-friendly reconfigurations of fandom as nonexclusive and multiple, suggesting that fans move from one franchise to another with relative ease and according to what suits their personal tastes and identity needs at any given point in time. Troika (2017, 11) claims that on average people are members of at least five fandoms, which works well for media franchises and licensed merchandise programs that depend on cyclical consumer engagements.

Where multiple interchangeable expressions of fandom feed the lifestyle Hot Topic sells to consumers, this ability to stand out among peers also translates into opportunities for both self-branding and brand advocacy via the kinds of curatorial mediation practices the retailer endorses as a way for consumers to show off their #HTFandom. If fandom is not franchise specific at Hot Topic, it is still meant to promote a particular brand: Hot Topic itself.

CURATORIAL MEDIATION AND THE TRANSFORMATIVE POTENTIAL OF AFFIRMING HOT TOPIC

In 2016 Hot Topic introduced #HTFandom as a way for its customers to link their shopping experiences to their selfies on Instagram and other social media platforms. The hashtag allowed shoppers to show off their fandom-themed acquisitions and express aspects of their personal style while also showing their appreciation for the retailer that sold them these items. Over forty-five thousand photos had been uploaded to Instagram using the hashtag as of December 2019. The hashtag identifies Hot Topic as a site that sells fandom accoutrements, and it links various property-specific fandoms under the auspices of the Hot Topic brand, which in turn generates its own fannish devotion for providing consumers with access to fandom as lifestyle.

Fandom as lifestyle is expressed within many of the uploaded photos through the privileging of individuals over community: almost all the #HTFandom photos are of people posing in their Hot Topic–acquired outfit, either by themselves or with a person as prop, like a mall Santa or a Disneyworld employee in a Mickey Mouse costume. It is also expressed through descriptions that link posters' acquisitions to expressions of their mood, attitude, and personal aspirations. This is what Brooke Erin Duffy and Emily Hund (2015) call "carefully curated social sharing," which offers seemingly intimate yet largely mundane access to a social media poster's private thoughts and feelings. For example, singer-songwriter Zoey Rebecca captioned a photo of herself adorned in a *My Neighbor Totoro* T-shirt: "I literally don't think I've ever had a cold this bad in my entire 21 years of life. I actually feel like I've been punched in the face there is just so much pain in my sinuses. I'm typing this

Figure 4.2. Hot Topic fandom Instagram post of *My Neighbor Totoro* T-shirt by Zoey
Rebecca (@zoeyrebecca_), December 15, 2019.

with a tissue stuck in my nose. Enjoy that mental picture. Probably going to
bed early again tonight. So here's a not-old-but-not-new picture from when
I was feeling cute and looking fine #Htfandom" (@zoeyrebecca_, December
15, 2019; figure 4.2). Zoey Rebecca's post taps into the affective economy of
social media through a combination of strategies that maximize engagement, including confessional, fannish, and sartorial labor designed to center
attention on her. Rarely is there any discussion of the entertainment franchise the social media user is repping. Rather, fandom as lifestyle emphasizes
how these franchises support fans in expressing their individuality/creativ-
ity/personality to potential followers, who constitute a network of individuals jockeying for approval, recognition, and status, rather than a community
with a shared investment in a particular story world.

Similarly, Laina posted a photo to Instagram of herself in a *SpongeBob
SquarePants* T-shirt featuring the character of Squidward Tentacles kneeling
over a tombstone with the epithet "Here Lies Squidward's Hopes and Dreams."
Laina captioned the photo: "Quarantine Thingz . . . #Viral #HTFandom" (@X.
Langg, May 22, 2020). Instagram user Logan posted a photo of himself sitting
on his bed, wearing an exaggerated sad expression as well as a T-shirt featuring Disney princesses in various distressed poses. The photo is captioned:

"Me: I'm not a dramatic person! Also me . . . this shirt from @hottopic is literally my life . . . #socialdistancing #HomewithHT #Htfandom, #Htfanatic" (@whatdoyousuppose, May 2, 2020). While both posts were responding to the COVID-19 pandemic occurring at the time of their upload and could be read as attempts to form community among people practicing similar social distancing, it is also apparent that (1) both posts foreground the styles and personalities of their uploaders as expressed through their choice and curation of branded T-shirts, essentially stressing how they stand out even while sheltering at home; and (2) these fandoms are minimally concerned with the actual entertainment properties they are repping in their photos. *SpongeBob SquarePants* and Disney princesses serve their posters' interests in self-expression through affiliation with a fan lifestyle facilitated by Hot Topic.

While Instagram helps promote Hot Topic as the source responsible for these acts of self-expression, the conversion of fandom into lifestyle brand is fulfilled on Hot Topic's website, where hashtag users are also encouraged to share their photos. On the Hot Topic site, selecting an #HTFandom image doesn't call up personal details about the individual bearing the outfit. Rather, as the site blithely states (as of December 2019), these photos "can be shopped." Selecting an image links users to the product page for the outfit on display. Images meant to show off one's individual style become shopping opportunities for others seeking access to fandom-themed merchandise to accomplish the same. This encapsulates Duffy and Hund's (2015) assertion that entrepreneurial femininity within a neoliberal economy is repeatedly defined as working for and through consumption. That is, the social capital of the predominantly (roughly 90 percent) female #HTFandom participants is dependent on both their successful articulation of their unique brand identities through the objects they've acquired and their ability to persuade others that they too can establish a unique brand identity by acquiring these same objects.

Hot Topic has also created an additional tier linking the retailer to the fandom-as-lifestyle brand: Hot Topic Fanatics (HTF). HTF is a program that offers opportunities for individuals to become Hot Topic brand ambassadors via social media. Criteria for becoming an HTF includes possessing a personal style/brand that demonstrates one's fan credentials, and having the ability to cultivate one's own fanbase. HTFs are described on the website (as of December 2019) as being "well-versed in the latest binge-worthy show, anime, up-and-coming band, or style trend before it is a thing," taking "creative and elevated photos" that exclusively feature their original content, and having already accrued at least five thousand followers on a "single major social media platform." In other words, HTFs are microcelebrities who have successfully cultivated fans of the fan lifestyles they share. The link to the HTF application page makes clear that not everyone will be accepted, reinforcing the notion that fandom is a competitive activity where differentiation among peers is essential.

Ultimately, these practices can be linked to acts of curatorial mediation, which involves the showcasing of branded merchandise in order to reveal something distinct about its owner. Curatorial mediation blurs distinctions between self-promotion and brand promotion as wearing licensed fan fashions to express something unique about oneself also expresses something unique about the brand being curated (namely its ability to serve this self-expressive function). Essentially, Hot Topic's fandom and fanatic programs are intended to promote opportunities for participants to adapt the retailer's everyday cosplay and franchise-inspired wares into expressions of individuality by showing off how they wear them in ways similar to but also different from other consumers, and by showing how they can take something available for anybody to buy and wear and somehow make it their own. This can involve linking the item worn to selective self-disclosures, mixing and matching separates in different configurations, or using makeup and hairstyles to intensify or soften a look. Or it can be about situating a look in different settings, from private to public, formal to informal, leisure to work environments. The fan body, in how and where it is posed, curates the merchandise and mediates how it can be used to evoke a range of personal styles and modes of self-expression.

This is perhaps best evidenced in the linking of uploaded #HTFandom photos to sales pages featuring models in similar outfits. The comparison between the purchaser and the model is often quite striking. While the purchaser and model typically mirror each other in looking directly at the camera and being the singular/central focus of the photo, #HTFandom photos adapt these items within a wide range of settings (in contrast with the white background for the models) and for a variety of personality traits, body types, and personal styles, demonstrating how these material expressions of fandom, which are interchangeable on Hot Topic models, can be transformed by consumers into unique expressions of their individuality (figure 4.3).

If fandom as lifestyle affirms that licensed and branded apparel offers possibilities for consumers to express their individuality, then curatorial mediation offers the opportunity to convert these expressions into marketable forms of self-branding. It does so by promoting acts of curation as entrepreneurial forms of creation that coproduce both the brand and the

Figure 4.3. *My Neighbor Totoro* T-shirt modeled on the Hot Topic website.

self, allowing them to inform each other as well as the opinions of followers. Curation and mediation are both practices perfectly attuned to the current neoliberal focus on constant self-promotion through social media and
the entertainment industry's efforts to exploit fandom's "contested utility"
(Murray 2004). If the entertainment industry has invested in lifestyle branding as a means of fostering both intimate and ubiquitous identification with
media properties, then the lifestyle it has sought to cultivate—predominantly
through apparel licensing at retail—is commensurate with a version of fandom that affirms official franchise installations while suggesting that those
texts offer transformational opportunities for actualizing an identity rooted
in the styles, attitudes, affectations, and practices of fan communities. For
example, Instagram user helloghostyx posted about how Hot Topic's publishing one of her selfies on its website affirmed her career aspirations to be a
fashion influencer whose style is expressed by pairing Tim Burton–themed
Hot Topic merchandise with clown-inspired makeup: "Story time of how I

was on the @HotTopic website and how it gave me the courage to follow my dreams.... I was really discouraged at the time and this moment changed my views on everything. #HTFandom" (@helloghostyx, May 23, 2020).

Fan lifestyle products complicate the binary relationship typically asserted by fan studies scholars between different groups of fans and the media industries. Fan studies has often valorized transformational fans, those who engage in activities such as writing fan fiction, making fan vids, creating merchandise, or participating in cosplay performances that defy the scriptural economy as set by industrial intellectual property (IP) owners (Helleckson and Busse 2006). These fans have historically been set up in opposition to affirmational fans, who supposedly uncritically consume only texts and things sold to them by brand owners and sanctioned licensees. This binary is also typically gendered, with transformational fandom being associated with feminist and queer politics and practices, and affirmational fandom being positioned as supporting patriarchal and heteronormative systems aligned with the interests of corporate brand owners (Hills 2014). Suzanne Scott (2019), Elizabeth Affuso (2018), Bob Rehak (2013), and others have begun to challenge this binary by demonstrating, on the one hand, how object-oriented fans often transform the things they buy through acts of curation and customization, and, on the other hand, how transformative possibilities have been built into the marketing of officially licensed products that also affirm their corporate owners' roles in making these playful opportunities possible for consumers.

In this essay, I have argued that Hot Topic sells fandom as a lifestyle that privileges self-expression through relationships consumers have with things they buy. I have also asserted that through the retailer's embrace of the aspirational labor of curatorial mediation, it has sought to "teach" consumers how fandom as lifestyle can potentially be monetized or rewarded. #HTFandom is presented as a vehicle for parlaying fan lifestyles into microcelebrity while recognizing Hot Topic as both a site for fandom lifestyles and a brand possessing its own fanbase. Still, while Hot Topic's approach to fandom may be exploitative, it should not be seen as inauthentic. Though the retailer has repeatedly been accused of commodifying counterculture, it serves as a visible nexus for complicating the distinctions made between affirmational and transformational fandoms, a nexus in which officially licensed fashion commodities are presented and perceived as offering transformative opportunities for self-expression. Hot Topic is certainly not the only retail space where fandom as lifestyle and curatorial mediation intersect, though it is likely one of the most visible and unapologetic in its promotion of these practices, marking it as an important site of investigation as fandom increasingly becomes a wearable category available for consumption.

REFERENCES

Affuso, Elizabeth. 2018. "Everyday Costume: Feminized Fandom, Retail, and Beauty Culture." In *The Routledge Companion to Media Fandom*, edited by Melissa Click and Suzanne Scott, 184–192. New York: Routledge.

Affuso, Elizabeth, and Avi Santo. 2018. "Mediated Merchandise, Merchandisable Media: An Introduction." *Film Criticism* 42 (2): 72–87.

Banet-Weiser, Sarah. 2009. "Home Is Where the Brand Is: Childhood Television in the Post-Network Era." In *Beyond Prime Time: Television in the Post-Network Era*, edited by Amanda Lotz, 75–93. New York: Routledge.

Blue, Morgan. 2013. "*D-Signed* for Girls: Disney Channel and Tween Fashion." *Film, Fashion & Consumption* 2 (1): 55–75.

Carter, Oliver. 2018. *Making European Cult Cinema: Fan Enterprise in an Alternative Economy*. Amsterdam: Amsterdam University Press.

Duffy, Brooke Erin, and Emily Hund. 2015. "'Having It All' on Social Media: Entrepreneurial Femininity and Self-Branding among Fashion Bloggers." *Social Media + Society*. https://doi.org/10.1177/2056305115604337

Gaines, Jane. 1989. "The Queen Christina Tie-Ups: Convergence of Show Window and Screen." *Quarterly Review of Film and Video* 11 (1): 35–60.

Geraghty, Lincoln. 2014. *Cult Collectors: Nostalgia, Fandom and Collecting Popular Culture*. London: Routledge.

Granshaw, Lisa. 2015. "How Geek Fashion Wants to Level Up Your Fan Wardrobe . . . and Where It's Going Next." SYFY.com. July 15, 2015. https://www.syfy.com/syfy wire/how-geek-fashion-wants-level-your-fan-wardrobeand-where-its-going-next

Hanks, Sarah. 2011. "Selling Subculture: An Examination of Hot Topic." In *Kinderculture: The Corporate Construction of Childhood*, edited by Shirley Steinberg, 93–114. Boulder, CO: Westview Press.

Hearn, Alison. 2008. "'Meat, Mask, Burden': Probing the Contours of the Branded 'Self.'" *Journal of Consumer Culture* 8 (2): 197–217.

Hebdige, Dick. 1979. *Subculture: The Meaning of Style*. London: Routledge.

Hills, Matt. 2014. "From Dalek Half Balls to Daft Punk Helmets: Mimetic Fandom and the Crafting of Replicas." *Transformative Works and Cultures* 16. https://doi.org/10 .3983/twc.2014.0531

Hot Topic, Inc. 2008. "Annual Report on Form 10-K for the Fiscal Year Ended February 2, 2008." US Securities and Exchange Commission. https://sec.report/CIK/00010 17712

Hot Topic, Inc. 2013. "Annual Report on Form 10-K for the Fiscal Year Ended February

2, 2013." US Securities and Exchange Commission. https://sec.report/CIK/00010
17712

Hsu, Tiffany. 2013. "Hot Topic Acquired by Private Equity Firm Sycamore for $600 Mil-
lion." *Los Angeles Times*, March 7, 2013.

Jung, Kacie Lynn, and Matthew Merlin. 2002–3. "Lifestyle Branding: As More Companies Embrace It, Consumer Opposition Grows." *Journal of Integrated Communications*, 40–45.

Kohnen, Melanie. 2014. "'The Power of Geek': Fandom as Gendered Commodity at
Comic-Con." *Creative Industries Journal* 7 (1): 75–78.

License Global. 2018. "Hot Topic Acquires Her Universe." April 6, 2018. https://www.lic
enseglobal.com/retail/hot-topic-acquires-her-universe

Licensing International. 2019. *2019 Global Licensing Survey.* New York: Licensing International. https://licensinginternational.org/get-survey/

Marwick, Alice. 2013. *Status Update: Celebrity, Publicity, and Self-Branding in Web 2.0.*
New Haven, CT: Yale University Press.

Meehan, Eileen. 1991. "'Holy Commodity Fetish, Batman!': The Political Economy of a
Commercial Intertext." In *The Many Lives of the Batman: Critical Approaches to a
Superhero and His Media*, edited by Roberta Pearson and William Uricchio, 47–65.
New York: Routledge.

Mullins, Paul. 2013. "Consuming Geeks: Subculture and the Marketing of Doctor Who."
Archeology and Material Culture (blog), March 1, 2013. https://paulmullins.word
press.com/2013/03/01/consuming-geeks-subculture-and-the-marketing-of-doct
or-who/

Murray, Simone. 2004. "'Celebrating the Story the Way It Is': Cultural Studies, Corporate Media and the Contested Utility of Fandom." *Journal of Media and Cultural
Studies* 18 (1): 7–25.

Newell-Hanson, Alice. 2017. "How Hot Topic Became America's Outsider Teen Haven."
i-D, November 21, 2017. https://i-d.vice.com/en_us/article/vb3abm/how-hot-top
ic-became-americas-outsider-teen-haven

Obsession Inc. 2009. "Affirmational Fandom vs. Transformational Fandom." *Obsession
Inc.* (blog), June 1, 2009. https://obsession-inc.dreamwidth.org/82589.html

PYMNTS.com. 2016. "The Reverse Aging of Retail." May 11, 2016. https://www.pymnts
.com/news/retail/2016/hot-topic-consumer-demographic/

Rehak, Bob. 2013. "Materializing Monsters: Aurora Models, Garage Kits, and the Object
Practices of Horror Fandom." *Journal of Fandom Studies* 1 (1): 27–45.

Santo, Avi. 2019. "Retail Tales and Tribulations: Transmedia Brands, Consumer Products, and the Significance of Shop Talk." *Journal of Cinema and Media Studies* 58
(2): 115–41.

Scott, Suzanne. 2019. *Fake Geek Girls: Fandom, Gender, and the Convergence Culture
Industry.* New York: New York University Press.

Troika. 2017. *The Power of Fandom.* Los Angeles: Troika. https://www.troika.tv/wp-con
tent/uploads/2019/11/FANDOM_REPORT.pdf

Wellman, Barry, Anabel Quan-Haase, Jeffrey Boase, Wenhong Chen, Keith Hampton, Isabel Díaz, and Kakuko Miyata. 2003. "The Social Affordances of the Internet for Networked Individualism." *Journal of Computer-Mediated Communication* 8 (3). https://doi.org/10.1111/j.1083-6101.2003.tb00216.x

YPulse. 2016. "Fandom Fashion: Why It's a Missed Opportunity." May 4, 2016. https://www.ypulse.com/article/2016/05/04/fandom-fashion-why-its-a-missed-opportunity/

5

Flying under the Radar

Culture and Community in the Unlicensed Geek Fashion Industry

Lauren Boumaroun

Starpuff Space is a private Facebook group for geek apparel brand Elhoffer Design, where "hardcore customers" discuss the clothes and other geeky topics, post photos, ask for care and alteration advice, and give feedback and suggestions to designer/CEO Catherine Elhoffer and her team, who personally respond to the comments and posts (Elhoffer, pers. comm., March 12, 2019). The group operates well beyond a simple customer service page; it is more like a community, where the clothes are merely a pretext bringing everyone together. The group's true value comes from the discussions circulating around the clothes and the media that inspire them. When a new product is released and someone does not understand the reference, other Starpuffs are happy to explain. Group members have even compiled a spreadsheet matching Elhoffer Design products with their source of inspiration. Starpuff Space embodies the gift culture ideals often associated with fandom and serves as a microcosm of the fan-run unlicensed geek fashion industry that emerged throughout the 2010s. This industry grew parallel to the much larger and officially sanctioned billion-dollar licensed merchandise industry, which often fails to meet the needs of women, nonbinary, and queer fans. Although fan-creators have legitimate concerns about their work "being corrupted or deformed by its entry into the commercial sphere" (De Kosnik 2009, 123), unlicensed brands have found a way to cheat the system and commodify fan production while keeping the power and profits within the fan community. By offering what licensed merchandise does not and catering to overlooked demographics, unlicensed geek fashion brands provide a gift to consumers, who reciprocate with financial and moral support. This creates a community that remains true to the tenets of a gift culture and uncorrupted by outside capitalist impulses.

For this project, I analyzed the online presence of six independent geek fashion brands and interviewed five of the brands' owners to gain insight into: how someone breaks into the industry, how they conceptualize their work, how they find and connect with customers, what the pros and cons are of working without licenses, and what support they receive from the geek community. I approach this group as a production culture, considering their shared sets of values and practices, the value they add through their labor, and the way this fosters a sense of community among all those involved (Caldwell 2008, 2). The brand owners interviewed—Paige Campbell (Quasar Creations), Arkeida Wilson (Classy Rebel Design), Sandra Botero (Heroicouture), Jordan Ellis (Jordandené), and Catherine Elhoffer (Elhoffer Design)—are at various stages in their careers, have different goals for their businesses, and create unique styles of clothing. Nevertheless, several recurring themes and statements emerged during our discussions, pointing to a shared set of values among the unlicensed geek fashion designers: adhering to the principles of bounding, treating design as translation, serving niche interests, placing an emphasis on authenticity, and supporting other women and nonbinary fans. Like John T. Caldwell (2008), I am not as interested in the object itself as I am in the creative labor, the way the object is perceived by its creator and consumer, and the culture surrounding it. In this paper, I look at how the shared values and practices of the unlicensed geek fashion industry foster community around clothing in a way that maintains the values of fandom's gift culture. Furthermore, I consider how this production culture (and the surrounding community) protects itself by operating parallel to the licensed industry rather than in competition with it.

In the unlicensed geek fashion community, clothes are imbued with meaning by the creator and speak to the consumer on a personal level. "Affect is . . . [the] distinguishing characteristic" that sets fan-made merchandise apart from the commodities sold by licensed brands (Busse 2015, 114). Rachael Sabotini (1999) likens fan culture to the potlatches held by Indigenous peoples of the Pacific Northwest, where status is not obtained through wealth or possessions but through the creation of "feast" objects and gifting. Fans that make original work, like art and fanfic, are granted the highest status, as these gifts are considered the most valuable. But a work of art is not automatically a gift—it is what we make of it. When we feel a personal connection to a work of art, even if we paid to experience it, we receive something in return that has nothing to do with price, for "a gift revives the soul . . . we are grateful that the artist lived, grateful that he labored in the service of his gifts" (Hyde 2019, xxxiii). Geek fashion consumers like Samara Trindade appreciate the brands for providing them with a way to "geek out loud" and giving them "a sense of pride in . . . what [they] wear" (pers. comm., July 20, 2021). The gift of geek fashion is not necessarily the clothing but the emotions it generates and the connections it creates. Geek fashionista Anika Guldstrand enjoys "the bliss of really liking what you're wearing," and the way geek fashion serves as "a secret call to your people" (pers. comm., August 3, 2021). That gratitude is the gift the customers return to the brands and share with others—discussing the brands on social media, tagging them in posts, and spreading the word to anyone who recognizes the true inspiration of their geeky apparel.

While the community's philosophy is aligned with gift culture, fans understand that tangible works of art cannot be given away. In fact, many are willing to pay more for geek fashion than regular clothing, especially from small, independent brands (Trindade, pers. comm., July 20, 2021; Janine Jones, pers. comm., August 4, 2021). Materials cost money, creation takes time, and the artist has to survive. People are merely "actor[s] in the marketplace," so it is near impossible to maintain a job that is a "pure" gift labor (Hyde 2019, 139). Thus, although unlicensed brands are anticommercial in that they adhere to the values of fandom's gift culture, the unlicensed industry has adopted a commercial model out of necessity. As Suzanne Scott (2009, 1.1) points out, scholarship on online gift economies has shown the unfeasibility of "engag[ing] with gift economies and commodity culture as disparate systems." However, while Scott's article is concerned with the industry "appropriating the gift economy's ethos for its own economic gain," here, I am interested in how a gift culture appropriates a commercial model while resisting commodity culture's ethos.

CULTURE AND COMMUNITY

Unlike mainstream licensed brands, which often replicate character costumes in the form of trompe l'oeil skater dresses (see Scott 2019, 184–219), unlicensed geek fashion designers prefer subtler references to the character, references that are based on the principles of bounding. Originally known as Disneybounding due to the popularity of Disney fan Leslie Kay's fan-inspired fashion blog *DisneyBound* (Borresen 2017), bounding seeks to create stylish outfits that capture the essence of fictional characters or media, without directly evoking the characters (figure 5.1). Like the fan beauty products discussed by Elizabeth Affuso (2018, 5), unlicensed geek fashions are subdued enough for spaces where costumes or cosplay would typically be inappropriate, such as a corporate office or a formal event.

Figure 5.1. Samara Trindade bounding as Rey from *Star Wars*.

Many unlicensed designers create what could be classified as "artisanal everyday cosplay," according to Scott's (2019, 202) taxonomy of everyday cosplay. The artisanal subcategory includes "fancrafted clothing items" that differ from mass-produced apparel not only in appearance but in principle. The creator is expected to be "a self-identified fan of the given media object . . . more engaged with and responsive to their customer base, in line with the reciprocal ethos of a fan community." As Brigid Cherry (2016, 170) has observed about indie yarn dyers in the fan handicrafting community on the fiber arts social media site Ravelry, "the interaction between indie dyer and customer/fan base . . . breaks down the usual barriers between producer and consumer." The shared fandoms and direct engagement on social media facilitate personal connections among fan-designers and geek fashion consumers, creating a geek fashion community.

Unbound by the terms of licensing agreements, unlicensed geek designers have the freedom to interpret the source material however they would like. Licensed fashion designers, on the other hand, are often required to incorporate certain branded elements into the design that make them overstated and more casual. Sandra Botero of Heroicouture initially made clothes using store-bought licensed fabrics but could not find designs that appealed to her, so she used the online site Spoonflower to design textiles that were a "bit more sophisticated." To honor Wonder Woman, Botero created a scarf with a grayish-blue background and alternating yellow-gold amphora print. The amphora itself features a sword design to pay tribute to Wonder Woman's Amazonian warrior origins. The colors echo the blue and yellow elements of Wonder Woman's costume but are neutral enough to coordinate with a variety of outfits. With Botero's designs, she ensures that each reference is clear enough that fans will recognize it, but "it doesn't come right out and scream at you either . . . I don't want it to look cosplay-ish" (pers. comm., March 20, 2019). The approach is not unlike the interpretive fan handicrafting discussed by Cherry (2016, 88), which constitutes "transformative work—inspired by but playing with the text," as opposed to mimetic production, which tends to be more affirmational.

While cosplay is often understood as rote replication of an original costume, Ellen Kirkpatrick's (2015, 2.3) theorization of cosplay as "translation" is an apt way to describe what geek fashion designers do—it is not about copying something word for word but about engaging in interpretation and problem-solving. While the garment remains true to the character's essence, it still allows space for the wearer's personal style to come through. For example, Elhoffer Design's Corps Dress is inspired by Captain Marvel, but unlike licensed brand Her Universe's Captain Marvel halter dress, there are no branded elements that easily mark it as such. The Her Universe dress is "cosplay-ish" and based on a clear and straightforward adaptation of Captain Marvel's supersuit onto a decidedly feminine silhouette. The short, flared navy halter dress features a red bustline and red sash that echo Captain Marvel's breastplate and belt while also accentuating the wearer's feminine curves. It is branded with Captain Marvel's signature eight-point gold star and is unmistakably meant to reference a superhero. Elhoffer's Corps Dress, on the other hand, uses fabric panels and piping in rich gem tones to mimic the lines of Captain Marvel's supersuit without replicating the design directly. The combination of the longer hemline, deeper colors, and creative interpretation results in a dress that subtly captures the essence of the character and enables fans to feel like Captain Marvel while still maintaining a sense of personal style. Starpuff Space is filled with posts and comments about people eager to wear their Corps Dress to work or a business casual event, and the excitement they feel when people at the event recognize the inspiration for the dress. As Kyra Hunting (2015, 133) explains, bodies are "a space within which one's passions and fandom can be made visible, unobtrusively, for oneself and one's fan community."

The personal and emotional nature of geek fashion is what makes the clothes more than commodities. The gift of geek fashion acknowledges consumers on a personal level while creating an emotional connection between designer and consumer and among consumers who celebrate the object together. Geek fashionista Janine Jones feels empowered by geek fashion and believes it can provide comfort for those with social anxiety, as it makes it easy to "find your people" (pers. comm., August 4, 2021). Trindade has similarly "used fandoms as a way of coping" with stress and appreciates being able to "carry that around with [her] on a day-to-day basis" through geek fashion (pers. comm., July 20, 2021). Geek fashion consumers share this happiness with the brands and one another on social media, creating emotional connections that exist outside the sales transactions and make fans more likely to buy from their brands. Trindade and her friends will share on social media about brands they like, buy matching products, and take photos together. Furthermore, geek fashion can serve as a "conversation starter" with new people (Jones, pers. comm., August 4, 2021). When someone recognizes a subtle design as representative of a beloved character, the shared knowledge creates a bond. The giving, receiving, and reciprocating of positive emotions, support, and validation between geek fashion designers and consumers align with the ethos of a gift culture, as a sense of community is valued above all else. The clothes are merely "an extension of that community" (Guldstrand, pers. comm., August 3, 2021).

In addition to offering styles not available from licensed brands, unlicensed designers often focus on lesser-known characters and moments in the text that licensed companies ignore. They fill a niche and invite fans into the process of poaching parts of the story and retelling them through clothing. Jordandené, for example, offers a series of products with the phrase "And Peggy" printed on them, a reference to the song "The Schuyler Sisters" from the Broadway musical *Hamilton*. Since Peggy Schuyler is not a main character in the musical (which is part of the humor of the "and Peggy" lyric), the official *Hamilton* merchandise does not feature her on her own. Licensed T-shirts feature the silhouettes of all three Schuyler sisters or a famous line sung by the eldest sister, Angelica, but Jordandené's Peggy shirt proved popular among fans. Jordan Ellis explains that "there are a lot of really cool moments . . . that aren't flashy, they're not like someone's catchphrase . . . they're a little bit deeper [which] fans appreciate but mainstream doesn't always" (pers. comm., February 28, 2019). It is like a shared inside joke, but without the exclusionary aspects. All are welcome to join the geek fashion community.

Another shared value in the unlicensed geek fashion community is devotion to and appreciation of authenticity. For the designers, their labor is a way to "communicate to other fans one's own commitment to the text and to the fandom" (Booth 2018, 2.1). Fan-made products like unlicensed geek fashions are authentic specifically because they are not "official, mass-produced commodities" (Hills 2014, 2.6). By isolating subtle details and showing their familiarity with a text's "deep cuts," these designers legitimize their status as real or authentic fans. In her discussion of pin trading and Disneybounding, Rebecca Williams (2020, 203) found that collecting, curating, and costuming "function as signifiers of forms of subcultural and symbolic capital" that aid fans in recognizing and connecting with one another. This recognition of a shared passion for the source material creates a feeling of belonging and understanding within the community and respect for the subcultural capital each member carries. Arkeida Wilson of Classy Rebel Design (formerly known as Chic Geek NYC) has taken advantage of the assumed subcultural capital of her followers, involving her customers in the design and naming process. On March 27, 2018, in a now-deleted Instagram post, Wilson (@classyrebeldesign) posted two dress designs inspired by upcoming film releases and asked her followers to guess what characters they were based on. In a way, the post served as an innocent test of authentic fandom: do you know enough to recognize the character? From a commercial standpoint, it enabled Wilson to connect directly with her consumers to gauge interest in the products.

Finally, the unlicensed geek fashion community is committed to uplifting women, nonbinary, and queer fans, thus supporting Scott's (2019, 185) claim that geek fashion provides a space "to challenge the androcentrism of the convergence culture industry." Despite the size of the licensed merchandise industry, the majority of the products are geared toward men, and women characters are often left out of licensed merchandise. Furthermore, men have historically been the most successful at professionalizing their fan work, in part because "masculine" fan practices like game modding and fan filmmaking are considered more viable for the commercial market (De Kosnik 2009, 120–21). When women are able to professionalize their fan labor, it is often not as well received (Scott 2015, 148). However, as I found in relation to costume designers working in animation, "the gendering of [clothing] design as female may actually create an entry point for women into a male-dominated field" (Boumaroun 2018, 27). Thus, the majority of geek fashion designers are women who have successfully transitioned their geeky hobby into a business with the help of their community. As Karen Hellekson (2009, 116) writes in relation to fanfic writers, these women operate on "a system of exchange based on symbolic gifts that represent the self while constituting the community." The focus on collaboration over competition creates bonds among designers and connects each individual customer base to a larger geek fashion community.

Members of the geek fashion community meet up at cons, engage with one another on social media, and mentor emerging designers. When Paige Campbell of Quasar Creations first considered transitioning from cosplay to geek fashion, she reached out to the participants of the 2015 Her Universe Fashion Show who had inspired her. They were happy to offer her advice on designing and creating geek couture and provided the trade knowledge and support she needed. At San Diego Comic-Con in 2018, just as Campbell was starting to transition her geek fashion hobby into a business, she met Catherine Elhoffer, who mentored her through the process. In addition to running her own geek fashion brand, Elhoffer spent years designing licensed apparel and knows the market well. When Quasar Creations officially started taking orders in January 2019, Elhoffer offered advice on how to grow the business, market unlicensed fashion, avoid licensing issues, and handle cease and desist letters if efforts to avoid infringement failed (Campbell, pers. comm., February 28, 2019).

Some unlicensed designers have even found guidance from within the licensed industry. Sandra Botero met Theresa Mercado at a con and started talking to her about Heroicouture, not realizing that Mercado was vice president of product development for licensed apparel and fashion at Hot Topic, BoxLunch, and Her Universe. The chance conversation turned mentorship ended up being beneficial for Botero, who is "very much one of the women that wants to help other women" and understands that "in helping others, you're also helping yourself." While the intervention of someone from outside the unlicensed community raises questions regarding the potential for cultivation and co-optation, Botero believes that people merely see the benefit in sticking together: "This is a very unique community . . . how many years were geeks and nerds ostracized? And now we're mainstream. So, we should celebrate each other" (pers. comm., March 20, 2019). This attitude pervades the geek fashion industry and ensures that it remains a community rather than a competition.

A PARALLEL INDUSTRY

Unlicensed geek fashion brands protect themselves and their interests by operating parallel to, rather than in competition with, the licensed merchandise industry. Although the relationship between licensors and unlicensed companies is not completely free of tension, the industry loosens up restrictions because, in many ways, the unlicensed industry supports the licensed industry and "there is money to be made" (Stanfill 2015, 137). In creating and selling products based on existing media properties, unlicensed brands provide free marketing for intellectual property (IP) owners and licensors. The social media discussions the community generates around these products offer information on what types of products consumers want and how much they are willing to pay. Tiziana Terranova (2000, 37) explains that while "excess productive activities," like Facebook comments and Instagram posts, are "pleasurably embraced," they can also be "shamelessly exploited." The community-building interactions that make unlicensed fashions a gift become free labor for the licensed industry and IP owners, providing marketing and ideas that are proven to reach the consumer on a personal level. Unlicensed brands also maintain a continuous market for fan apparel, as their customer base is likely to buy licensed merchandise to pair with their subtler pieces. Although flying under the radar and working without a license limits how large these companies can scale, the designers are happy staying small, since it allows them to maintain the sense of community that is so important to their brands' identities.

The unlicensed geek fashion community provides free marketing for studios' IP as well as market research for licensors and licensees trying to better understand what their customers are looking for. Just as fanfic "works as advertising for mass-marketed media products" (De Kosnik 2009, 124), so does fan-created fashion. In fact, the media industry is becoming increasingly conscious of the free labor it can get from fans, "especially those who identify as Disney lifestylers or 'influencers' on social media" (Williams 2020, 200), like Whosits & Whatsits founder Tiffany Mink. Although she is no longer associated with Whosits, Mink founded the unlicensed geek fashion brand while occasionally working with Disney as an influencer and sharing sponsored content to her twenty-eight thousand YouTube subscribers and forty-eight thousand Instagram followers. In fact, many people discovered Whosits & Whatsits through her other social media channels. Thus, her sponsored content for Disney indirectly promoted her unlicensed Disney products. Disney was likely aware of the Disney-inspired T-shirts Mink designed while at Whosits but never served the company a cease and desist, presumably because, in sharing her own fandom and disseminating her unlicensed products, Mink also promoted Disney and its sub-brands. Disney seems to understand one of the basic characteristics of fandom's gift culture: "Many people talking about a gift make it seem more valuable; therefore it *is* more valuable, no matter what the objective quality" (Sabotini 1999). Moreover, fans like Mink have direct access to the market, and one glance at the comments on their Instagram pages can save studios money on market research. There is information on what customers are requesting, which designs are most popular, and what types of prices people are willing to pay. Unlicensed designers have personal, direct contact with consumers that gives them an advantage over disconnected IP owners.

Unlicensed designers promote fan-driven consumption more generally by creating this parallel industry and maintaining a base of customers who, though loyal to their independent brands, will buy from licensed brands as well. Fan-made merchandise will never take the place of the original text or branded merchandise, "they can only whet the appetite for more" (Tushnet 2007, 144). Unlicensed designers maintain fan consumption and, therefore, demand for licensed merchandise, which has become increasingly important in a time when studios are pressed to rely on ancillary revenue sources (Lothian 2015, 141). While licensed merchandise brands generally coordinate their product releases with film releases, unlicensed geek fashion brands

Figure 5.2. Screenshots from the Whosits & Whatsits and Hot Topic e-commerce sites comparing the unlicensed Neverland Beanie to a similar licensed product now sold by Hot Topic.

carry designs for a specific fandom even if there are no associated releases at that time. Elhoffer Design, for instance, regularly releases new merchandise inspired by older films. It released two dresses inspired by *Hercules* (dir. John Musker and Ron Clements, 1997) in 2019, and an entire collection of apparel inspired by *Anastasia* (dir. Don Bluth and Gary Goldman, 1997) in 2020. Whosits & Whatsits carries a T-shirt inspired by Halloween favorite *Hocus Pocus* (dir. Kenny Ortega, 1993) year-round. Drawing on Walter Benjamin's "Task of the Translator," Shannon K. Farley (2013, 4.1) states that "it is the rewritings of literature that ensure its afterlife." Geek fashion designers who translate texts into everyday clothing ensure the survival of these texts and their associated imagery through their continuous rewritings.

In addition to providing direct access to consumers, free marketing, and design inspiration, unlicensed brands seemingly provide inspiration for licensed products. Whosits & Whatsits' Neverland Beanie propelled the company to popularity in 2011. Ten years later, Hot Topic introduced a Disney-licensed green knit beanie with a red embroidered feather that looks suspiciously similar to the original Whosits design (figure 5.2).

While I cannot prove conclusively that Hot Topic designers were inspired by the Neverland Beanie, the likelihood is high given the similarities between the products and the pervasiveness of copying within the fashion industry. Unlike media companies, which own their IP, fashion brands are generally unprotected by copyright laws, as fashion is considered too "utilitarian" to qualify as an artistic work under US copyright law (Scafidi 2006, 122). Thus, independent designers—especially those who already operate within a legal gray area like unlicensed geek fashion designers—rarely push back against larger brands.

Due to the normalization of copying within the fashion industry and unlicensed geek fashion's marginal legal status, most of the designers accept the idea that Disney and other IP owners may look to them for inspiration. Williams (2020, 201) has noticed that despite accusations of Disney "parasitically 'borrowing' from Disney fans to commercialize and sell their own ideas back to them, the majority of fans remain uncritical of this." As Terranova (2000, 47) explains, not all free labor is "necessarily exploited labor." For some designers and fans, there is a sense that they receive something in return. In addition to the gift of the original media products on which their fandom is based, they get a relative amount of freedom to create and enjoy unlicensed merchandise. But this "co-optation and colonization of fan creations" has replaced past generations' "fears of litigation and cease-and-desist orders" (Busse 2015, 112), and not every unlicensed designer is as accepting. Catherine Elhoffer has heard of her designs being discussed at Disney and does not think it is fair for the company to take inspiration from her. From her perspective, if she is respecting Disney by creating quality clothing that pays homage to its IP without using any of its branding, it should respect her work. However, Elhoffer is also aware that she has no legal recourse against studios and licensors and thus relies on the quality of her products to stand apart from mass-produced licensed products (pers. comm., March 12, 2019).

Overall, unlicensed designers are uninterested in using design details that would encroach on licensors' IP. As Elhoffer states, "I will respect your IP, but I don't need to use it. I don't need the symbols to go on things" (pers. comm., March 12, 2019). The subtlety of their designs and tendency toward obscure references should not and do not require a license. In choosing less flashy moments of the text, adapting character looks in subtler ways, and avoiding the use of character names in their marketing, these brands protect themselves from legal action and abstain from competing with licensed merchandise. Furthermore, they do so in a way that does not feel limiting. Arkeida Wilson says that she is "very happy not working with licenses . . . because I try not to copy any designs directly from the movie or comic. I like to keep it as an inspiration . . . because that's kind of how geek-bounding is" (pers. comm., March 6, 2019). Although working without licenses limits how large their brands can grow, scaling would destroy the personal connections that are key to their businesses. Most unlicensed brands are happy remaining small enough to "fly under the radar" (Campbell, pers. comm., February 28, 2019). Not only would licenses limit their creative freedom, mass production would force them to lower the quality of their work. Most importantly, they would lose their tight-knit community. Lewis Hyde (2019, 115–16) explains that "when emotional ties are the glue that holds a community together, its size has an upper limit." Unlicensed designers' main goal is to connect with the community and provide their customers with the clothing they always wished licensed brands had offered.

CONCLUSION

As I have shown, an independent, fan-run geek fashion industry emerged throughout the 2010s, running parallel to the billion-dollar licensed merchandise industry, remaining (mostly) uncorrupted by outsiders, and operating in alignment with fandom's gift culture. Unlicensed geek fashion designers can be viewed as a production culture, operating on a shared set of values and practices that are anticommercial, align with fandom's gift culture, and foster community among designers and their customers. Although the designers cannot give their work away for free and must participate in the commercial market to a degree, the objects remain gifts, because they are infused with affect by their creators and speak to consumers on a personal level. The geeky apparel these designers create lets people integrate fandom into their everyday lives in ways that licensed merchandise often does not. The designers are also fans and their brands are relatively small, so they are able to connect with customers on an individual level. Working without a license gives these designers the freedom to interpret the source material as they would like and pull from moments in the story that are not as well known by the mainstream. In doing so, they invite their customers to join in playful poaching and bond over shared subcultural capital. These shared passions lead the designers to befriend and mentor one another, focusing on collaboration rather than competition.

The engagement among the designers and consumers that create and maintain this community becomes free labor for the IP owners and licensed merchandise industry. Through the creation of media-inspired objects and social media conversations surrounding them, the unlicensed community provides free marketing for IP owners and their licensees. They increase the value of the IP by talking about it, and their conversations provide direct information on what customers want. In addition to promoting fan consumption, designers ensure the afterlife of media products by continuously rewriting them through their clothing. However, their creative labor can be exploited and used as inspiration for licensed merchandise. Some unlicensed designers are uncritical of this practice and others find it frustrating, but it is understood to be part of the industry. Although operating without a license limits how large a brand can scale, they would prefer to stay small and connected to the community. As such, the unlicensed industry has commodified fan production while still adhering to the essence of a gift culture. Customers pay for materials and labor and get a T-shirt or a dress, but along with that they get gifts that do not have monetary value: the opportunity to connect with their favorite stories and characters on a personal level, recognition of their fan identity, and, perhaps most importantly, acceptance into a community.

REFERENCES

Affuso, Elizabeth. 2018. "Everyday Costume: Feminized Fandom, Retail, and Beauty Culture." In *The Routledge Companion to Media Fandom*, edited by Melissa A. Click and Suzanne Scott, 184–92. New York: Routledge.

Booth, Paul J. 2018. "Framing Alterity: Reclaiming Fandom's Marginality." *Transformative Works and Cultures* 28. https://doi.org/10.3983/twc.2018.1420

Borresen, Kelsey. 2017. "'Disneybounding' Is the Dress-Up Trend Creative Fans Are Obsessed with." *HuffPost*, November 15, 2017. https://www.huffpost.com/entry/disneybounding-ideas-for-disney-lovers_n_59e5185ce4b02a215b325a30

Boumaroun, Lauren. 2018. "Costume Designer/Everything: Hybridized Identities in Animation Production." *Framework* 59 (1): 7–31.

Busse, Kristina. 2015. "Fan Labor and Feminism: Capitalizing on the Fannish Labor of Love." *Cinema Journal* 54 (3): 110–15.

Caldwell, John T. 2008. *Production Culture: Industrial Reflexivity and Critical Practice in Film and Television*. Durham, NC: Duke University Press.

Cherry, Brigid. 2016. *Cult Media, Fandom, and Textiles: Handicrafting as Fan Art*. London: Bloomsbury Academic.

De Kosnik, Abigail. 2009. "Should Fan Fiction Be Free?" *Cinema Journal* 48 (4): 118–24.

Farley, Shannon K. 2013. "Translation, Interpretation, Fan Fiction: A Continuum of Meaning Production." *Transformative Works and Cultures* 14. https://doi.org/10.3983/twc.2013.0517

Hellekson, Karen. 2009. "A Fannish Field of Value: Online Fan Gift Culture." *Cinema Journal* 48 (4): 113–18.

Hills, Matt. 2014. "From Dalek Half Balls to Daft Punk Helmets: Mimetic Fandom and the Crafting of Replicas." *Transformative Works and Cultures* 16. https://doi.org/10.3983/twc.2014.0531

Hunting, Kyra. 2015. "Fashioning Feminine Fandom: Fashion Blogging and the Expression of Mediated Identity." In *Cupcakes, Pinterest, and Ladyporn: Feminized Popular Culture in the Early Twenty-First Century*, edited by Elana Levine, 116–36. Champaign: University of Illinois Press.

Hyde, Lewis. 2019. *The Gift: How the Creative Spirit Transforms the World*. New York: Vintage Books.

Kirkpatrick, Ellen. 2015. "Toward New Horizons: Cosplay (Re)Imagined through the Superhero Genre, Authenticity, and Transformation." *Transformative Works and Cultures* 18. https://doi.org/10.3983/twc.2015.0613

Lothian, Alexis. 2015. "A Different Kind of Love Song: Vidding Fandom's Undercommons." *Cinema Journal* 54 (3): 138–45.

Sabotini, Rachael. 1999. "The Fannish Potlatch: Creation of Status within the Fan Community." *Fanfic Symposium*, December 20, 1999. http://www.trickster.org/symposium/symp41.htm

Scafidi, Susan. 2006. "Intellectual Property and Fashion Design." *Intellectual Property and Information Wealth* 115:115–31.

Scott, Suzanne. 2009. "Repackaging Fan Culture: The Regifting Economy of Ancillary Content Models." *Transformative Works and Cultures* 3. https://doi.org/10.3983/twc.2009.0150

Scott, Suzanne. 2015. "'Cosplay Is Serious Business': Gendering Material Fan Labor on *Heroes of Cosplay*." *Cinema Journal* 54 (3): 146–54.

Scott, Suzanne. 2019. *Fake Geek Girls: Fandom, Gender, and the Convergence Culture Industry*. New York: New York University Press.

Stanfill, Mel. 2015. "Spinning Yarn with Borrowed Cotton: Lessons for Fandom from Sampling." *Cinema Journal* 54 (3): 131–37.

Terranova, Tiziana. 2000. "Free Labor: Producing Culture for the Digital Economy." *Social Text* 18 (2): 33–58.

Tushnet, Rebecca. 2007. "Payment in Credit: Copyright Law and Subcultural Creativity." *Law and Contemporary Problems* 70:135–74.

Williams, Rebecca. 2020. *Theme Park Fandom: Spatial Transmedia, Materiality and Participatory Cultures*. Amsterdam: Amsterdam University Press.

6

Droids on the Runway

Fandom, Business, and Transmedia in *Star Wars* Luxury Fashion

Nicolle Lamerichs

As a form of labor and production, fan fashion is best understood as a range of business models that are closely aligned to the official creative industries. Historically, fan fashion developed as precarious, fan-driven labor, where fans themselves created costumes (cosplay), and outfits based on the stories that they love (Crawford and Hancock 2019, 6–10). These grassroots fan fashion practices are increasingly commodified, and have become a part of both the official creative industries and the more exclusive realms of the fashion industry. This phenomenon is similar to what Dick Hebdige (1979) has described as "incorporation" in his work on subculture and style, where punk aesthetics moved from the streets to the shops and eventually the runway. Within this process, subcultural styles and aesthetics become commodified and disassociated from their political context. Fan-oriented fashion, in other words, becomes part of the official, mainstream economy, as "a fan practice alongside contemporary industrial efforts to route [predominantly] female fans toward neoliberal modes of consumer engagement" (Scott 2019, 15).

For the purpose of this study, I define fan fashion as an aesthetic system of dress that mediates popular texts. In my previous work, I have studied several forms of fashion, namely costuming, cosplay, and pop-cultural apparel and collections inspired by existing media, such as *The Hunger Games* (Lamerichs 2018a, 2018b). These forms of fashion connect deeply to embodiment, affect, and fan identity. Because fans move betwixt and between material, fictional, visual, and corporeal texts, one way to view these media relationships is through the concept of transmediality, which is often defined as content or stories that "flow . . . across multiple media platforms" (Jenkins 2006, 2). Such "transtexts" can be officially authored by the creative industries, or initiated by fans themselves (Derhy Kurtz 2014; Stein 2017). From the official clothing that Disney sells at its theme parks to licensed *Harry Potter* clothing lines, fan fashion allows its consumers to explore existing franchises and stories as a form of "tactical transmedia" (Gilligan 2011). In theorizing these "embodied transmedia extensions" (Williams 2020, 181), we also need to acknowledge that these are not neutral processes of mediation, but practices deeply connected to our own identity and lived experiences.

In this chapter, I frame fan fashion as an example of how design, fan identity, and business models interlace. Within the creative industries, fan fashion is a niche, but one that is steadily growing and in need of attention. As a system, fan fashion is a sliding scale between official business models and forms of entrepreneurship (see also Carter 2018; Einwächter 2017; Scott 2019). This chapter focuses on *Star Wars*–inspired luxury fashion, which is a particular type of fan fashion, market, and couture. In analyzing this high-end fashion, I combine insights from fan studies and fashion theory.

Through its transmedia references, *Star Wars* luxury fashion has the potential to draw different "brand fans" (Hutchins and Tindall 2016), namely *Star Wars* fans, fashion fans, and consumers who are both. The results of this study show, however, that these luxury goods co-opt popular culture as a form of branding, while the actual fans are commonly excluded from participation. In line with Hebdige's (1979) analysis of incorporation, this study shows how high fashion commodifies *Star Wars*, its culture, and its imagery. These brands do not exclusively target the fan as a main consumer, and their affinity with the culture may be minimal. Fashion lines even create a strategic distance from fans in terms of pricing and accessibility, and discursively in their marketing campaigns. These cultural dynamics, created by the commodification of fan culture, are at the heart of this chapter.

FAN FASHION, EMBODIMENT, AND BUSINESS

As a medium, fashion is best captured as an aesthetic system that is both consumed and produced. As Joanne Entwistle writes (2015, 43 [qtd.], 47) in *The Fashioned Body*: "The fashion system not only provides garments for wear, it endows garments with beauty and desirability, sometimes making direct contact with art. In doing so, it weaves aesthetics into the daily practice of dressing." Moreover, fashion demands regular and systematic change of garment and thereby has an element of choice for consumers. Clothing is not only produced and marketed but worn, making it more than "a thing." In fact, the fashion system cannot be read without the body that it produces.

Academic discourses on media often give the impression that the body has become obsolete, transparent, or wired. The fan's body, however, is playful and present in many fan practices, and fan fashion is but one example. The body is a medium in and of itself, and practices of fashioning and embodying media are emblematic of our current consumer culture, where the body is part of a larger media network (Featherstone 2010).

The relationship between popular culture and high fashion is complex. As Monica Geraffo (2019) emphasizes in her study on *X-Men* comics from the 1980s, the casual attire of the heroes outside of their costume was especially meaningful as it solidified their double identity and made them more human. Their casual wear was explicitly based on fashion of that time. Examples of such cases are many. Naoko Takeuchi's *Sailor Moon* designs drew from Western high fashion and brought this style to Japan, where fans now amply cosplay these designs (Koide 2016). Princess Serenity's dress, for instance, is literally a Dior dress. When fans costume such character versions, the relationship with fashion becomes layered. Through their own cosplays, fans directly mimic haute couture, which is often unavailable to them. However, all fans may not be aware that some costume designs in *Sailor Moon* are references to high-end fashion brands, in which case they may frame such dresses in relation to repertoires that they know from manga and anime.

Fashion, produced both by fans and in official productions, is an aesthetic system as well as a business model. Fan fashion in particular can be understood as an "object-oriented fandom" (Rehak 2014). Fans use objects, wearables, and fashion to represent and reinforce their fan identities in a performative way, but certain objects, such as exclusive pins, signal hierarchy (Geraghty 2014). This is even more the case for luxury fashion, where scarcity and exclusivity drive up the economic value. High fashion increasingly incorporates popular culture and imagery, creating a complex fandom where fashion fans and geek culture meet. This is emblematic of a wider trend in which fandom increasingly spills over into other industries, cultures, and modes of production.

APPROACH

In this chapter, I analyze different practices in relation to *Star Wars* fashion with overlapping spheres of production and consumption within fan culture. I conduct a close reading of different *Star Wars* garments in relation to the source text. I understand fan fashion as a system intimately tied to the transmedia franchising of the story (e.g., Hassler-Forest and Guynes 2018). While fashion conveys meaning and can be read as a text (Barthes 1985; Hebdige 1979), it should not be reduced to its textuality. Fashion is lived, performed, and constructed (Entwistle 2015). In the case of fan fashion, identity and subculture cannot be excluded from the conversation.

This chapter explores fashion as an embodied form of transmedia, and analyzes its mediation of specific themes from *Star Wars* and its story world. The case studies in this chapter include the *Star Wars* collections by Rodarte, Rag & Bone, and Preen. The context of these designs, including their branding and pricing strategies, is analyzed to see how designers position their fashion in relation to fandom. The reception and circulation of the collections across social media platforms such as Instagram are also taken into account.

As the close reading reveals, Rodarte mediates *Star Wars* as an archetypal myth with nostalgic themes. By contrast, Rag & Bone mediates *Star Wars* as future-forward streetwear. Its collection is inspired by the technology, vessels, and uniforms in *Star Wars*, as well as Imperial and First Order styles. Preen, finally, frames *Star Wars* above all as an iconic franchise in a pop art collection with an emphasis on recognizable characters like Darth Vader. In other words, these three brands each have their own unique approach to the *Star Wars* franchise and story world.

RODARTE'S *STAR WARS* GOWNS

During New York Fashion Week in 2014, the well-received finale of Rodarte's catwalk show consisted of several beautiful *Star Wars* gowns, using film stills printed onto silk textiles (Ratcliffe 2014). For the designs of a collection of chic *Star Wars* gowns, Rodarte's founders, the sisters Laura and Kate Mulleavy, mined their nostalgic feelings and their "fascination with storytelling and cinema." For these designers, fashion clearly functions as both a visual and a narrative expression. In an interview with *PAPER* magazine (Cole 2014), the designers explained the relationship of *Star Wars* to their own youth, but also emphasized the films' canonical status:

> More than anything, this collection is about the limitless possibilities of youth and how our imagination transformed our backyard into a great adventure. In the end, the dresses represent something intangible—the instantaneous and overwhelming moment of impact that changes the way you see the world. They represent the instant where you learn to keep your eyes wide-open to

the vast potentiality of everything. The *Star Wars* films seem to have become a part of who we are. In a broader sense, they have melded with the collective conscious of our cultural DNA.

In this interview, *Star Wars* is painted affectively, as a moment of transformation for the sisters. The dresses represent this intensity—an "intangible" moment of play and imagination. The Mulleavy sisters associate *Star Wars* with growing up and with seeing the world in a different way. *Star Wars* is described as a contemporary myth and part of the "cultural DNA." This fondness of play and imagination is in line with Rodarte's earlier work, such as its medieval spring collection (Phelps 2012).

The *Star Wars* collection was marketed in collaboration with the official brand, with Rodarte organizing a special photo shoot at the Skywalker Ranch (Lucasfilm's movie ranch) for *PAPER* (Cole 2014). This was the first time George Lucas had granted access to the property for a specific *Star Wars* shoot, and the shoot was organized with the help of a mutual friend (Khan 2014). Hosting the shoot at Skywalker Ranch clearly aligns the dresses with the figure and authorship of George Lucas, and even adds an aura of authenticity to the dresses by connecting them to this official *Star Wars* space rather than the catwalk.

The sisters still post photographs of these dresses frequently on their Instagram, and the fan response has been positive. When the official Rodarte Instagram account (@rodarte) posted a picture of a model in the C-3PO dress (May 4, 2016), posing with the actual robot, it received 3,177 likes. A May 4, 2018, post to the same account of the Luke Skywalker gown from the *PAPER* photo shoot (figure 6.1) got 5,648 likes (both stats as of May 30, 2019). What stands out is that both dresses were posted on Star Wars Day, May 4 (or "May the Fourth"), a fan holiday and major consumer event for merchandise. While many brands seize this day to sell their *Star Wars* merchandise, for Rodarte, this is primarily a moment of branding. The dresses are not for sale and are only available for fans through pictures. In line with the designers' statement, the access to the dresses is quite literally intangible.

In a close reading of the dresses in the Rodarte collection, their nostalgic and mythological qualities clearly stand out. The long gowns consist of light fabrics for the most part. Different materials are combined: soft photographic prints with portraits of Yoda and C-3PO at the bottom, rougher fabrics and long scarves at the top. The prints are of iconic characters and scenes of the original trilogy. While the dresses seem very different at first sight because of their color schemes, they do have similar cuts and designs. Each has a V-neck

Figure 6.1. Skywalker
dress by Rodarte.
Photograph from
PAPER magazine, 2014.

created partly by folding the fabric, and features a floor-length sheath silhouette. The characters and prints are most prominent from the waist down, while the top is framed in a complementary color scheme. Classic *Star Wars* is central in the collection.

Note the Luke Skywalker gown, for instance. A detailed full-bodied photograph of Luke Skywalker makes up most of the bottom part of the dress. It is an iconic still of the moment that Luke decides to leave Tatooine and embarks on his hero's quest. The viewer's eye is directed to Luke, the waist of the model, and the hem of the dress. This is characteristic of the whole collection since the upper part of each dress is fairly sober while they are printed from the waist down. The only exception is perhaps the Tatooine dress, which consists of different black fabrics contrasted with the purple sky and moons at the bottom. The upper part of the dresses is layered, with a long scarf wrapped around the model for the runway presentation. The design is classical and long, a typical and timeless column silhouette. The pairing of iconic images with the classic silhouette gives *Star Wars* a historical dimension and symbolizes fans' ongoing attachment to the original trilogy. Tapping into nostalgia and the iconography of *Star Wars*, the Rodarte sisters timed their dresses perfectly to the release of the new franchise.

Overall, this collection combines old and new materials in beautiful ways. Details like a few rhinestones almost seem symbolic of the stars and galaxy. The collection is not futuristic; it is a bricolage of materials, including prints that explicitly refer to *Star Wars*. The color palettes are related to the environments and characters of *Star Wars*, with the fabrics and color schemes coordinated for each dress (e.g., black-purple for Tatooine, beige for Luke). With its classic and elegant gowns, this collection frames *Star Wars* as an archetypal myth.

Though fans expressed interest in the gowns, they were only available for photo shoots and exhibits (Donnelly 2014). The dresses belong to an exclusive few, such as Willow Bay (wife of Disney's CEO, Bob Iger), who wore the Yoda gown to the eighty-seventh Academy Awards. In an interview with *Tech Times*, she noted, "What I find so fascinating is how the image appears in photographs. Yoda is crystal clear, wise and strong, even draped along the column of a dress" (Parrish 2015). This example also reveals that high-end fan fashion exists largely outside of fandom. The Yoda dress is worn and marketed by those that own *Star Wars*, while the fans have little opportunity to buy the gowns and can only admire them. Since many fans are avid collectors of merchandise, this scarcity of high fashion also subverts the logic of fandom as a consumer space where items can be readily bought, traded, and procured.

Overall, the gowns are framed as fashion and art through and through—a system to which fans have little access. The *Kessel Runway* (2014c), a blog for *Star Wars* fashion, comments: "Even if they were available, they would be outside of most fan's [*sic*] price range. A similar style dress from the same collection has a retail price of US$6,325, though they could have been a lovely wedding dress for a dedicated fan!" In other words, as part of the fashion system, these dresses exist largely outside of fan culture. They are objects to be admired and circulated on Instagram as images, or in YouTube runway videos, but fans can never have the lived experience of wearing them. However, some luxury fashion is made available to fans, and the Rag & Bone collection discussed below is the perfect example.

RAG & BONE X *STAR WARS* COLLECTION

In the 2021 *Star Wars* collection by Rag & Bone, *Star Wars* is not framed as nostalgic at all, but rather framed as minimalist and futuristic. The designers started working on this collection around the time of the release of *Rogue One: A Star Wars Story* (dir. Gareth Edwards, 2016), but it really came together when Rag & Bone chief executive and creative mastermind Marcus Wainwright did a short film with Mark Hamill (who portrays Luke Skywalker in the franchise) to promote the fashion brand. In the film, Hamill emphasizes the cinematic qualities and heroism of *Star Wars*: "I wish my life was a nonstop Hollywood movie show, a fantasy world of celluloid villains and heroes. Because celluloid heroes never feel any pain. And celluloid heroes never die" (Rag & Bone 2016).

The theme of heroism and the Force is evoked in the fashion itself, as well. Different fabrics are used throughout the collection, giving each piece a unique look. Some pieces allow fans to almost embody the Resistance, such as Echo (a white hooded women's jacket, originally sold for US$1,295) and Hope (a white knitted sweater with high collar and large sleeves, originally sold for US$450). That the design of these pieces is inspired by Princess Leia shows in the color scheme and hood, among other elements. Other designs have a Stormtrooper aesthetic, most particularly the "Storm Trooper tee," which is completely white with a few black stripes that reference the helmet.

Unlike the items in the Rodarte collection, the Rag & Bone pieces (including, e.g., an X-wing T-shirt) emphasize the technology and costume design of *Star Wars*. An Obi-Wan hoodie is the most character-oriented piece in the collection, and is heavily inspired by the Jedi costumes. The beige color scheme and the hood clearly mediate the costume design of Obi-Wan, but translate this into more general streetwear. Aside from this hoodie, the designs are subtle and minimalist. The collection was launched parallel to *Star Wars: The Last Jedi* (dir. Rian Johnson) in December 2017, as a "limited-edition lineup that nods to the franchise's functional, futuristic style but steers clear, very clear, of anything resembling cosplay gear or fanboy merch," as fashion critic Matt Sebra (2017) aptly summarized in *GQ*. What is particularly interesting in this quote is how the critic distances fan fashion from fan merchandise (even disdainfully calling it "fanboy merch") and practices like cosplay. Designers and critics create a discursive distinction between fandom and fashion, even as they aim to capitalize on the popularity of geek culture.

The collection has mid- to high-range prices. Some items are even sold in the official Disney store, such as the Obi-Wan hoodie (for US$350). In terms of segmentation, *Star Wars* fans are part of the target audience, and the fashion is marketed as licensed *Star Wars* merchandise in collaboration with Disney. Part of the profits of the collection go to the Star Wars: Force for Change initiative, a charity program to improve the lives of children around the world, which is officially connected to the brand (Starwars.com, 2017). By framing the collection as part of the well-known charity, Rag & Bone creates a deeper connection between official *Star Wars* initiatives and its own brand.

By remixing the aesthetics of *Star Wars* with streetwear, Rag & Bone has produced a unique collection. The connection with storytelling is minimal, and can rather be described as evocative. This collection presents fans with the military *Star Wars* of Stormtroopers, Resistance fighters, and Jedi knights. Strong black and white colors function as references to troopers, drones, and ships. The beige and soft brown outfits evoke the style of the rebellion. Like in Rodarte's collection, color mediates the values of the Empire and the Resistance, but Rag & Bone goes beyond the typical heroic dichotomy. The fashion brand presents *Star Wars* designs that echo its technology, space ships, troopers, and droids. In terms of mediation, this can be understood as a futurist interpretation of what *Star Wars* is. Even the marketing campaign with Mark Hamill emphasizes the technological and filmic aspects of *Star Wars* (the "celluloid heroes"), which is a different approach to heroism than the character-specific and archetypal approach of Rodarte.

However, this minimalist approach to *Star Wars* suits Rag & Bone as streetwear that is inspired by "American workwear" and aims to create "timeless" and sustainable outfits that last for years (Rag & Bone, n.d.). The designs are distinctively Rag & Bone and recognizable to the company's fans, while a *Star Wars* fan may not read these outfits as part of the franchise. Rag & Bone's minimalist white hoodies, after all, are quite different from the Rodarte dresses, with their iconic stills from the films. The Rag & Bone collection is set apart from merchandise quite explicitly. There are no quotes, characters, or stills inspired by the films. A *Star Wars* fan might not even recognize these pieces as references to the franchise. The average fan, in other words, is excluded not only by the pricing of these pieces, but also by their design and messaging.

PREEN BY THORNTON BREGAZZI AND DARTH VADER

Appearing on *Jimmy Kimmel Live!* in May 2014, Julia Roberts sported a Darth Vader blouse created by the label Preen from designers Justin Thornton and Thea Bregazzi. This white shirt features a prominent, dark gray, pop art image of Darth Vader. The blouse is part of a larger collection of shirts and dresses with large, similar prints of Darth Vader's helmet. When the collection debuted during London Fashion Week in 2014, models strutted the runway to the Imperial March, Darth Vader's theme (Brown Thomas 2014; *Kessel Runway* 2014a).

Star Wars is presented as iconic in this collection. The garments in this collection all feature the same image of Darth Vader's helmet. When examined closely, the iconic image of the helmet is revealed to be a collage of galaxy stills and cutouts of TIE fighters from the *Star Wars* films. The images are chosen purposefully, too, and are aligned with the Empire and Darth Vader's backstory. For instance, there is a shot of Luke fighting reflected in the lens of the helmet, which connects Vader to his son, whom he is seemingly watching over (figure 6.2).

It is striking that Preen picked Darth Vader as a key figure for this collection. Vader's image is combined with other pop art patterns, which frames *Star Wars* above all as mainstream, popular culture. Vader's helmet is similar to Andy Warhol's images of Marilyn Monroe (1962–67), a recognizable icon that can be remixed endlessly. Vader is the face of a generation, an image that audiences must recognize. Such an image can be reproduced, remixed, and embedded in different contexts and colors, but it still retains its meaning. Just like the image of Monroe signified the birth of the modern celebrity and film, this helmet represents current consumer culture and its vast, continuously remixed story worlds.

In contrast to the other two collections, these designs present *Star Wars* as pure pop art by using patterns consisting of lines, repeated X-wings, colored fields, and filters. The colors of this collection pop out immediately. For instance, the Saber dress from this collection has psychedelic red lines and blocks and sports the Vader image at the top. The Vader dress has a similar image, but the color scheme is mostly black, with red details and curvy white lines. The dresses fit the eclectic mix of punk and vintage that Preen is known for.

In terms of pricing, the collection positions itself as a premium luxury brand. The pricing of the Padme shirt, for instance, was reported at £355 or US$560 (*Kessel Runway* 2014b). The dresses sold for between £850 and £1,200 in retail (roughly US$1,360–US$1,920 in 2014). While the Darth Vader collection has exclusive fashion items, Preen has also been involved with other *Star Wars* collaborations. For instance, it released a more affordable Stormtrooper shirt that was related to the *Star Wars: Force for Change* charity initiative and retailed for £55 (US$88). These shirts are available more widely, and are more

Figure 6.2. Darth Vader blouse from the 2014 Preen collection by Thornton Bregazzi.

akin to streetwear. As in the case of Rag & Bone, charity is an opportunity to connect the fashion to the *Star Wars* franchise and its values, which opens the doors to a larger consumer market.

While this collection uses *Star Wars* imagery explicitly, it may lack the proper references and nuance to appeal to many *Star Wars* fans. Despite their different coloring, the pieces in the collection are similar in terms of design. Each item in the collection uses similar images, even the Padme top, which features the same Vader stills and TIE fighters on its sleeves. The shirt has little to do with Padme, save for perhaps its bright yellow and red color scheme, reminiscent of her Queen Amidala attire. A piece like the Padme shirt thereby also shows the limits of fan fashion. Designers mediate an existing story or property with limited knowledge of the story, and come up with generic concepts for widely different characters.

CONCLUSION

This chapter reveals fan fashion to be a complex system, one that can even be disconnected from fandom altogether. As embodied transmedia, these collections appeal to fans through their references to *Star Wars* characters and stories. Designers clearly capitalize on subcultural knowledge about *Star Wars* and on feelings toward the franchise. For example, Preen's runway debut was accompanied by Stormtroopers, while Rag & Bone involved Mark Hamill in its campaign. Fashion brands mobilize affect, such as nostalgia, for *Star Wars* but always pair this with the expectations of their own consumers.

While the brands in question capitalize on the popularity of geek culture, they firmly position their collections as luxury fashion rather than merchandise. The pieces in these collections are framed as scarce and exclusive through their pricing strategies and marketing, which present barriers to fans' access to them. The fact that Rodarte's dresses circulated widely in fandom but were not even for sale is an important example of how the fashion system can operate. *Star Wars* is interpreted by the fashion designers as part of the North American culture and canon, rather than a cult property. The relationship with Disney and its stores is primarily visible in the context of more affordable pieces, those designed for charity. This estrangement from fandom also shows in the circulation of these pieces on social media. It is nearly impossible to find images of actual fans wearing or unboxing these items on Instagram, YouTube, or other platforms. Instead, celebrities, bloggers, and models marketed and wore the dresses.

Critically, these examples show how fan capital can be transformed into exclusive art and designs—a commodification of characters and images, separated from their original context and meaning. These results are in line with Hebdige's (1979) concept of incorporation, which always implies a shift to mainstream contexts and ways of operating. Here, the logic works in reverse. Mass products and merchandise are adapted to be more exclusive designs, fit for the runway. In many of these cases, fans are not the primary target audience anymore, and the market has shifted to other consumers altogether. While fan fashion has the potential to serve as a mode of subcultural identity expression, this is by no means the norm. Even when dedicated fans have the access or resources to purchase these pieces, they are often discursively excluded by the fashion brands themselves. To analyze fan fashion means to study these tensions fully in terms of culture, branding, and business.

REFERENCES

Barthes, Roland. 1985. *The Fashion System*. London: Cape.
Brown Thomas. 2014. "PREEN Autumn Winter 2014." Uploaded July 9, 2014. YouTube video, 5:21. https://www.youtube.com/watch?v=ety5fOQqL3A
Carter, Oliver. 2018. *Making European Cult Cinema: Fan Enterprise in an Alternative Economy*. Amsterdam: Amsterdam University Press.
Cole, Todd. 2014. "Rodarte at the Skywalker Range." *PAPER*, September 3, 2014. http://www.papermag.com/rodarte-at-skywalker-ranch-1427376423.html   (article removed from site).
Crawford, Garry, and David Hancock. 2019. *Cosplay and the Art of Play*. London: Palgrave MacMillan.
Derhy Kurtz, Benjamin. 2014. "Transmedia Practices: A Television Branding Revolution . . . and It's Just Getting Started." *Networking Knowledge* 7 (1): 1–6.
Donnelly, Tim. 2014. "Rodarte's 'Star Wars' Dresses Are the Droids You're Looking For." *New York Post*, February 11, 2014. https://nypost.com/2014/02/11/rodartes-star-wars-dresses-are-the-droids-youre-looking-for/
Einwächter, Sophie. 2017. "Negotiating Legal Knowledge, Community Values, and Entrepreneurship in Fan Cultural Production." *Media in Action* 2:93–112.
Entwistle, Joanne. 2015. *The Fashioned Body: Fashion, Dress and Modern Social Theory*. Cambridge: Polity.
Featherstone, Mike. 2010. "Body, Image and Affect in Consumer Culture." *Body & Society* 16 (1): 193–221.
Geraffo, Monica. 2019. "Secret Identities: Marvel Superheroes, Fashion Trends, and Subcultural Streetwear, 1975–1995." Paper presented at Comics/Fandom, Cologne, March 29, 2019.
Geraghty, Lincoln. 2014. *Cult Collectors*. New York: Taylor and Francis.
Gilligan, Sarah. 2011. "Heaving Cleavages and Fantastic Frock Coats: Gender Fluidity, Celebrity and Tactile Transmediality in Contemporary Costume Cinema." *Film, Fashion & Consumption* 1 (1): 7–38.
Hassler-Forest, Dan, and Sean Guynes. 2018. *Star Wars and the History of Transmedia Storytelling*. Amsterdam: Amsterdam University Press.
Hebdige, Dick. 1979. *Subculture: The Meaning of Style*. New York: Routledge.
Hutchins, Amber, and Natalie Tindall. 2016. Introduction to *Public Relations and Participatory Culture: Fandom, Social Media and Community Engagement*, edited by Amber Hutchins and Natalie Tindall, 3–8. Milton Park, UK: Taylor and Francis.
Jenkins, Henry. 2006. *Convergence Culture: Where Old and New Media Collide*. New York: New York University Press.

Jimmy Kimmel Live! 2014. "Julia Roberts vs. Sally Field in Celebrity Curse Off." Uploaded May 6, 2014. YouTube video, 4:04. https://www.youtube.com/watch?v=0swXMgM 2840

Kessel Runway. 2014a. "Preen by Thornton Bregazzi." December 2, 2014. http://www.th ekesselrunway.com/preen-by-thornton-bregazzi/

Kessel Runway. 2014b. "Review—Preen 'Padme' Shirt." December 3, 2014. http://www .thekesselrunway.com/review-preen-padme-shirt/

Kessel Runway. 2014c. "*Star Wars* Dresses by Rodarte." December 22, 2014. http://www .thekesselrunway.com/star-wars-dresses-by-rodarte/

Khan, Bonita. 2014. "*Paper* Feature Rodarte's *Star Wars* Collection." *Hit the Floor*, September 4, 2014. http://www.hitthefloor.com/lifestyle/fashion/paper-feature-roda rtes-star-wars-collection/

Koide, Jamie. 2016. "Sailor Moon Character Outfits Modeled on High-Fashion Designs (Pics)." *Sora News 24*, June 13, 2016. https://soranews24.com/2016/06/13/sailor -moon-character-outfits-modeled-on-high-fashion-designs

Lamerichs, Nicolle. 2018a. "Fan Fashion: Re-Enacting Hunger Games through Clothing and Design." In *Companion to Media Fandom and Fan Studies*, edited by Paul Booth, 150–72. New York: Wiley Blackwell.

Lamerichs, Nicolle. 2018b. *Productive Fandom. Intermediality and Affective Reception in Fan Cultures.* Amsterdam: Amsterdam University Press.

Parrish, Robin. 2015. "Exclusive: The 'Yoda Dress' from the Oscars, Explained." *Tech Times*, February 25, 2015. https://www.techtimes.com/articles/35440/20150225/

Phelps, Nicole. 2012. "Spring 2013 Ready-to-Wear Rodarte." *Vogue*, September 10, 2012. https://www.vogue.com/fashion-shows/spring-2013-ready-to-wear/rodarte

Rag & Bone. 2016. "Rag & Bone Men's Project—Mark Hamill." Uploaded by Rag & Bone Films, October 17, 2016. YouTube video, 0:43. https://www.youtube.com/watch?v= XcRPOy1SKII

Rag & Bone. n.d. "Story and Values." Accessed June 15, 2021. https://www.rag-bone .com/our-company/story-values.html

Ratcliffe, Amy. 2014. "*PAPER* Magazine Features Rodarte *Star Wars* Collection at Skywalker Ranch—Exclusive!" StarWars.com, September 3, 2014. https://www.starw ars.com/news/paper-magazine-features-rodarte-star-wars-collection-at-skywal ker-ranch-exclusive

Rehak, Bob. 2014. "Materiality and Object-Oriented Fandom." *Transformative Works and Cultures* 16. https://doi.org/10.3983/twc.2014.0622

Scott, Suzanne. 2019. *Fake Geek Girls: Fandom, Gender, and the Convergence Culture Industry.* New York: New York University Press.

Sebra, Matt. 2017. "*Star Wars* x Rag & Bone Is the Actually Stylish Movie Merch We've Been Waiting For." *GQ*, November 6, 2017. https://www.gq.com/story/star-wars -rag-and-bone-collection

StarWars.com. 2017. "Rag & Bone Celebrates the *Star Wars* Saga with New Collection." November 6, 2017. https://www.starwars.com/news/rag-bone-celebrates-the-star -wars-saga-with-new-collection

Stein, Louisa. 2017. "Fandom and the Transtext." In *The Rise of Transtexts: Challenges and Opportunities*, edited by Benjamin Derhy Kurtz and Melanie Bourdaa, 71–89. New York: Routledge.

Williams, Rebecca. 2020. *Theme Park Fandom: Spatial Transmedia, Materiality and Participatory Cultures.* Amsterdam: Amsterdam University Press.

7

"I Am Not in a Cult"

Poppy and the Gendered Implications of Ironic Beauty Fan Cult(ure)

Paxton C. Haven

"I am not in a cult" is the irreverent rallying cry of beauty influencer turned electropop musician turned fictional cult leader Poppy and her adoring followers, the Poppy Seeds. This motto, which is plastered all over Poppy's official branded merchandise and promoted across her social media channels, playfully suggests the type of fannish humor that provokes an ironic indulgence in all things Poppy. Originally uploading short videos on YouTube under the username That_Poppy in 2014, Poppy would engage in exaggeratedly memetic activities such as brushing her hair or petting a plant, speaking in a whispery monotone with a piercingly high tonality that is at once saccharine and eerily bone chilling, and offering a parodic android performance. She never once broke character in any official music video, interview, or social media post, and so the blurred boundary between human being and mediated technology also functioned to comment on the constructed nature of digital influencers. Counter to the conventional appeals to authenticity that permeate influencer economies of personality and lifestyle branding, Poppy's plasticity quickly garnered attention for its satire of contemporary internet culture, thereby creating a cultish fan base whose basis of participation was being in on the joke. This "joke," however, quickly developed from ironically stunted performance of YouTuber fan engagement to a pop star persona with multiple albums and international tours, two graphic novels, and a large dedicated fan base with its own virtual world, Poppy.Church. As branding a fan platform as a church implies, Poppy's satire of influencer appeals to authenticity has evolved into a pop music cult. Poppy's instructive hailing of the cult fan, therefore, reveals the neoreligious aspects of "influence," allowing us to explore the ways these rituals of affect structure the increasingly interwoven sites of the popular music industry, social media platforms, and beauty influencer economies.

Through babydoll-style dresses and large bow barrettes in every hue of pastel, Poppy's sartorial work satirizes the concept of an "industry plant," or an artist whose cultural production and persona are seen as blatantly commercial and artificial (an accusation that is often directed at conventionally feminine commercial pop musicians) (Rindner 2020). Poppy's form of subversively infantilized style carries significant weight in the production of anticorporate alternative femininities within pop music history, particularly in reference to riot grrrls. Gayle Wald, coauthor of *Smells Like Teen Spirit: Riot Grrrls, Revolution and Women in Independent Rock*, argues that riot grrrl's sartorial articulation, "was wearing girl style, but doing it slightly off-kilter. Not like when Britney Spears came out in her schoolgirl uniform (and braided pigtails) that sexualized girlhood in a pretty familiar way" (qtd. in Euse 2017). Whereas Poppy's music is aesthetically more akin to the commercial bubblegum pop of Britney Spears, the various intertextual layers of her android influencer persona produce a disjuncture of image and music text that is reminiscent of the transgressively feminine symbolism of the riot grrrl, albeit seeming at first like typical industry fare. In the past decade, the concept of industry plant has disproportionately been used to categorize pop musicians who leverage their large digital followings to get record deals. Enacting the artificiality of industry intervention through these exaggerated markers of hyperfeminine style, Poppy draws attention to the gendered constructs of authorship and legitimacy that lead music journalists and fans to categorize internet success stories as premeditated products of publicists and producers. When first introduced to Poppy's bright, synthy, formulaic pop music, her hyperconsumerist lyrics such as, "Pop is on the radio, and who decides we'll never know, somebody told me I should follow where the money goes," appeared condescending of female-driven pop music (Poppy 2017b, track 11). Likewise, it is easy to read the repeated sartorial and rhetorical references to Poppy's "cult" as an ironic social commentary on obsessive fans in the pop music "stan wars" era. However, this does not adequately reflect the manifold ways Poppy's fans internalize these sartorial appeals to irony. The subversive nature of Poppy's beauty influencer persona, instead, relies on style as an unspoken, highly interpretive site of textual negotiation.

In framing the story of Poppy's rise to microcelebrity fame against the context of industry plant, I argue that the industrial and cultural power of these hegemonic scripts is countered by Poppy's self-reflexive parodic strategies of cutely cult branding. This polysemic mix of humor, neoreligiosity, and gendered critique reflects the politics of ambivalence at the center of Sarah Banet-Weiser's (2012) conceptualization of brand culture. As the media industries become gradually structured by social media strategies of self-branding and multiplatform content circulation, the work of digital influencers is increasingly incorporated into the promotional operations of legacy media. Yet only a choice few get to reap the benefits of industrial legitimation, while the remainder of these innovative cultural producers are creatively exploited, industrially unprotected, and culturally invalidated (Duffy 2017). Poppy's rise to internet celebrity through the fan engagement strategies that she satirizes, therefore, does not point the sardonic finger at the individual influencers or even the audience of this content, but instead examines the implicit systems of social and industrial power that construct contemporary frameworks of "influence." When Poppy's satire is positioned as a critique of the ways beauty influencer strategies of self-branding get incorporated into inequitable productions of gender within mainstream promotional tactics, the sacredness of influence becomes the ultimate articulation of power within these concurrent media industries. Poppy performs these processes of legitimation to reflect the disproportionate orientations of power within these cultural and economic contexts, and the collective hailing of a fan community contingent on subversive infiltration from within these normative scripts of pop star celebrity and influencer beauty cult(ure).

THE DOCTRINE OF "BLEACH BLONDE BABY"

> *My eyelashes are seven feet long, people stop, they stop and stare*
> *They wanna know if I got 'em glued on but I woke up and they were there*
> *I was born with makeup on, mani-pedi, and everything*
> *Normal babies whine and cry, but I could only sing*
>   —Poppy, "Bleach Blonde Baby"

The music video for "Bleach Blonde Baby" begins with an extreme close-up of Poppy's perfectly lined, glossy pastel pink lips, with her bottom false eyelashes peeking from the top of the frame. As she sings the first line, the video cuts to Poppy standing in the center of a blank white room in a beige tulle dress cinched at the waist, countered in silhouette by a ridiculously large black satin bow (figure 7.1). With two men dressed in white morphsuits hovering around her figure and digitally imposed seven-foot lashes that fill the top half of the frame, the viewer is immediately drawn to the sartorial absurdity. This absurdity is further communicated through the lyrics, which speak of constant perfection and the innate effortlessness of her aesthetic. These opening

Figure 7.1. The sartorial absurdity of Poppy's "Bleach Blonde Baby" is established within the first seconds of the music video (0:12). Still from music video, uploaded to YouTube.

moments immediately establish the broader context of the song's parody, at once invoking the unattainable beauty standards of pop music celebrities, with reference Beyoncé's "Flawless" lyrics, and appealing to beauty product advertising the likes of "Maybe she's born with it, maybe it's Maybelline." Whereas on the surface the lyrics present the bleached blonde baby aesthetics as a "cotton candy dream" of God's creation, the video's visual framing of setting and style frustrate these saccharinely sacred declarations of self. The video for "Bleach Blonde Baby" positions bleach, blonde, and baby as three sartorial categories of the music industry's insidious formula of hypernormative femininity. The visual frameworks of this video directly reflect the title of the song as each setting is *bleach*ed white and Poppy's pin-straight *blonde* wig fills every frame, while her pastel bows and endless bundles of tulle construct an adult woman trapped in a state of infantile (*baby*) innocence and robotically stunted emotionality. Narratively, the video re-creates Poppy's meteoric rise from banal content creator dreaming of success in her bedroom to pop star standing at the altar of her church looking down at her adoring followers and basking in the glow of immense virtual influence (figure 7.2). Through her parodic embodiment of the industry plant within this video, Poppy

Figure 7.2. Intense contrast lighting within this establishing shot of Poppy's "Bleach Blonde Baby" music video draws the viewer's attention to the juxtaposition of the bare white church setting and Poppy's ornate stylings (3:26). Still from music video, uploaded to YouTube.

reveals the complex negotiation of sexuality, performance, and power that bears disproportionate weight on female pop musicians' self-fashioning and their subsequent branding within the media industries.

The Discursive Artifice of "Bleach"

Central to Poppy's beauty influencer satire is the tension between authenticity and artificiality, exhibited in the video for "Bleach Blonde Baby" within the symbolism of bleached hair and bare white sets. To bleach hair is to radically strip the original hair color to create a blank slate for further artificial coloring using dye and toner. Poppy establishes within the lyrics that she came out of the womb with this pin-straight hair of aesthetic intervention, claiming an innate authenticity within this blatant artificiality. With deliberate reference to the semiotic history of blondeness and pop stardom, the beginning chords of "Bleach Blonde Baby" sample the iconic opening chord progression of Madonna's 1985 "Material Girl," a song whose music video in turn re-creates Marilyn Monroe's "Diamonds Are a Girl's Best Friend" number from *Gentlemen Prefer Blondes* (dir. Howard Hawks, 1953). In a song that boasted a tongue-in-cheek materialism during the Reagan years of political conservatism and backlash against mainstream feminist discourses, Madonna's sartorial re-creation of one of Hollywood cinema's most troubled starlets provides a rich text of gender, industry, and reception. Richard Dyer (2003, 40), in his chapter on Monroe's star text as a representation of discourses of sexuality and feminine agency within 1950s Hollywood, argues that Monroe, "conforms to, and is part of the construction of, what constitutes desirability in women." Central to these symbols of desirability is Monroe's peroxide blonde hair. Dyer (2003, 42) positions blondeness as the ultimate symbol of white women's desirability as constructed by Hollywood's patriarchal and racist regimes of representation, "the most prized possession of white patriarchy . . . the symbolism of sexuality itself." Madonna, quite cleverly satirizing her star text of sex provocateur, evokes these sartorial markers of desirability and celebrity to transform the inherent innocence of Monroe's sexual iconography into unabashed reclamation. Poppy's "Bleach Blonde Baby," through sonic reference to "Material Girl," similarly situates her satire of the gendered constructions of industry plant during a moment of increasing encroachment of beauty influencer economies and infrastructures of influence within the mainstream pop music industry. While the lyrics of "Bleach Blonde Baby," taken at face value, seem to perpetuate the sexist, racist, and capitalist regimes of beauty representation promoted through normative influencer culture, the visual storytelling of the music video's set and style invokes a certain type of industry satire that encourages a more discursive reading.

Positioned within this lineage of popular culture icons whose self-reflexive infantilization is communicated through subtle aesthetic gestures of subversive agency, the sartorial humor of Poppy's absurdist eyelashes, tremendous bundles of tulle, and ginormous bows prompts a certain knowingness of its audience. For some, the invitation to dissect and construct meaning provides the quintessential fan experience of participating outside of the normative constructs of the pop music industry, while for others, willfully submitting to the spectacle of excess and artifice provides similar enjoyment. Central to John Fiske's (1997, 79) discussion of Madonna fandom is the role of style, reproduction, and feminist reimaginations. Arguing against the "cultural dupe" connotation of young girls' ideological and industrial manipulation by pop music consumerism, Fiske positions these "wannabe" re-creations of Madonna's style as a critical "site of semiotic struggle between the forces of patriarchal control and feminine resistance, of capitalism and the subordinate, of the adult and the young." Poppy's industry plant satire is akin to what Fiske understands to be the central tensions of Madonna's sartorial fandom practices. This contrast between the blatant banality of the lyrics and the meticulous construction of the video's visual storytelling instructs a certain type of fannish interpretation, a discordant production of meaning that taunts the self-reflexive cult fan through its semiopaque signs and symbols.

The Signified Contexts of "Blonde"

The dual projects of the music industry's forceful codification of hypernormative female pop musician aesthetics and the sexist derision of these signifiers as formulaic or inauthentic are prevalent throughout popular music history. For the music genres and styles that Poppy most directly references, early aughts bubblegum pop and Y2K pop-punk, early popular press constructions of Avril Lavigne provide an interesting example of how blondeness operates within the sexist industry plant classifications. When Lavigne came on the scene, she and her marketing team made sure to brand her, as Nekesa Mumbi Moody (2004) wrote in 2004, as "a brash teen who didn't dye her hair blond, wear tight outfits or bounce to a bubble-gum beat." Moody's article, titled "The Anti-Britney," instead positions Lavigne as a guitar-wielding singer-songwriter, with her Doc Martens on the throat of bubblegum pop banality. This example points to a lineage of pop music journalists who reproduced the gendered constructs of legitimacy through opposition to the "girly" women of mainstream pop music.

In more contemporary contexts, the pop music fan subreddit r/Popheads is teeming with debates over the current state of industry plants, often using sartorial practices as evidence of inauthenticity. Ava Max, whose 2018 lead single "Sweet but Psycho" held the number-one spot on the UK pop charts for four weeks, was a constant reference in the thread "Artists Who Are Obvious 'Industry Plants'?" (r/Popheads, January 6, 2021). Max is known for her signature "Max Cut," an asymmetrical peroxide blonde wig with one side chopped as short bob and the other side left long and loose, and much of her popular press coverage discusses this sartorial choice as a genuine expression of her quirky self (see, e.g., Zipper 2020). Users on this Reddit thread, however, were much more critical of this self-fashioning. Bre3ent argued that Max's "most recent persona seems focus grouped by a bunch of suits," to which Meerk4T later responded, "Ava is def incredibly manufactured. Her personality is her wig, and then in interviews when she's asked to describe how she came up with the songs, she literally says things that make no sense in the context of the actual song." Other artists mentioned in this thread included Lorde and Billie Eilish, who initially differentiated themselves from the effervescent teenage pop stars of the previous generation through moodier color palettes and structurally ambiguous silhouettes, and who later went blonde to signal a new era of artistic production. Lorde's momentary blondeness was featured in the 2021 music video for "Mood Ring": a lyrical commentary on pseudospiritual wellness culture, where the blatant artificiality of her blonde wig visually positions Lorde's character in the video as a primary candidate for the insidiously charismatic appeals of this form of lifestyle branding. Eilish's "platinum plunge" launched the promotional cycle for her second studio album, *Happier Than Ever* (2021), and was immediately met with critiques that she was selling out her previous androgyny for a more sexualized, and therefore industrially normative, mode of pop star sartorial articulation (Snapes 2021). Together, these examples illustrate the persistence of these gendered scripts of authenticity as artists, fans, and critics alike perpetuate proximity to blondeness as the ultimate signifier of industrially enforced artificiality.

Whereas Moody (2004) points the finger at artists like Britney Spears and Christina Aguilera for their more provocative style and suggestive choreography, Poppy's video suggests through the various stagings of her fashion that a pop star's framing, often the product of a director or stylist on set, works in collaboration with the artist but should not fall on their shoulders alone. Poppy repositions the process of persona construction as a complex site of negotiation between the artist, their creative teams, the record label, and the fans. Sartorially based excess of meaning, within Poppy's work, makes visible the various layers of industry intervention within the pop spectacle while also cleverly embedding hints of agency to subtly assert her awareness and prompt her fans to do the same. It is within these visual frameworks that the eerie juxtaposition of cute and cult signals a knowingness about her interpellation within these regimes of normative representation, a sartorial wink to the audience that constructs an in-community joke with her imagined fandom.

The Subversive Interrogations of "Baby"

To argue that Monroe's story, and therefore Madonna's intertextual appropriation and Poppy's subsequent reference, is purely one of patriarchal exploitation would be to discredit the type of work her performances contributed to redefining the dumb blonde trope within American cinema. Richard Dyer (2003, 34) describes the humor that is central to the dumb blonde trope as the irrational tension between sexual innocence and sexual impact: "Monroe knows about sexuality, but she doesn't know about guilt and innocence—she welcomes sex as natural." Poppy's approach to the inherent artificiality of the bleached blonde industry plant similarly teases at the irrational boundaries

Figure 7.3. The deep focus on Poppy's direct stare into the camera turns the infantilized gaze back onto the viewer to further interrogate how youth sexualization functions in dominant sartorial scripts of pop star femininity (1:42). Still from "Bleach Blonde Baby" music video, uploaded to YouTube.

of her highly gendered texts and their cultural connotations of banal super-ficiality and hypercommodification through humor. The industry plant's implicit youth, and the context of "barely legal" sexualization of mainstream pop stars, is subverted through such a deliberate infantilization. The insidi-ous misogyny of the industry, and our eventual expectations as consumers of these normativities, is flipped on its head. Sexualization is not absent from this project but is an unspoken and invisible boundary object through which Poppy's evocation of actual babies causes the viewer to examine more implicit or insidious ways that we've come to expect a certain level of aes-thetic refinement, "just enough, but not too much" sex appeal, and an acces-sible artificiality. With Poppy framed within re-creations of a birthing ward and a childhood bedroom, the eeriness of her infantile monotone and soft blank stare interrogates the structures of patriarchy that sexualize youth cul-ture, particularly within the tumultuous industry plant pipeline of child star turned adult pop provocateur (figure 7.3).

Poppy's purposeful infantilization, however, communicated through lace bonnets adorned in multicolor pastel flowers and knee-high socks, is juxtaposed with her ability to demand attention from a group of elderly followers. The climax of each chorus within the music video shows Poppy in a rhinestone white prayer robe made of overflowing tulle as she stands

Figure 7.4. Poppy's cutely cult style is on full display as elements from each outfit in the "Bleach Blonde Baby" music video converge to resignify markers of trivial femininity within the context of praise, adoration, and worship (2:04). Still from "Bleach Blonde Baby" music video, uploaded to YouTube.

at the altar in front of a glowing stained-glass mosaic triangle branded in her P insignia, an appropriation of the Illuminati's Eye of Providence (figure 7.4). As her onlooking elderly congregation applauds from the pews of this completely white facsimile of a church building, the stark contrast of the ages depicted instructs the viewer to think critically about the ways age, influence, and celebrity operate within this video's satirical appropriation of the industry plant. Poppy reconstitutes the signifying functions of passivity inherent within large bows, white tulle, and rosy blush cheeks to assert their ability to command the reverence of her adoring followers and structure an entire world of virtual influence. Further, in exposing the sexist double bind of young pop star sexuality and branding within the mainstream industry through these eerie evocations of youth culture, Poppy makes the viewer sit in these moments of uncomfortable infantilization. With fan YouTube comments like, "All of the dislikes are from the people who don't get the sarcasm" (Creep Queen), "so it's about how pop culture basically treats pop stars like theyre [sic] perfect gods. Love it" (asteroids), and "She's never been weird, she just exposes the weird side of the music industry" (sofia cunha), Poppy's fans not only understand the humor but also extrapolate the various industrial and cultural contexts of this satire (Poppy 2017a). The expressive space of critical interpretation within Poppy's image is therefore contingent not on liberation of its female fans' sexuality from the constraints of patriarchy, such as Fiske (1997) argued about Madonna, but on a liberation of the patriarchal cultural assumptions of cuteness and bubblegum pop as inherently banal expressions of hyperfeminine style. However, as much of this video also plays with cultish markers of neoreligiosity, such as the church setting or the mosaic glass insignia, part of Poppy's thesis relies on this context of celebrity worship to legitimate her subversive commentary. With lyrics that tout the immense influence of these hypernormative markers of beauty, the video's final shots of her adoring congregation dancing around with massive furry letters that spell out "everybody dies" once again remind the viewer of the project's cultural critique and cheekily point to the absurdity of the entire surrealist experience of microcelebrity fame.

In exaggerating the neoreligious context of her pop music cult persona through a construction of audience built on a parody of age, Poppy hails the viewer through self-reflexive humor. Matt Hills (2000, 82–83) takes the performance of irony seriously in his discussion of cult fandoms. Satire is more than simply a joke, it evokes a "politics of double coding" that legitimizes as much as it subverts its subject of ridicule to offer "an internalized sign of certain self-consciousness about our culture's means of legitimation." The rituals surrounding cult fandoms function as a collective discursive struggle, as Hills writes, "over what constitutes 'rational' and 'proper' behavior within contemporary media culture." The double coding of Poppy's industry plant embodiment teases at the gendered rationale of the music industry's processes of cultural legitimation. The pop persona, who disproportionately bears the weight of these sexist and racist pressures from industrial framing, is also a product of audience expectations surrounding the "Bleach Blonde Baby" formula of industry plant. In retelling the narrative of her accumulation of influence, or rise to microcelebrity fame, through this ambivalent lens of gendered critique, Poppy reveals how the cult of beauty informs these cultural and industrial scripts of feminized pop music production. The double work of this pop music cult, however, does not end with the conversation of representation. As user Single Unicorn astutely pointed out in the YouTube comments section of the "Bleach Blonde Baby" video, "the idea of poppy for a brand is so smart. People get confused and do conspiracies about her, therefore more people know about her. Because people are so fascinated by her, they keep watching her, and because of that, the company/brand makes a lot of money. They keep expanding and make even more money. It's perfect" (Poppy 2017a). It is within this never-ending loop of accumulation of influence, built into Poppy's parody of brand cult(ure), that the android influencer herself is eventually incorporated—signaling a new, sentient phase in persona construction and satirical performance.

"I AM PROUD OF MY BARE FACE"

On December 28, 2019, Poppy posted a statement regarding the rumored split from her primary creative partner, Titanic Sinclair, to her Facebook page. This statement presents Sinclair as a manipulative egomaniac who uses real-life trauma as a tactic within his social experiments, with specific reference to his faking a suicide attempt to elicit a reaction from Poppy's fans. In a particularly poignant part of the statement, Poppy (2019b) claims, "He weaved himself into a storyline, wanting the public to believe he was a puppeteer, which is far from the truth." Over the next couple months, Sinclair defended himself on Reddit and eventually leaked unreleased demos and photos of Poppy without makeup: a direct attempt to delegitimize the meticulously opaque persona and image the two artists had created together. After remaining silent on the creative and romantic split since her initial post in December 2019, Poppy uploaded the seventh short video in a series of makeup tutorials to her YouTube page on May 5, 2020, titled, "Makeup Removal with Poppy." As she removes a highly feminized tool of sartorial expression as a reclamation of the character she has built since 2014, makeup is not a mirage of artifice or a performance of normative beauty standards but an exercise of authorial agency within and through a highly feminized format of digital labor and intimate fan engagement. Here, the seams of this methodically woven tapestry of artificial authenticity begin to unravel, and new threads of gendered critique must be sewn to prevent further tears in the fan base. This moment of vulnerability is a critical turning point in Poppy's storytelling that uses the fandom surrounding her image and style to retroactively assert her creative sovereignty as the thematic architect, musical genius, and embodied spectacle of her pop music persona.

This seismic shift in persona through more conventional appeals to branded authenticity was further communicated by a return to her natural brunette hair color. While many fans remarked on the apparent happiness and independence communicated through Poppy's return to pre-android form, others asserted Titanic's authorial claim to Poppy's lyrics, concepts, and, most importantly, image. It is through this rupture in Poppy's cultish fandom that the true semiotic function of the bleached blonde baby sartorial construction reveals itself. For some fans, Poppy's project relied on the satirical appropriation of music industry artificiality for the purpose of critiquing the doubly gendered scripts of authentic persona and musical legitimacy. For others, Poppy's hyperfemme imagery was merely a canvas of artificiality created by a man who deployed ideologies of authenticity and musical legitimacy to poke fun at the silly world of pop music consumerism. With this new sartorial transformation, both sides of this interfandom rift position the bleached blonde wig as this site of patriarchal control. Yet the oppositional perspectives reflect the trouble of cult fandom's "double coding" (Hills 2000, 82). Ultimately, Poppy's work constructed this polarizing fan arena of highly subjective affect and the subsequent gendered discourses of beauty cult(ure) through unique appeals to sartorial storytelling and self-reflexive branding. When the real-life conflicts of this artificially blonde branded persona necessitated a genuine declaration of selfhood, Poppy made a choice to become sentiently brunette. In this process, Poppy provided a more definitive reading of her previous android character's sartorial articulations to set the stage for the next era of persona construction.

In the age-old tale of artists who begin their careers by deconstructing celebrity culture, Poppy's rise in popularity soon began to replicate the fraught structures of influence and consumption that her initial character satirized. With a new record deal from Sumerian Records, an indie label specializing in heavy metal and progressive rock, Poppy ditched the subversive strategies of girly pop cult satire and embraced her popular press construction as the "face of Nu-Metal" (Poppy 2019a). The "face" is instructive: her image is still foregrounded in her industrial positioning, but this time the industry has hailed her sartorial articulations, not the other way around. The trouble of cult fandom's double coding reveals itself differently here as the processes of industry legitimation through capitalist accumulation incorporate the once-discursive aspects of the project's self-reflexive weaponization of influence. As she trades in her pastel bows and knee-high socks for spiked chokers and black latex bodysuits, gone is the sartorial wink of her subversively infantilized style. Instead, the thematic residue of her previous projects' neoreligious "influence" now reifies these more masculinized markers of self-fashioning as convincing symbols of authentic persona and legitimate authorship. Her strategic femininity within the hypermasculinist genre of nu metal is similarly concerned with gender and power, but individual sentience now subsumes the broader industrial and societal implications of her previous satire of beauty cult(ure).

REFERENCES

Banet-Weiser, Sarah. 2012. *Authentic™: The Politics of Ambivalence in a Brand Culture*. New York: New York University Press.

Duffy, Brooke Erin. 2017. *(Not) Getting Paid to Do What You Love: Gender, Media, and Aspirational Work*. New Haven, CT: Yale University Press.

Dyer, Richard. 2003. *Heavenly Bodies: Film Stars and Society*. 2nd ed. London: Routledge.

Euse, Erica. 2017. "Revisiting Riot Grrrl's Perverse Love of Infantilized Hair." *i-D*, June 22, 2017. https://i-d.vice.com/en_uk/article/7xbvga/revisiting-riot-grrrls-perverse-love-of-infantilized-hair

Fiske, John. 1997. *Reading the Popular*. London: Routledge, 1997.

Hills, Matt. 2000. "Media Fandom, Neoreligiousity, and Cult(ural) Studies." *Velvet Light Trap* 45:73–84.

Lorde. 2021. "Mood Ring." Uploaded August 17, 2021. YouTube video, 3:44. https://www.youtube.com/watch?v=P103bWMdvtA

Moody, Nekesa Mumbi. 2004. "The Anti-Britney." *Spokesman Review*, May 30, 2004. https://www.spokesman.com/stories/2004/may/30/the-anti-britney/

Poppy. 2017a. "Bleach Blonde Baby (Official Video)." Uploaded December 13, 2017. YouTube video, 3:29. https://www.youtube.com/watch?v=6FbdqwlR0H4

Poppy. 2017b. *Poppy.Computer*. Mad Decent, 2017, compact disc.

Poppy. 2019a. "Poppy Is the Face of Nu-Metal in 2019." Interview. Uploaded by BUILD Series, June 11, 2019. YouTube video, 19:44. https://www.youtube.com/watch?v=usF1v6HtEvE

Poppy. 2019b. "To whom it may concern." Facebook, December 29, 2019. https://www.facebook.com/Poppy/photos/a.866022383414853/3237272802956454

Poppy. 2020. "Makeup Removal with Poppy." Uploaded May 5, 2020. YouTube video, 1:24. https://www.youtube.com/watch?v=OhpDnvrmsYk

Rindner, Grant. 2020. "What Is an Industry Plant?" *Complex*, March 31, 2020. https://www.complex.com/pigeons-and-planes/2020/03/what-is-industry-plant/

Snapes, Laura. 2021. "'It's All about What Makes You Feel Good': Billie Eilish on New Music, Power Dynamics, and Her Internet-Breaking Transformation." *British Vogue*, May 2, 2021. https://www.vogue.co.uk/news/article/billie-eilish-vogue-interview

Zipper, Marni. 2020. "Ava Max's Definition of Success Is All about Being Authentically You." *Audacy*, September 13, 2020. https://www.audacy.com/im-listening/ava-maxs-definition-of-success-is-about-being-authentic

8

In the Navy

Savage X Fenty's Fandorsement Work

Alyxandra Vesey

In early February 2017, Rihanna posted an Instagram selfie of Mariah Carey posing on a climbing machine in black-and-white Fenty x Puma booties, with the caption, "Yo I made it!!!" (@badgalriri, February 2, 2017). The post illustrated Carey's significance in Rihanna's origin story. The younger singer won her high school beauty pageant with a rendition of Carey's "Hero" a year before signing a contract with Def Jam that catapulted her to 250 million global record sales, 54 million downloads, and fourteen *Billboard* Hot 100 chart-topping singles (Molanphy 2019). It also telegraphed Rihanna's pivot from pop stardom to beauty mogul. Rihanna supplemented her early recording career with endorsements from Secret, Nike, and CoverGirl. With a string of blockbuster albums, she transitioned into what Kristin J. Lieb (2013, 42) categorizes as a "career artist," or a recording act with over three multiplatinum albums in their catalog, by supplementing her hit records with lucrative brand partnerships with Parlux Fragrances, Puma, and MAC Cosmetics. Roughly a decade into her recording career, Rihanna filed to trademark her surname, Fenty, for use on "clothing, swimwear, lingerie, cosmetics, skincare, and computer software" (Sharkey 2014). This proprietary decision facilitated her launch of several lifestyle companies, starting with Fenty Beauty in fall 2017. Thus, the timing of the Carey selfie also anticipated how Rihanna and her team would use celebrity fandom as a promotional strategy. While Rihanna continued to post selfies and tutorials to boost new products by reinforcing her personal connection to them, her Instagram account began highlighting musicians' product engagement and repositioned her as the fulcrum between generations of Black female pop stars. For example, Rihanna posted a picture of Lizzo in a Savage X Fenty bra from *ELLE*'s Women in Music issue (@badgalriri, September 5, 2019). *ELLE* published this issue a few months after Lizzo's performance of "Truth Hurts" at the 2019 BET Awards, which went viral after crowd footage of Rihanna clapping during her flute solo recirculated online.

Rihanna reinforced their connection by including Lizzo as a runway model for Savage X Fenty's fall 2020 collection. She also replicated her own pop star trajectory by naming Normani as Savage X Fenty's first brand ambassador in September 2019, a month after the former Fifth Harmony member released her first solo single, "Motivation."

In this chapter, I recognize such promotional efforts as fandorsement work, or established celebrities' sharing social capital with their nascent counterparts by enlisting them as spokespeople for their branded goods through mutual fan affinities. I use Savage X Fenty to illustrate this phenomenon by examining how its race-, size-, and gender-inclusive runway shows and its recruitment of Normani and Megan Thee Stallion as brand ambassadors are constructed as intergenerational exchanges between Rihanna and her protégées. Normani's Savage X Fenty deal echoes the first phase of Rihanna's career as a spokesmodel and accords with other contemporary pop stars' promotion of their mentors' extramusical ventures, as when Chloe x Halle promote their association with Beyoncé's management company, Parkwood Entertainment, by posting pictures of themselves in Ivy Park clothing. In a sense, fandorsement work adheres to the promotional logic of stan culture, a digital remediation of fan communities wherein celebrities' devoted followings use social media to make their allegiances legible online by assembling themselves into squads with hashtaggable team names. For example, Rihanna Navy takes its name from "G4L," the pop star's anthem in which she describes her female listeners as a navy capable of world domination. Yet at the same time, Savage X Fenty's fandorsement work also positions Rihanna's protégées as beneficiaries of the pop star's lucrative brand, thus creating opportunities for intergenerational wealth that have historically been foreclosed to Black female pop stars in the US recording industry.

THEORIZING FANDORSEMENT WORK

Celebrity studies pioneer Richard Dyer (1979, 35) defines stardom as "an image of the way stars live." Glamour is an inextricable part of this lifestyle, especially for female and feminine celebrities whose fame depends on their ability to spectacularize themselves through iconic style. Dyer (1979, 38) claims these beauty ideals are meant to be "shared by star and fan" through filmographies and ephemera like fan magazines that offer tips and beauty secrets to fans who cannot afford luxury goods but want to access some part of their screen idols' extraordinary allure to add sparkle to their everyday lives. For pop stars who use performance to translate their musical recordings into mediated spectacle, stage wear is a crucial component of their singular yet replicable glamour. This was true for girl groups and girl singers who emerged during rock 'n' roll's first decade (1955–64), a period overlapped by the rise of television, teen magazines, and youth-oriented advertising. As ambassadors for feminine youth culture, these young women were compelled by their management teams and the public to present themselves as aspirational figures who gracefully navigated adult sexuality and the gendered and racialized expectations of adolescent innocence while executing choreography in coordinated dresses, confectionary hairdos, and winged eyeliner (Warwick 2007; Apolloni 2021).

Music video remediated spectacular glamour for female pop stars during its commercial ascent in the 1980s. Lisa A. Lewis (1991, 109) posits that music video's integration into artists' promotional strategies allowed female pop stars like Cyndi Lauper to showcase their idiosyncratic style while negotiating domestic and public spaces in short-form narratives about personal discovery "that resonate[d] with [offscreen] female cultural experiences." Music video also helped artists announce personal transformations and new projects to maximize fan engagement. For example, Janet Jackson used the video for "Love Will Never Do (without You)" (1990), which featured the pop star frolicking on the beach in ripped jeans and a bustier, to declare her evolution from dancing tomboy to lithe bombshell. Music videos' ubiquity throughout the late twentieth century also allowed fans to carefully study and mimic their idols through extensive screen time and the medium's integration into advertising and shopping malls. John Fiske (1992, 38) identifies such fan behavior as enunciative productivity, or public fan activities that construct identities and assert community membership through speech or appearance. Fiske (1989, 77–92) arrived at the concept by interrogating his daughter's adoption of Madonna's style as a model for feminine empowerment. Thus, enunciative productivity is a useful framework not only for understanding fan identification through self-presentation but specifically for examining pop divas' engagement with sartorial fandom. A diva's endurance as a public figure often relies on her ability to distill her brand sensibility into a shared symbolic language with fans. Madonna fans wore stacked rubber bracelets to approximate her early-career club-kid aesthetic. Brandy idealized Black girlhood by popularizing braided hairstyles. More recently, Lorde, Alessia Cara, and Billie Eilish have rejected pop's propensity for female objectification by using baggy clothing to reclaim bodily autonomy for themselves and their young fans.

In addition to making television appearances and music videos, contemporary female pop stars are also expected to create what Lieb (2013, 22) describes as "compelling narrative constructions . . . with brand-specific details" on social media. This expectation coincides with the rise of "Instafame," Alice E. Marwick's (2015, 137) term for "the condition of having a relatively great number of followers on the [Instagram] app." Rihanna's Instagram account, @badgalriri, had 134 million followers as of August 2022. Like many of her contemporaries, she and her team regularly post a mélange of intimate tableaux and promotional content. In particular, her makeup tutorials and product selfies respond to, replicate, and reinforce her fans' online engagement with beauty culture. Social media and digital communication inform Savage X Fenty's recruitment of prominent influencers as models and brand ambassadors, many of whom appear on both Rihanna's account and their respective platforms, and its partnership with TechStyle Fashion Group, an online-only fashion retailer. This feedback loop illustrates Marwick and danah boyd's (2011, 140) claim that digital-age celebrity is an "organic and ever-changing *performative practice* rather than a set of intrinsic personal characteristics or external labels." For Marwick and boyd, celebrity is based on "a set of circulated strategies and practices that place fame on a continuum, rather than as a bright line that separates individuals." Rihanna's crafted candid glamour also illuminates the platform's confluence of mundane and spectacular content, which Marwick (2015, 142) attributes to users' varying degrees of fame: "'regular' selfies often emulate celebrity-related media, while celebrity selfies often closely resemble those of the nonfamous."

In many ways, contemporary female pop stardom affirms the advancement of what Sarah Banet-Weiser (2018, 16) identifies as popular feminism, a neoliberal framework for gender equality that commodifies liberation and empowerment through "a trajectory of capitalist 'success'" by optimizing and individualizing women's professional achievement, personal esteem, and social currency. Popular feminism shapes performers' careful brand management and stan armies' impulse to elevate their favorite pop idols. It contextualizes female pop stars' work as lifestyle moguls and impresarios, a development that links Rihanna to businesswomen like Madonna, who helped cultivate Meshell Ndegeocello's and Alanis Morissette's talent by launching Maverick Records. It also informs Taylor Swift's decision to appear with her female celebrity friends in concert and on social media during *1989*'s rollout (2014), a practice that critic Jude Doyle (2015) described as "girl squad feminism" and that ultimately reasserted her authority over the group and marginalized female celebrities of color.

However, girl groups negotiated professional sisterhood with personal ambition long before popular feminism emerged as a contemporary ethos. Diana Ross's post-Supremes solo career created a template for crossover solo stardom that influenced Beyoncé's and Rihanna's trajectories as their vocal groups' breakout stars. By contrast, acts like Labelle adopted a more heterogenous approach to showcase individual talent within the collective, influencing subsequent personality-driven pop groups like Salt-N-Pepa, TLC, and the Spice Girls (Grieg 1989; Bertei 2021). Furthermore, popular feminism's implicit whiteness cannot fully account for how Black female pop stars utilize entrepreneurialism as a tactic to build generational wealth. In her book about soul music's formal aesthetics, Emily J. Lordi (2020, 35) locates soul's etymology as a marketing term for Black business owners to telegraph racial pride and radicalism to their customers during the late 1960s. Thus, soul's celebration of authentic self-expression was "in keeping with, not opposed to, soul artists' desire to get paid." Hip-hop, a genre built from soul's earthen foundation, advanced sampling and boasting as two citational practices that connected contemporary artists to their elders and highlighted rappers' rhyming prowess and material worth through their lyricism. It is also a genre with its own vetting process for up-and-coming talent, through rap crews, guest verses, and features.

As a genre, hip-hop exhibited minimal anxiety about "selling out" during its commercial rise in the 1980s. Dan Charnas (2010, x) posits that "if hip-hop has four elements (DJing, MCing, graffiti, and breaking), and perhaps a fifth (style), then I argue for the recognition of a sixth: marketing." Thus, rappers like Adidas fans Run-DMC used enunciative productivity to declare their ambitions as consumers and entrepreneurs. While both hip-hop and pop are often denounced by critics as "materialistic" (McLeod 2002), such commentary ignores Black artists' economic disenfranchisement under white supremacy and companies' and advertisers' reticence to align their brands with "urban" music. For example, in 1986, Run-DMC's manager, Lyor Cohen, wore down Adidas into signing hip-hop's first million-dollar endorsement deal after executives saw fans hold up their shoes during a live performance of "My Adidas" on the group's *Raising Hell* tour (Charnas 2010, 185). In 2003, Jay-Z became the first rapper to design his own sneaker, the S. Carter, as part of a brand partnership with Reebok's RBK line. A few years later, Adidas acquired Reebok and tapped 50 Cent, Nelly, and Missy Elliott to create their own sneaker collections (Welty 2016a). But the German athletic company wanted its own hip-hop designer, and so it recruited Kanye West in 2013 to launch Yeezy, a venture that initiated the company's pursuit of partnerships with producer Pharrell Williams and rapper Kendrick Lamar, the latter through Reebok's parent company (Greene 2014; Welty 2016b). In 2019, Beyoncé relaunched her Ivy Park athleisure line with Adidas after severing ties with her previous business partner, Topshop, after its owner, Philip Green, was accused of sexual misconduct (Elibert 2020).

While early endorsement deals facilitated hip-hop's rise and eventually resulted in profitable brand partnerships, many rappers created their own brands at the turn of the twenty-first century in order to demonstrate to a risk-averse fashion industry scaffolded by white supremacy that hip-hop had global commercial reach. In 1998, P. Diddy (then Puff Daddy) launched Sean John, a clothing line that quickly outsold his recorded output and accounted for over 60 percent of his US$160 million annual gross (Davis 2001). A year later, Jay-Z started Rocawear, which he would sell almost a decade later for over US$200 million (Reuters 2007). Such entrepreneurial hustle informed rappers' celebration of their own branded goods in verse. But their female counterparts rarely boasted such abundance. In 2019, *Forbes* published a list of the twenty highest-paid rappers, which included Diddy and Jay-Z in the top five, behind Kanye West's US$150 million annual gross. Nicki Minaj and Cardi B were the list's only female rappers, with a combined annual salary of US$57 million (Greenburg 2019). These women follow in the footsteps of pioneers like Queen Latifah, one of the few female rappers to enjoy a sustained career as an actress, television/film producer, and spokeswoman. Exceptionalism also limits female rappers' commercial success. Charts analyst Chris Molanphy (2017) observes that the music business only supports "one rap queen . . . at a time, while a handful of others hang on at a lower commercial tier." These limits are often reinforced by ginned-up rivalries, though artists like Missy Elliott have pushed against them by collaborating with multiple female rappers and singers and mentoring younger artists like Aaliyah and Tweet.

These conditions inform Beyoncé's and Rihanna's lyrical product placement as performers who grew up on hip-hop, a genre that is now at the center of popular music, and who apply its swagger to their own songs. Beyoncé's 2011 hit "Single Ladies (Put a Ring on It)" includes a line about the pop star rebounding at a club with someone who clings to her like a pair of Deréon jeans, a reference to the clothing line she launched with her mother in 2006. And in 2013's strip club anthem "Pour It Up," Rihanna revels in how much people love her smell, an allusion to her Reb'l Fleur signature fragrance, which generated over US$80 million (Born 2011, 9). Furthermore, unlike their white female and Black male contemporaries, they embody their brands' appeal to Black feminine beauty. Robin James (2015, 161) interprets "Pour It Up" as a refutation of the judgment passed on Black women's "frivolous" spending in the absence of systemic investment in their quality of life. Such lyricism reclaims rap's masculine swagger and promotes products that facilitate what Suzanne Scott (2019, 185) describes as "hyperfeminized expressions of fannish affect," a guiding principle in Savage X Fenty's fandorsement work.

PHRESH OUT THE RUNWAY

In September 2019, Amazon Prime released a backstage documentary for Savage X Fenty's Fall/Winter 2019 collection that was filmed at the Barclays Center during New York Fashion Week by directors Alex Rudzinski and Sandrine Orabona. The event followed the brand's inaugural runway show (at the 2018 New York Fashion Week), which YouTube livestreamed. That inaugural show was a twenty-minute presentation that attracted two million viewers and drew headlines for its diverse cast of models, including Slick Woods, who strutted down the runway in a lace bodysuit before going into labor with her son (Instagram, @slickwoods, September 14, 2018). Savage X Fenty made films for its 2019 and 2020 collections in exchange for online distribution (Binkley 2019). Amazon Studios head Jen Salke proclaimed that Savage X Fenty reinvented "what fashionable lingerie should be" by celebrating "inclusivity, body positivity, and fun" (Weinberg 2019). However, Kellie Ell (2019) of *Women's Wear Daily* questioned its inventiveness by noting that many lingerie companies offered a range of sizes and that Victoria's Secret remained intimate apparel's leader in sales and online engagement. What Savage X Fenty had going for it was a willingness to leverage Rihanna's glamorous image and sizable following by booking supermodels, as well as a wide range of microcelebrities, influencers, and nascent pop stars, many of whom had not been included in a runway show. According to style blogger Cora Harrington, the brand's appeal "[was] very much Rihanna" (Ell 2019).

To some extent, the Victoria's Secret annual fashion show was an important precursor for the Savage X Fenty runway shows. In particular, its fifteen-year run on CBS (2002–17) solidified the brand's proximity to pop stardom by presenting the fashion show as a music revue led by male heartthrobs who crooned to and ogled the runway models during their performances in order to help position the brand as an integral part of heterosexual seduction. The fashion show also usually booked at least one pop diva to appeal to female consumers and model less complicated underwear. For example, Rihanna debuted her seventh album, *Unapologetic*, at the 2012 fashion show.

She coordinated with the event's costuming by wearing black garters to perform "Diamonds" and layering a gauzy kimono over white underwear for "Phresh Out the Runway." However, by the late 2010s, the ratings for the Victoria's Secret annual fashion show were in free fall. In 2018, CBS declined to renew its contract after a 40 percent drop in eighteen-to-forty-nine-year-old viewers, and the show ran its final broadcast on ABC later that year (O'Connell 2018). Furthermore, Victoria's Secret battled accusations of exclusionary casting practices against plus-size, transgender, and nonbinary models that made the brand seem conservative and antiquated. Savage X Fenty differentiated itself by booking BIPOC (Black, Indigenous, and people of color), fat, and gender nonconforming influencers, some of whom identified as Navy members, alongside established models like Cara Delevingne. Savage X Fenty cast plus-size model Paloma Elsesser, body-positive influencers Margie Plus and Raisa Flowers, and transgender model Isis King and dressed them and the thin cisgender supermodels in the same undergarments. Victoria's Secret responded to Savage X Fenty's inclusive bookings by hiring Elsesser for its Spring 2021 swimwear campaign (Betancourt 2021).

Amazon's 2019 and 2020 Savage X Fenty shows used pop stardom as brand differentiation by fusing music video's iconographic visual language with the concert documentary's mediated communion between musicians and fans and the selfie's intimate digital portraiture. Aided by Rudzinski, who had directed multiple MTV Video Music Awards (VMAs) ceremonies and live broadcast network musicals, the shows' immersive production design and emphasis on dance and spectacle allowed the Savage X Fenty films to merge concert staging with music video world-building. The 2019 show introduced these concerns with an opening sequence that gave viewers a glimpse of Rihanna's team developing a live runway show that highlighted, as Rihanna put it, "unique characteristics and people that aren't usually highlighted in the world of fashion and what society perceives as sexy" (Rudzinski and Orabona 2019). The curation of these "unique characteristics and people" on the catwalk and behind the scenes replicated the Navy's recruitment logic of gathering a wide range of women, femme, and nonbinary people to promote and elevate Rihanna as a global brand. While the 2019 film introduced the collection with a montage detailing Rihanna's input during meetings, fittings, and rehearsals, Amazon's 2020 film worked around the runway show's remote shoot at the Los Angeles Convention Center in early fall during the COVID-19 pandemic by organizing the production thematically. Rihanna introduced each segment in voice-over while journaling about how concepts like inspiration and sexuality shaped the collection, and the models elaborated on the show's major themes in interviews that reinforced the brand's "reputation as the #MeToo answer to Victoria's Secret," as Booth Moore (2020) of *Women's Wear Daily* surmised.

Savage X Fenty fashion shows borrowed from the sound design of the Victoria's Secret shows by combining live performances with prerecorded remixes that sustained an energetic mood for would-be consumers. Furthermore, some musicians followed in Rihanna's footsteps and performed at both events. However, they were less beholden to upholding conventional femininity while wearing Rihanna's lingerie. For example, Halsey's performance of "Graveyard" at Savage X Fenty 2019 was comparably looser than their stiff rendition of "Without Me" at the 2018 Victoria's Secret fashion show. At the Barclays Center, Halsey relished their pansexuality by caressing the models while frolicking on stage in a black robe. Such production decisions illustrated Savage X Fenty's inclusion of female, femme, and gender nonconforming models to "queer" lingerie beyond compulsory heterosexuality and the male gaze and make its branded image of aestheticized desire applicable to a wider range of bodies and orientations.

Rihanna's team continued to draw from the pop world for Savage X Fenty's 2020 runway show by booking Puerto Rican rapper Bad Bunny and Spanish singer-songwriter Rosalía as performers. The show also included a segment with Lizzo twerking before a mirror to D'Angelo's "Brown Sugar" in an electric blue bodysuit. The brand also strengthened its queer credentials by hiring *Pose* actress Indya Moore and *Drag Race* queens Jaida Essence Hall, Shea Couleé, and Gigi Goode as models. Their inclusion demonstrates how drag queens, particularly trans femmes of color, have reimagined the catwalk, historically one of the fashion industry's most exclusionary gatekeeping mechanisms, into inclusive spaces for queer creative expression and community-building. It also reveals drag queens' engagement with pop stardom through lip sync battles and celebrity impersonation, a development accelerated by *Drag Race*'s popularity and the program's expectation that successful contestants follow host and producer RuPaul's example by launching their own recording careers and pursuing endorsement contracts and brand partnerships. Furthermore, Ru girls are often cast based on their ability to cultivate and maintain devoted online followings, particularly among teenage girls, to strengthen the show's fanbase (Framke 2017). For example, Hall, Couleé, and Goode have nearly 3.5 million Instagram followers between them. Their Instafame bolsters Savage X Fenty's online presence as their product selfies and behind-the-scenes footage recirculate on the platform and generate hundreds of thousands of likes, views, and comments. But Rihanna and her team prioritize recruiting up-and-coming Black female recording acts who can use their proximity to her brand as a springboard for their own success. This dynamic was dramatized at the end of the 2019 runway show, when Rihanna embraced Tierra Whack backstage after her closing medley with DJ Khaled, Fat Joe, and Fabolous and asked "you know how much I love you, right?" (Rudzinski and Orabona 2019). While Whack is not yet a household name, her 2018 debut, *Whack World*, pioneered the Instagram video album as a distribution strategy by providing her surreal microsongs with candy-coated visuals that inventively adhered to the platform's video length and aspect ratio requirements. This dynamic also informs the cultivation of Normani and Megan Thee Stallion as Savage X Fenty's brand ambassadors.

STAY UP ON MY INSTAGRAM: NORMANI AND MEGAN NEGOTIATE FANDORSEMENT WORK

Normani was among the coterie of models who appeared in both of the Amazon runway shows. In November 2019, she turned to Instagram to announce her selection as Savage X Fenty's "first ever brand ambassador," posting a selfie before a mirror in a scarlet bra-and-panty set and rhinestone-branded thigh highs. However, she telegraphed the endorsement deal not on social media but in the middle of the 2019 runway presentation, dancing a short, intricate routine to Sean Paul's "Get Busy." The performance highlighted Normani's athleticism, an asset that Rihanna specifically asked her to showcase and that prompted her to exclaim "Ugh why can't I be you?!" on Twitter after several clips of Normani's performance recirculated on social media (Yotka 2019; @rihanna, September 22, 2019). Normani's dancing skills distinguished her from the rest of Fifth Harmony, the vocal group she joined as a contestant on FOX's singing competition *The X Factor*. After cutting three albums with Epic in the 2010s, Normani signed a solo deal with RCA that removed her from the racist trolling she had withstood from Harmonizers as the lone Black group member and repositioned her as "a big-voiced dance machine with a flair for diva-like showmanship," according to *Rolling Stone*'s Brittany Spanos (2020). Normani honored this legacy by restaging Janet Jackson's routine to the 1986 "Pleasure Principle" video at the 2018 BMI R&B/Hip-Hop Awards for the performer's lifetime achievement award. She also executed elaborate routines for her video and the 2019 VMAs performance of "Motivation," which evoked Jackson's rigorous choreography and erotic self-possession. Though "Motivation" peaked at number 33 on the *Billboard* Hot 100, such promotional

decisions were designed to position Normani as an extension of Black wom-
en's commercial and cultural lineage in pop music. While discussing how it
felt for Rihanna to choose her as Savage X Fenty's first brand ambassador,
Normani enthused that she "is somebody I've looked up to for a very, very
long time. She's had so much influence on me" (Yotka 2019).

Normani went into 2020 planning to release her debut album and capitalized on her moment by gracing two *Rolling Stone* covers early in the year.
In addition to her first feature with the magazine, she posed with SZA and
Megan Thee Stallion for its second annual Women Shaping the Future issue.
Normani also released "Diamonds," a collaboration with Megan, as the lead
single to Warner Bros.' Harley Quinn vehicle, *Birds of Prey*. However, the song
stalled at number 16 on the *Billboard* Bubbling under Hot 100 chart, and *Birds
of Prey* was pulled from theaters a month after its release due to the COVID-19
pandemic. Like for many in the music industries, Normani's recording and
touring plans were jettisoned for the immediate future. She kept a low profile on social media, occasionally posting Savage X Fenty selfies on Instagram along with candid shots, signal boosts for Black Lives Matter, and an
announcement that she was selected to be cosmetic company Urban Decay's
new "global citizen." Such partnerships were a lifeline during the COVID-19
pandemic, which disrupted most performers' touring prospects throughout
2020. Normani also briefly appeared in Savage X Fenty's 2020 show as part of
a segment set to N.E.R.D's "She Wants to Move," where she preened in white
lingerie and a bridal veil. However, she subtly indicated some discomfort with
her career trajectory on social media. In July, she posted a #savagexambassa-
dor selfie in an orange thong with the caption "yes, I swear I still make music"
(@normani, July 12, 2020). Such a post illustrates the limits of Savage X Fenty's
fandorsement work strategies. Normani, a young Black woman raised in the
Christian faith and a survivor of racist trolling, may not feel empowered by
sharing selfies in her idol's branded underwear. Yet the digital economy she
inherited from her heroines, women who benefit from her admiration, values her visibility over her artistry. This emphasis on brand visibility reveals
fandorsement work's limitations. Normani is a talented and seasoned enter-
tainer nearly a decade into her recording career. She released three albums
with Fifth Harmony but has released only a handful of singles since going solo
in 2018. While fandorsement work keeps her name in circulation through her
alignment with Savage X Fenty, it cannot provide her with the resources to
cement her own identity.

While Normani's intermittent and ambivalent posting may illustrate the ennui of a rising star born a few decades too late, her "Diamonds" collaborator cannily embraced Instafame. Days before US COVID-19 fatalities surpassed a hundred thousand lives lost, Savage X Fenty announced Megan as the brand's new spokesmodel. The campaign was part of Megan's broader promotional strategy for *Suga* (2020), the EP she dropped as a follow-up to her 2019 debut mixtape, *Fever*. Megan began promoting her upcoming EP's lead single, "B.I.T.C.H.," an empowerment anthem in the mold of Missy Elliott's "She's a Bitch" that celebrated Black female rappers' reclamation of misogynistic language for professional autonomy and personal dignity. Such triumphal gestures took on a deeper significance when Megan revealed on Instagram Live that her label, 1501 Certified, had decided to delay *Suga*'s release after the rapper requested to void her contract after meeting with her management team at Roc Nation (Kiefer 2020). *Pitchfork* reported that 1501 and its distributor, Atlantic subsidiary 300 Entertainment, took nearly 75 percent of Megan's recording profits and "a 50 percent share of Megan's publishing, 30 percent of her touring income, 30 percent of her merchandising, control of her merchandising, and a cut of such 'passive income' as sponsorships and endorsement deals" (Hogan 2020). Megan considered it "unconscionable" that she earned only US$15,000 after generating roughly US$7 million in streaming and download sales (Lamarre 2020).

Megan released *Suga* by filing a restraining order against 1501, and the EP rounded out the *Billboard* Hot 100's top ten when it debuted in mid-March. During *Suga*'s release week, a Black teenager named Keara Wilson created a dance for its third single, "Savage," and uploaded her routine to TikTok while fiddling with the video-sharing app. It quickly went viral (@keke.janajah, March 3, 2020). A few days later, Megan and her friend Kelsey Nicole uploaded their version of Wilson's dance to Instagram, where Megan captioned it "#savagechallenge" (@theestallion, March 16, 2020). Megan had already proven her savvy use of hashtags to create interactive content for fans that quantified engagement. She had turned her "hot girl shit" ad-lib on the song "Cash Shit" into #hotgirlsummer, a hashtag that helped boost *Fever*'s streaming sales. Megan capitalized on the "hot girl summer" meme by branding her followers "Hotties" on social media and distilled her complicated legal battle into #freetheestallion, a succinct phrase that made it easy for her fans to rally around her without knowing the inner workings of contract law. Her savvy challenged 1501's implicit sexism in undervaluing her talent by seeking to control interest of her "Hottie" merchandise and by framing as "passive" Puma, Coach, and Revlon's endorsements with her to boost their digital reach.

Megan's first #savagechallenge video also demonstrated her resourceful-ness. The post's other caption, "#quarantineandchill," visualized by Megan and Kelsey's decision to stage the shoot in Megan's kitchen in gray sweats, signposted the pandemic's early existential threat. Megan's team canceled the concert and festival dates they had booked to promote *Suga*. Further-more, the pandemic threw a wrench in Megan's ability to safely make a video for the song. Megan used #savagechallenge to drum up streams for "Savage" in the absence of the recording industry's conventional promo-tional methods. She hosted four different versions of the video on YouTube, including an animated lyric video that reproduced Wilson's original "Sav-age" dance, an animated video that won the VMA for Best Hip-Hop Video, and two videos for the "Savage" remix that Megan recorded with Beyoncé for Megan's debut studio album, *Good News* (2020), one of which supple-mented preexisting footage from the stars' videographies and profiles with intercut shots of Megan and her fans doing the #savagechallenge dance. Megan took the challenge to TikTok with a series of videos that telegraphed contemporary pop stars' need to be fluent across Web platforms in order to be legible within a digital economy. As a result, several Instagram and TikTok users circulated their own versions of the #savagechallenge dance. This challenge also presaged "WAP," Megan and Cardi B's Internet-breaking ode to desire with a video cameo from Normani, as the rapper's second viral sensation during an especially cruel summer.

Furthermore, Megan, twerked in Savage X Fenty sweats for her first #savagechallenge video, demonstrating her ability to seamlessly integrate other artists' products into her social media presence. She already had some experience with this, having shot an unboxing video earlier in the year for Beyoncé's Ivy Park x Adidas athleisure line as part of its promotional blitz of gifting the collection to a smattering of influencers. Many of the cam-paign's unboxing videos were synched to Beyoncé songs, including Megan's minute-long twerk session to "Crazy in Love" (Megan Thee Stallion 2020a). However, while Megan did not actually model Ivy Park x Adidas merchan-dise in her unboxing video, she announced her brand ambassadorship to Savage X Fenty by posting multiple Instagram and TikTok videos that fea-tured the rapper posing in branded lingerie to "Savage" (Heching 2020). These clips, which received upward of a million views on their respective platforms, demonstrated Megan's ability to reframe her unapologetic artis-tic statement into a jingle for another Black pop star's products in order to multiply both of their fortunes.

PLANNING FOR THE FUTURE

In March 2021, Megan Thee Stallion accepted the Grammy Award for Best New Artist. The moment was significant for a few reasons. For one, she was the second Black female rapper to win the award in the Recording Academy's history, after Lauryn Hill's historic win in 1999. She was also the third Black woman in this century to win a Best New Artist Grammy, a form of industry recognition that had eluded performers like Rihanna and Beyoncé. While Beyoncé achieved a Grammy milestone later that evening for her work with Megan on "Savage," which won Best Rap Song and resulted in the pop star receiving the most career wins of any recording artist in Grammy history, neither she nor Rihanna were nominated for Best New Artist at the beginning of their careers. They have primarily been recognized in "genre" categories, while Best New Artist is one of the four "main" categories that the Recording Academy often bestows on white artists working in pop and rock. For another, Megan concluded her emotional speech by thanking her mother, Holly Thomas, a former rapper who managed her daughter's early career and died from brain cancer two months before the release of Megan's *Fever* mixtape. She also received this award from Lizzo, a friend, collaborator, and fellow Houstonian who lost in the category to Billie Eilish in 2020. Finally, she capped her speech by noting that "it's been a hell of a year, but we made it" (Hamilton 2021).

The offhand remark was undoubtedly an allusion to COVID-19, which required the Recording Academy to stage the event outside during the first vaccination wave. But it also nodded to Megan's having to balance a professional breakthrough with personal hardship. In July 2020, she was shot by rapper Tory Lanez at a party, an incident she used to reinterpret "Savage" as a protest anthem on *Saturday Night Live* a month before the 2020 US presidential election. Halfway through the performance, Megan and her dancers stopped twerking and raised their fists to a recording of activist Tamika Mallory excoriating Kentucky attorney general Daniel Cameron for the grand jury's failure to indict the police who killed Breonna Taylor. In front of a bullet-ridden red screen, Megan exclaimed that "we need to protect our Black women" (King 2020). She elaborated on this statement in a *New York Times* op-ed that recognized Black women as American democracy's saviors, who "are entitled to our anger about a laundry list of mistreatment and neglect that we suffer" (Megan Thee Stallion 2020b).

The setbacks of 2020 seemed to fuel Megan's ambition. In December 2021, she graduated from Texas Southern University with a BS in health administration. She also followed "Savage" with a dozen new singles, including *Good News* cuts "Girls in the Hood" and "Body," "Thot Shit," a remix of BTS's "Butter," and the lascivious Dua Lipa duet "Sweetest Pie," all of which were accompanied by eye-popping music videos and dance challenges that helped the songs go viral online. She also expanded her portfolio as a businesswoman by promoting her own hot sauce as part of a partnership with the Popeyes Chicken franchise, appearing in Cash App commercials as its new spokeswoman, and working with these companies and other corporations like Amazon Music and Fashion Nova to create scholarships, educational resources, and financial contributions for female students and entrepreneurs of color, particularly in cities with sizable Black communities, like Atlanta and her hometown of Houston. Similarly, in spring 2022 Lizzo returned to the spotlight with three new projects to promote: her forthcoming album, *Special*; a dance-based competition reality show for Amazon, *Watch Out for the Big Grrrls*, part of her multiyear development deal with the company; and her new plus-size shapewear line for Fabletics, Yitty. Such relentless hustle demonstrates how these women learned the lessons of fandorsement work by creating and pursuing musical projects and extramusical ventures in their own image.

While Megan and Lizzo seized their moment, their mentor continued to cultivate her brand. By summer 2019, Rihanna was named the wealthiest woman in pop music, having amassed US$600 million primarily as a beauty mogul (Robehmed 2019). In July 2020, she and her team launched Fenty Skin and enlisted male rappers A$AP Rocky and Lil Nas X as brand ambassadors in order to target male customers as a growing demographic group within the skincare market. She also leveraged her inclusive lifestyle brand's economic pull by aligning it with the fight for racial justice. In March 2020, her nonprofit donated US$5 million to various organizations dedicated to fighting the spread of COVID-19, a virus that has disproportionately affected Black and Latinx people (CLF 2020). After George Floyd's murder in May 2020, Fenty's lifestyle companies participated in Blackout Tuesday, and Savage X Fenty donated funds to Black Lives Matter (Potter 2020). She also appeared to be preparing to extend her legacy in other ways. In February 2022, Rihanna announced on Instagram that she and A$AP Rocky were expecting their first child together (@badgirlriri, February 2, 2022). This life event perhaps best distills fandorsement work's potential as a tactic for Black performers' acquisition of intergenerational wealth: a couple who fell in love while he was promoting her skincare line, a child who will be the benefactor to one of contemporary pop music's most sizable fortunes, and a mother who turned her iconic glamour into a business empire.

REFERENCES

Apolloni, Alexandra. 2021. *Freedom Girls: Voicing Femininity in 1960s British Pop*. New York: Oxford University Press.

Banet-Weiser, Sarah. 2018. *Empowered: Popular Feminism and Popular Misogyny*. Durham, NC: Duke University Press.

Bertei, Adele. 2021. *Why Labelle Matters*. Austin: University of Texas Press.

Betancourt, Bianca. 2021. "Paloma Elsesser on Redefining Sex Appeal." *Harper's Bazaar*, September 28, 2021. https://www.harpersbazaar.com/fashion/models/a37758024/

Binkley, Christina. 2019. "How Jennifer Salke Turned Amazon Studios into a Storytelling Powerhouse." *ELLE*, October 14, 2019. https://www.elle.com/culture/movies-tv/a29461367/jennifer-salke-amazon/

Born, Pete. 2011. "Rihanna Expands Scent Offerings with Rebelle." *Women's Wear Daily* 202 (106): 9.

Charnas, Dan. 2010. *The Big Payback: The History of the Business of Hip-Hop*. New York: New American Library.

CLF (Clara Lionel Foundation). 2020. "CLF Donates $5 Million to Fight COVID-19." March 20, 2020. https://claralionelfoundation.org/news/rihanna-donates-5-million-to-fight-covid-19/

Davis, Alisha. 2001. "Puffy's Fur Is Flying." *Newsweek*, February 11, 2001. https://www.newsweek.com/puffys-fur-flying-155325

Doyle, Jude. 2015. "Taylor Swift, Nicki Minaj, and the Limits of Girl Squad Feminism." *Verge*, July 23, 2015. https://www.theverge.com/2015/7/23/9025695/

Dyer, Richard. 1979. *Stars*. London: British Film Institute.

Elibert, Mark. 2020. "Laced Up: Beyoncé's First Ivy Park x Adidas Collaboration Foreshadows Her Sneaker-Culture Dominance." *Billboard*, January 13, 2020. https://www.billboard.com/music/music-news/laced-up-beyonce-ivy-park-adidas-breakdown-8547744/

Ell, Kellie. 2019. "Taking Lessons from Rihanna." *Women's Wear Daily*, November 12, 2019. https://wwd.com/fashion-news/intimates/rihanna-savage-x-fenty-changing-lingerie-world-1203346655/

Fiske, John. 1989. *Reading the Popular*. New York: Routledge.

Fiske, John. 1992. "The Cultural Economy of Fandom." In *The Adoring Audience: Fan Culture and Popular Media*, edited by Lisa A. Lewis, 30–49. New York: Routledge.

Framke, Caroline. 2017. "How RuPaul's Drag Race Went from Cult Favorite to Inspirational Teenage Dream." *Vox*, June 26, 2017. https://www.vox.com/culture/2017/6/26/15845792/

Greenburg, Zack O'Malley. 2019. "Highest-Paid Hip-Hop Acts 2019: Kanye Tops Jay-Z to Claim Crown." *Forbes*, September 19, 2019. https://www.forbes.com/hip-hop-cash-kings/

Greene, Tasha. 2014. "Adidas' Music Gamble: Why They're Betting on Pharrell Williams and Kanye West." *Billboard*, April 22, 2014. https://www.billboard.com/music/music-news/adidas-music-gamble-why-theyre-betting-on-pharrell-williams-and-6062768/

Grieg, Charlotte. 1989. *Will You Still Love Me Tomorrow? Girl Groups from the 50s On*. London: Virago Press.

Hamilton, Hamish, dir. 2021. *The 63rd Annual Grammy Awards*. CBS, March 14, 2021.

Heching, Dan. 2020. "Megan Thee Stallion Heats Up TikTok and Instagram in Lingerie Sets by Rihanna's Savage X Fenty Line." *Daily Mail*, June 19, 2020. https://www.dailymail.co.uk/tvshowbiz/article-8439057/

Hogan, Marc. 2020. "Why Is Megan Thee Stallion Suing Her Record Label?" *Pitchfork*, March 6, 2020. https://pitchfork.com/thepitch/megan-thee-stallion-suing-record-label-suga/

James, Robin. 2015. *Resilience & Melancholy: Pop Music, Feminism, and Neoliberalism*. New York: Zero Books.

Kiefer, Halle. 2020. "Label Drama over Contract Dispute Has Megan Tweeting #FreeTheeStallion." *Vulture*, March 1, 2020. https://www.vulture.com/2020/03/megan-thee-stallion-claims-label-drama-blocking-album-drop.html/

King, Don Roy, dir. 2020. *Saturday Night Live*. Hosted by Chris Rock. Musical guest Megan Thee Stallion. NBC, October 3, 2020.

Lamarre, Carl. 2020. "Carl Crawford Denies Megan Thee Stallion's Claims." *Billboard*, March 3, 2020. https://www.billboard.com/pro/carl-crawford-megan-thee-stallion-1501-label-denial/

Lewis, Lisa A. 1991. *Gender Politics and MTV: Voicing the Difference*. Philadelphia: Temple University Press.

Lieb, Kristin J. 2013. *Gender, Branding, and the Modern Music Industry*. New York: Routledge.

Lordi, Emily J. 2020. *The Meaning of Soul: Black Music and Resilience since the 1960s*. Durham, NC: Duke University Press.

Marwick, Alice E. 2015. "Instafame: Luxury Selfies in the Attention Economy." *Public Culture* 27 (1): 137–60.

Marwick, Alice E., and danah boyd. 2011. "To See and Be Seen: Celebrity Practice on Twitter." *Convergence* 17 (2): 139–58.

McLeod, Kembrew. 2002. "Between a Rock and a Hard Place: Gender and Rock Criticism." In *Pop Music and the Press*, edited by Steve Jones, 93–113. Philadelphia: Temple University Press.

Megan Thee Stallion. 2020a. "Beyonce Gifts Megan Thee Stallion Ivy Park Package!" Uploaded January 23, 2020. YouTube video, 0:47. https://www.youtube.com/watch?v=9n-OqOAfrc4

Megan Thee Stallion. 2020b. "Why I Stand Up for Black Women." *New York Times*, October 13, 2020. https://www.nytimes.com/2020/10/13/opinion/megan-thee-st allion-black-women.html

Molanphy, Chris. 2017. "Will the Mainstream Support More Than One Rap Queen at a Time?" *Pitchfork*, April 13, 2017. https://pitchfork.com/thepitch/1487-will-the-ma instream-support-more-than-one-rap-queen-at-a-time-a-charts-investigation/

Molanphy, Chris. 2019. "Rolling in God's Royal Uptown Road Edition." *Hit Parade*, November 27, 2019. Podcast, 1:37:40. https://slate.com/podcasts/hit-parade/2019 /11/the-decade-in-charts-2010-to-2019

Moore, Booth. 2020. "First Look at Savage X Fenty Fall 2020." *Women's Wear Daily*, October 1, 2020. https://wwd.com/fashion-news/fashion-features/rihanna-sava ge-fenty-fall-2020-first-look-1234611968/

O'Connell, Michael. 2018. "ABC Move Does Nothing for Victoria's Secret Fashion Show." *Hollywood Reporter*, December 3, 2018. https://www.hollywoodreporter.com/tv /tv-news/victorias-secret-ratings-hit-new-low-fashion-show-s-move-cbs-abc-11 65810/

Potter, Logan. 2020. "Rihanna's Three Brands Are Opening Their Wallets for Blackout Tuesday." *PAPER*, June 2, 2020. https://www.papermag.com/rihanna-pullup-blac kout-tuesday-2646147520.html

Reuters. 2007. "Iconix to Buy Rocawear, Jay-Z's Clothing Brand." *Reuters*, March 7, 2007. https://www.nytimes.com/2007/03/07/business/07clothes.html

Robehmed, Natalie. 2019. "How Rihanna Created a $600 Million Fortune—and Became the World's Richest Female Musician." *Forbes*, June 4, 2019. https://www.forbes .com/sites/natalierobehmed/2019/06/04/rihanna-worth-fenty-beauty/amp/

Rudzinski, Alex, and Sandrine Orabona, dirs. 2019. *Savage X Fenty*. Amazon Prime. Film, 51 min.

Scott, Suzanne. 2019. *Fake Geek Girls: Fandom, Gender, and the Convergence Culture Industry*. New York: New York University Press.

Sharkey, Linda. 2014. "Rihanna Trademarks Her Name for Use on a Clothing Empire." *Independent*, August 8, 2014. https://www.independent.co.uk/lifestyle/fashion/ne ws/rihanna-trademarks-her-name-9656814.html

Spanos, Brittany. 2020. "Normani: A Pop Perfectionist Makes Her Move." *Rolling Stone*, February 28, 2020. https://www.rollingstone.com/music/music-features/norma ni-motivation-fifth-harmony-solo-album-950372/

Warwick, Jacqueline. 2007. *Girl Groups, Girl Culture: Popular Music and Identity in the 1960s*. New York: Routledge.

Weinberg, Lindsay. 2019. "Rihanna's Savage X Fenty Lingerie Show to Stream on Amazon." *Hollywood Reporter*, August 26, 2019. https://www.hollywoodreporter.com /news/rihannas-savage-x-fenty-lingerie-nyfw-show-stream-amazon-1234446

Welty, Matt. 2016a. "Jay Z's Reebok Deal Changed the Sneaker Industry Forever." *Complex*, December 4, 2016. https://www.complex.com/sneakers/2016/12/jay-z-reeb ok-influence

Welty, Matt. 2016b. "Kendrick Lamar Answers Important Questions about Reebok Deal." *Complex*, March 16, 2016. https://www.complex.com/sneakers/2016/03/kendrick-lamar-reebok-interview-manchester-england

Yotka, Steff. 2019. "I Feel Great, Empowered, Fearless, and Beautiful." *Vogue*, November 21, 2019. https://www.vogue.com/article/normani-savage-x-fenty-brand-ambassador-interview

PART III

Fans of Fashion + Fashion as Fan Expression

9

Drop Culture

Masculinity, Fashion Performance, and Collecting in Hypebeast Brand Communities

Elizabeth Affuso

Since the 2005 founding of sneaker blog *Hypebeast*, the slang term to which it gives its name has emerged as a robust global fashion subculture positioned at the intersection of hip-hop, sports, and street style. Hypebeast communities are centered on particular fashion brands, notably Supreme, A Bathing Ape (or BAPE), Off-White, and Yeezy. Hypebeasts are, quite literally, beasts for the hype, and the subculture is rendered around a system of product drops. "Hype" is generated when limited-edition merchandise is released as an event, creating physical community spaces at stores and online communities centered on sharing product knowledge, collecting, and reselling. Historically male and centered in Hong Kong, Japan, and the United States, hypebeast culture has spread rapidly worldwide through the proliferation of style blogs, internet forums, and Instagram feeds devoted to it. Through textual analysis of hypebeast influencer feeds and related hashtags such as #WDYWT (What Did You Wear Today?), online forums, and retail merchandise events, this chapter investigates how digital space alters fashion subcultures. It situates hypebeasts within the globally connected commodity marketplace to consider how race and masculinity operate in fashion transnationally, and it applies fan studies discourse to fashion cultures broadly to think about the relationship of fashion subcultures to celebrity fandom in sports and hip-hop specifically. Finally, it explores cultures of collecting around fashion goods in a masculinized fashion subculture. While much of collecting discourse in fan studies is centered on the idea of it as a gendered practice, it has not historically been theorized as such in relation to male fashion consumers. By applying existing literatures of collecting (Baudrillard 1994; Geraghty 2014) and fashion digital cultures (Marwick 2013; Phạm 2015) to a case study of the brand A Bathing Ape (BAPE), this chapter theorizes an approach to fashion collecting, digital knowledge communities, and sartorial social media performance that accounts for transnational flows.

CHASING STATUS

In 2005, college student Kevin Ma started a sneaker culture blog called *Hypebeast* to, in his own words, "keep track and share information about sneakers such as when they were released, where to buy, background stories of sneakers, and what was happening in sneaker culture" (Newton 2011). The original impetus for the blog was to provide a centralized repository of information about sneaker culture as a way of sorting content from message boards and web forums. In this initial iteration, the site was primarily of interest to members of the sneakerhead subculture, a group of sneaker collectors that emerged "in the late 1970's/early 1980's and the introduction of the hip-hop era. During this time, footwear became synonymous with streetwear, and notable sneakers, such as the suede Puma Clydes, Adidas Shell Toes, Converse Chuck Taylors, and Pony David Thompsons were introduced to the streets. . . . Yet, a large majority of Sneakerheads attribute their introduction to the sneaker community to the 1985 release of the Nike Air Jordan 1s" (Matthews, Cryer-Coupet, and Degirmencioglu 2021, 2–3). Nike Air Jordans are unquestionably the most important streetwear item ever created, and Nike's collaboration with Michael Jordan is among the most lucrative in fashion history, doing US$4.7 billion in sales in fiscal year 2021. The continued growth of the Jordan product line (up 31 percent for 2021) points to two trends that hypebeast culture engages with: an interest in retro or lifestyle products, and a focus on celebrity and status items (Coffey and Badenhausen 2021). This culture of lifestyle and status has been further exacerbated by the rise of digital culture, and it is within this model that the hypebeast subculture spins off from sneakerheads. Like sneakerhead style, hypebeast looks are rooted in the aesthetic of streetwear, with a focus on sneakers, hoodies, baseball caps, down jackets, and sweatpants. Beyond style, the two subcultures share several elements, including a focus on knowledge, cultures of collection, scarcity, and community. Where they are ideologically dissimilar is in the perceived authenticity of purchasing/collecting, with concern—from sneakerheads—that hypebeasts, "buy only hype stuff . . . they are like hype over shoes, not really knowing the true history of a shoe. They buy them just to resell them and overcharge [people]" (Matthews, Cryer-Coupet, and Degirmencioglu 2021, 10).

This tension around authenticity and entrepreneurialism is seen over and over in fan communities. The focus on the production of economic capital around clothing is a concern for both scholars and sneakerheads because of its fixation on luxury objects and the impact that has on young people. The streetwear brands that hypebeasts are centered on fall into the luxury arm of this sector, creating exclusivity not just in rarity, but also in price. As Amelia Widjaja, Samuel Afiat, and Desideria L. D. Leksmono (2019, 7) have noted of hypebeasts, "this phenomenon uses digital marketing to promote the rise of 'conspicuous consumption' in which the youth are 'hyped up' to consume high-end brands and luxury goods in order to feel included and increase their social status." Status in hypebeast communities requires both the funds to acquire goods and the leisure time to support the temporal demands of waiting in line for product drops. Some tensions around hypebeasts are linked to larger moves within digital culture toward the representation of status and the neoliberal tendency toward self-branding. Of this self-branded status, Sarah Banet-Weiser (2012, 44) has noted that "in the neoliberal era they [consumers] are reimagined to even more relentlessly focus on an individual person, one who has access to customized products and can become an entrepreneur of self." In digital culture, style subcultures provide endless opportunities to leverage subcultural position into entrepreneurship. This could be participation in forums where product knowledge is privileged or accounts on Instagram and TikTok where style can be shown off. Minh-Ha T. Phạm (2015, 3) has noted that these spaces "represent an individual's taste. Unlike the clothing featured in fashion magazines or in retail spaces that is displayed on mannequins or on hangers, the clothes on style blogs are personal. They are worn on a real person's body and convey an idea of self-composure." Social media sites, in particular, provide a forum for individuals to generate fans in the form of followers as part of the entrepreneurial microcelebrity or influencer economy.

Due to the international positionality of the big hypebeast brands, including A Bathing Ape (BAPE) in Japan, Supreme in New York, and Off-White in Milan—and the regionalism of sneaker launches by Nike, Puma, and Adidas—forums have proven particularly useful to hypebeast communities. Members on brand-specific forums like BAPETalk, NikeTalk, and the now-defunct Simply Supreme can share information about release dates (drops) and provide a peer-to-peer marketplace to access items not available in a collector's home region. In the early years of forums, the focus "wasn't on getting a piece to flip, but on collecting and expressing personal fashion and a passion. Sub-threads on how to achieve certain looks for denim, DIY projects, customization and restoration, and styling outfits were authentic and built the foundation for what makes streetwear so appealing to the masses nowadays" (Peng 2018). This ongoing fixation on authenticity within participants' discussion of the subculture reflects a larger cultural trend "from 'authentic' culture to the branding of authenticity" (Banet-Weiser 2012, 5).

The internet forums that birthed hypebeast culture have also been essential to spawning larger contemporary trends to perform everyday fashion on social media. Forums like NikeTalk, Simply Supreme, and BAPETalk, as well as others on websites such as Hypebeast and ISS/Sole Collector, launched the What Did You Wear Today? posts (#WDYWT) that originated Outfit of the Day (#ootd) selfies, which have gone mainstream in spaces like Instagram and TikTok. In both, users take selfies of their daily outfits to perform their styling for the digital audience and elicit affective responses. These outfit selfies demonstrate how to style clothes and link looks to brands through tagging practices. Documenting this early history, Matt Peng (2018) writes:

> The now widely popular "What Did You Wear Today" (WDYWT) trend that you see all over social media was born and perfected first on forums. "I remember seeing the first WDYWT thread appear on NikeTalk in the general forum and one of the first comments on that thread were people saying 'who cares what you wore today' . . . fast forward to today and you have a massive online trend on #ootd. Crazy how it all ends up right," comments [Greg] Lam of [sneaker shop Image NY]. Within the WDYWT domain, the eventual marriage between high-end fashion and streetwear that we take for granted today also started to blossom.

The initial forums, and the social media content that evolves from them, do two important things: they create a transnational style community, and they provide a public outlet for the performance of subcultural style. This public outlet is distinctly contemporary in the desire not only to show outfits off for those within physical space, but also to perform style for digital communities. Digital culture has produced a context collapse. People are wearing outfits not necessarily for their lived environment, but for their digital audiences. Additionally, digital culture has reorganized style icons away from models, celebrities, and designers toward influencers.

Within this influence economy, streetwear and street style have proliferated, and hypebeast culture has exploded. Social media allows individuals to gain clout through their access to retail goods and their skills at styling. This plays into what Alice E. Marwick (2015, 139) has labeled "Instafame," which "demonstrates that while micro-celebrity is widely practiced, those successful at gaining attention often reproduce conventional status hierarchies of luxury, celebrity, and popularity that depend on the ability to emulate the visual iconography of mainstream celebrity culture." The shift from forums to social media streamlined the brand communities and cultures of collecting, notably providing an updated design and integrated marketplace that have allowed simpler navigation and more visibility (Peng 2018). Hashtags emerging from the forums like #WDYWT are paired with brand hashtags or subcultural ones allowing for easier sorting and searching. Notably, while #ootd is more popular on social media, #WDYWT remains the hashtag of choice for hypebeasts. Meanwhile, hypebeast brands have leveraged their brand communities into robust social media followings. On Instagram as of July 2022, for example, there are 13.3 million followers for @supremenewyork, 4.9 million for @bape_us, and 10.7 million for @off___white. In a classic symbiosis, much of the drop information that hypebeasts used to turn to forums for is now centralized by brands on their official pages. For example, Supreme uses Instagram to promote its weekly drops (Saturdays in Japan and Thursdays in the rest of the world). The weekly schedule of drops allows for in-person communities to be made as fans wait in line at brick-and-mortar retail stores for access to limited-edition goods. Hypebeast brands rely on the logic of scarcity to drive sales and hype. New styles and colorways are constantly being introduced and once sold out don't return, driving a robust secondary market. In January 2021, when much of Los Angeles was shut down amid the COVID-19 pandemic, lines could still be found outside Supreme, BAPE, and RipNDip on Fairfax Avenue, pointing to the ways that drop culture provides ritualized engagement for members even in isolated times.

SARTORIAL COSMOPOLITANISM

While online shopping enables wider participation, brick-and-mortar store locations of hypebeast brands are typically centered in high-end urban shopping districts such as Fairfax Avenue in Los Angeles, SoHo in New York, Shibuya in Tokyo, and the Marais in Paris. These locations are also central to street style and to the performance of fashion. Within the Japanese and Hong Kong contexts, the shopping districts where hypebeasts are centralized are also those associated with various forms of cosplay. Anne Peirson-Smith (2013, 82) roots both cosplay and streetwear within the "evolving entertainment landscape in Southeast Asian cities where Cosplayers are expressing themselves as active consumers of manga and anime." She continues: "This transcultural tendency is also evident in the Hong Kong fashion scene, where Japanese anime-inspired brands such as A Bathing Ape, by Japanese designer and DJ, Nigo, have recently been obsessively popular amongst the Hong Kong youth market, with regular queues forming outside of the main store every weekend." While Peirson-Smith positions this "transcultural tendency" within the Southeast and East Asian marketplace, the larger interest in Japanese brands within European and North American markets can be linked to the same explosion of global interest in manga and anime, along with fandom of the hip-hop stars who regularly wear brands like BAPE. Henry Jenkins (2006, 152–72) refers to these cultural flows as "pop cosmopolitanism." Here, I use a case study of BAPE to propose a sartorial cosmopolitanism that relies on fans to network within subcultural communities and to create a global style flow.

Of course, "hypebeasts are highly influenced by celebrity figures such as rappers, and [they] buy and wear sneakers endorsed by popular celebrities because they see those sneakers as trendy and fashionable" (Choi and Kim 2019, 151). Streetwear brands such as BAPE have leveraged their relationship to hip-hop stars such as the A$AP Mob, Kanye West, and Pharrell Williams to push interest in their products. Signature BAPE styles like Ape Head camo shark hoodies have become nearly ubiquitous in hip-hop videos; and the label is referenced in songs such as Soulja Boy's "Crank That," with its "I got me some Bathin' Ape" lyric. The interest of a Japanese brand such as BAPE in hip-hop culture points to the transnational positionality of streetwear, which roots itself in the global fetishization of Black music cultures and street fashion. This fetishization connects with the larger lineage of streetwear, which can be traced to basketball and the global rise of the NBA in the 1980s and 1990s, and to hip-hop artists who integrated fashion from the start, with songs such as "My Adidas" by Run-DMC (Rizzo 2015, 108). In the music business, fashion partnerships leverage celebrity brands into a larger and more lucrative business, but as Alyxandra Vesey notes elsewhere in this collection, it is often something that male hip-hop celebrities are able to do with greater success. As Ian Condry (2006, 114–16, 129) has noted, Japanese consumption cultures produce a particular relationship to fandom and music cultures and to the increased massification and nichification of Japanese society, pushing the interest both in hip-hop and (in neighborhoods such as Shibuya) in streetwear. While hip-hop is linked to fashion cultures worldwide, the central positionality of fashion is significant in the Japanese context, where clothing sales of hip-hop-related brands significantly outnumber record sales.

The Japanese streetwear brand A Bathing Ape (BAPE) is born from this moment in which fandom of hip-hop produces a fashion brand that then becomes a fandom culture within itself. BAPE was founded by Nigo in 1993 in Ura-Harajuku, the backstreet section of Tokyo's Harajuku district and an area that is associated with more independent brands. The name A Bathing Ape is taken from the Japanese phrase "a bathing ape in lukewarm water," which "describes youth who lead complacent and sheltered lives, whose only concerns deal with passing midterms and making it into prestigious institutes of higher education" (Underline 2016). BAPE styles—with their focus on pattern, cartoon images, and bright colors—rebel against these norms and stand in stark contrast to the black and navy blue of Japanese school uniforms and corporate attire. Nigo later became the DJ in Japanese hip-hop band Teriyaki Boyz and collaborated with Pharrell Williams on his Billionaire Boys Club clothing line, among many other projects. In 2021, he was appointed head of Kenzo as part of a larger move by LVMH Moët Hennessy Louis Vuitton to bring streetwear into the luxury sector and capitalize on the importance of these brands within the global fashion economy. Other examples of this move on the part of LVMH include naming the late Virgil Abloh of Off-White as Louis Vuitton artistic director in 2018, and Rihanna's Fenty fashion maison partnership from 2019 to 2021.

Iconic BAPE products include the Ape Head camo pattern emblazoned on hoodies and sneakers, shark hoodies with a shark mouth screen printed on a hood that zips over the face, and BAPE STA sneakers, which take much of their profile from Nike's Air Force 1, but with a star logo shooting up the side in lieu of the swoosh (figure 9.1).

The Ape Head camo, which is a camouflage print with the monkey head that makes up the brand's logo interspersed within the pattern, points to BAPE's luxury positionality, akin to such signature prints as Louis Vuitton's LV monogram and Damier Ebène check, Fendi's FF monogram, and Goyard's interlocking Y Goyardine. These recognizable prints are central to luxury brands' ability to project status to the public, and they point to Thorstein Veblen's (2004, 278) assertion that "the commercial value of the goods used for clothing in any modern community is made up to a much larger extent of the fashionableness, the reputability of goods than of the mechanical service which they render in clothing the person of the wearer. The need of dress is eminently a 'higher' or spiritual need." In the case of luxury goods, the need is about projecting social, economic, and knowledge capital. To the uninformed spectator, someone wearing an Ape Head camo sweatshirt might appear to be wearing any old camo, but to other subcultural community

Figure 9.1. Ape Head camo shark hoodie and BAPE STA sneakers for sale, as shown off by r/bapeheads member u/pallettetown on Reddit, October 3, 2021.

members or fashion insiders, the distinction is clear. That the signature print is camo only adds to the significance, as the fabric is designed—in its military function—to "conceal, deceive and distort" (Wilson 2008, 280). The iconography of BAPE products makes them easily recognizable to consumers, and BAPE often combines signatures together—as in the twentieth-anniversary BAPE STA Low Color Block Shark sneaker, which merges the BAPE STA style with the shark-head design. The signature styles are also easily adapted into fan-targeted collaborations such as BAPE x Marvel, which featured Iron Man, Spider-Man, and Hulk BAPE STA sneakers (figure 9.2). Collaborations such as these tap fandom of both BAPE and Marvel for maximum collectability, and shoes from these limited collections go for more than US$1,000 on the secondary market.

Figure 9.2. BAPE x Marvel Hulk BAPE STA sneaker, 2005.

The prices of these products also point to luxury positioning, with T-shirts running US$259, hoodies US$335 and up, baseball hats US$155, and sneakers US$389 as of October 2021. There's also women's wear, kids' wear, and a professional line called Mr. Bathing Ape that sells BAPE camo ties (US$199) for when hoodies won't do. There is no comparable professional line for women, pointing to the centrality of men to hypebeast brands. This centrality is also reflected in the number of products on offer, with sixteen shopping pages of women's products and fifty-two of men's.

Like many brands associated with hypebeasts, BAPE centralizes drop culture, releasing new products every Saturday at its shops worldwide and online. In the early years of the brand, before the rise of social media, Nigo would make fifty shirts a week and give half to style influencers. Meeting only 10 percent of demand became a hallmark of BAPE's production and led to the logics of scarcity that are central to hypebeast subcultures (Underline 2016). Information about these drops appears in digital brand communities, most notably BAPETalk. BAPETalk started as an internet forum in 2006 and had garnered more than 947,200 posts and 39,300 members as of October 2021. Subforums on BAPETalk include the Weekly Drop List, which provides information for the Saturday product drops; Legit Check, where members provide detail shots of garments to authenticate them for purchase or sale on secondary markets; A Bathing Ape Official News and Release Info, where members discuss official brand information and new lookbooks; and General Discussion, which hosts informational topics such as the rarity of a given item or rumored collaborations. The Weekly Drop List also links to an informational post that has existed in some form since 2007. This "Beginner's Guide to Buying BAPE from Japan" is designed to help forum members work through international purchases, including through the use of a proxy service. This type of guidance is not as essential now as it might have been in the past due to the normalization of internet shopping and the proliferation of services such as Google Translate, but it points to the ways that fans share knowledge to help their fellow fans make legitimate purchases. We especially see these communities emerge around transnational sartorial fandom to assist with language issues or to help fans navigate retailers and avoid scams. For example, on Reddit, r/KitSwap (for soccer jerseys and apparel) has lists of trusted retailers to aid subreddit users. In the early years of BAPE's global popularity, the company did not have shops outside of Asia, which made this especially important (shops opened in New York and Los Angeles in 2005 and 2006, respectively).

Stand-alone forums like BapeTalk have dropped in popularity as social media has risen, but these sites have managed to leverage their communities on Instagram and other platforms. On Instagram, for example, @bapetalk_worldwide had roughly ten thousand followers as of July 2022, with more than one thousand posts tagged #BapeTalkWorldwide. Much of what this Instagram page does is post images from BAPE fashion influencers as a curator of BAPE style content. And the two BAPE subreddits, r/Bape and r/bapeheads, had 7,900 and 22,930 members, respectively, as of that same month. Drop culture has become so cutthroat with bots that subscription app services like Drop o'Clock and bot license services like Cybersole have developed professional drop services, while e-commerce companies like Shopify are spending millions on bot-defeating protocols (Wakabayashi 2021). The existence of apps like these speaks to the ways that fan practices have been commodified by digital culture.

CAN BRAND COMMUNITIES BE FANS?

Fashion brands are not typically talked about in the language of fandom unless they are celebrity brands; instead, fandom for retail brands is termed brand loyalty. Brand communities are "defined as a type of consumer community in which members share interests and/or passion with respect to a specific brand" (Choi and Kim 2019, 143). Importantly, "brand communities are participants in the brand's larger social construction and play a vital role in the brand's ultimate legacy" (Muñiz and O'Guinn 2001). This chapter claims that many of the brand communities that we see within contemporary economies operate within the language and logics of fandom. Late capitalism and its push toward consumer citizenship point toward a brand fandom that is different from brand loyalty. While this idea of "brandom" is often centered on entertainment companies like Disney and Apple, and sports teams that position themselves as lifestyle brands (Guschwan 2012; Williams 2020, 69–73; Holt 2004), I want to position fashion brands as entertainment and hypebeast style as a fan practice due to the ways that style is an expressive practice that cannot be contained by brands.

Sneakerheads broadly, and hypebeasts specifically, provide an interesting case study for thinking about how to apply the logics of fandom to consumer goods in a way that makes sense in neoliberal, late capitalism, where everything has the potential to be commodified. Hypebeasts typically center their community relationships on the wearing and collecting of specific models or brands, such as Nike Air Force 1s or the streetwear brands Supreme and BAPE. Within these communities members display both their hierarchies of knowledge in relation to commodity goods, and certain forms of productivity (semiotic, enunciative, textual) that are essential to fandom (Fiske 1992). While fan studies often distances itself from merchandise and the purchase of commodity goods, preferring a gift economy logic, scholars have started to intervene in this model (Affuso and Santo 2018). Streetwear companies play to their fan base with the release of nostalgic items and limited-edition goods. The detailed knowledge displayed in these communities goes beyond the brand loyalty we expect in brand communities and is more akin to fandom. Style is also an adaptive practice that seeks not to mimic what fashion brands put forth, but rather to combine and reuse in ways that are specific to individuals. Hypebeasts who have clout within the community, whether on forums or on social media, are those who have styling skills or product knowledge that is seen as unique. It seems the inevitable outcome of neoliberal, late capitalism that fandom would move beyond media texts or celebrities toward brands.

Sneakerheads and hypebeasts are among the most significant users of digital culture to create style communities, starting with internet forums and moving into social media spaces. Internet forums are a place for community, but also a way to build and show off collections. In *Cult Collectors*, Lincoln Geraghty (2014, 2) argues that "collecting has been overlooked in fan studies and . . . devalued as a fan practice because of its basis in consumption rather than production." Geraghty additionally points to memory and nostalgia as the "driving influences" for fan collecting. Within fashion collecting, much of this memory- and nostalgia-driven collecting comes from fans who lacked the financial resources to purchase the item the first time around (Matthews, Cryer-Coupet, and Degirmencioglu 2021, 6–7), or those who are looking to refer to styles from previous eras of their life as a youthful nostalgia type of positionality. As Jin Woo Choi and Minjeong Kim (2019, 143) have noted, "sneakerheads are not only avid consumers, but also collectors who collect consumer goods. Collectors collect items as an investment, for reasons of security or nostalgia, or because they are addicted to it." Where sneakerheads make a subcultural distinction with hypebeasts is around the issue of "security or nostalgia," with sneakerheads seeing these factors as the primary motivations for collecting. Sneakerheads perceive that hypebeasts view investment as the top priority instead. As with so many distinctions of this type, this doesn't apply to all members of either group, but in its slang usage, the term *hypebeast* "tends to mock someone as an attention-seeking poseur," pointing to a sense that members of the subculture are inauthentic in their collecting (Dictionary.com, n.d.). As a subculture associated primarily with young men, hypebeasts operate in categories that fan studies has often perceived as "masculinized modes of fan engagement (textual mastery, collecting, trivia, etc.)" (Scott 2019, 77). As Geraghty (2014, 60) notes, "female fans are seen as more productive and transformative in practices such as fan fiction writing and male fans affirm their fandom through the buying and collecting of memorabilia."

Hypebeasts are interesting because they bring this masculinist fan collecting to an arena—fashion—that has historically been feminized. With fashion, the stakes of this are even higher because of larger histories of dress and gender. As Elizabeth Wilson (1990, 32) has noted, oppositional subcultural styles such as mods and teddy boys (and dandies, zoot-suiters, and to some extent punks) were the province of men: "Sartorial excess and deviance readily equates with rebellion for men. It *can* [but does not always] signify revolt for young women." It is within this larger history of masculinized, subcultural fashion rebellion that hypebeasts exist. In particular, the common practice of lining up on the street to purchase goods is derided as hysterical when done by female consumers, while this same claim is not leveraged at men.

While hypebeasts celebrate consumerism in ways that are often seen as antithetical to fandom, knowledge sharing within digital forums points to similarities to the gift and affect economy models that are central to fan communities. The depth of knowledge about colorways, editions, styles, release dates, and quantities demonstrated by many hypebeasts goes far beyond that of brand loyalty and speaks to a depth of engagement that is closer to fan practice. The transcultural flows of this subculture also point to the ways that fan knowledge and the sharing of that knowledge enable transnational style communities such as this to exist.

REFERENCES

Affuso, Elizabeth, and Avi Santo. 2018. "Mediated Merchandise, Merchandisable Media: An Introduction." *Film Criticism* 42 (2). https://doi.org/10.3998/fc.137612 32.0042.201

Banet-Weiser, Sarah. 2012. *Authentic™: The Politics of Ambivalence in a Brand Culture.* New York: New York University Press.

Baudrillard, Jean. 1994. "The System of Collecting." in *The Cultures of Collecting*, edited by John Elsner and Roger Cardinal, 7–24. Cambridge, MA: Harvard University Press.

Choi, Jin Woo, and Minjeong Kim. 2019. "Sneakerhead Brand Community Netnography: An Exploratory Research." *Fashion, Style & Popular Culture* 6 (2): 141–58.

Coffey, Brendan, and Kurt Badenhausen. 2021. "Jordan Brand Leads Nike Resurgence in Sales and Shares." *Sportico*, June 24, 2021. https://www.sportico.com/business /sales/2021/nike-earnings-beat-estimates-1234632741/

Condry, Ian. 2006. *Hip-Hop Japan: Rap and the Paths of Cultural Globalization.* Durham, NC: Duke University Press.

Dictionary.com. n.d. "Hypebeast." Accessed October 24, 2021. https://www.dictionary .com/e/slang/hypebeast/

Fiske, John. 1992. "The Cultural Economy of Fandom." In *The Adoring Audience: Fan Culture and Popular Media*, edited by Lisa A. Lewis, 30–49. London: Routledge.

Geraghty, Lincoln. 2014. *Cult Collectors: Nostalgia, Fandom and Collecting Popular Culture.* London: Routledge.

Guschwan, Matthew. 2012. "Fandom, Brandom and the Limits of Participatory Culture." *Journal of Consumer Culture* 12 (1): 19–40.

Holt, Douglas B. 2004. *How Brands Become Icons: The Principles of Cultural Branding.* Boston: Harvard Business School Press.

Jenkins, Henry. 2006. *Fans, Bloggers, and Gamers: Exploring Participatory Culture.* New York: New York University Press.

Marwick, Alice E. 2013. *Status Update: Celebrity, Publicity, and Branding in the Social Media Age.* New Haven, CT: Yale University Press.

Marwick, Alice E. 2015. "Instafame: Luxury Selfies in the Attention Economy." *Public Culture* 27 (1): 137–60.

Matthews, Delisia, Qiana Cryer-Coupet, and Nimet Degirmencioglu. 2021. "I Wear, Therefore I Am: Investigating Sneakerhead Culture, Social Identity, and Brand Preference among Men." *Fashion and Textiles: International Journal of Interdisciplinary Research* 8 (1). https://doi.org/10.1186/s40691-020-00228-3

Muñiz, Albert M., Jr., and Thomas C. O'Guinn. 2001. "Brand Community." *Journal of Consumer Research* 27 (4): 412–31.

Newton, Matthew. 2011. "Hypebeast Founder Talk 'Influencers' and Authenticity." *Forbes*, September 8, 2011. https://www.forbes.com/sites/matthewnewton/2011/09/08/hypebeast-founder-talks-influencers-and-authenticity/

Peirson-Smith, Anne. 2013. "Fashioning the Fantastical Self: An Examination of the Cosplay Dress-Up Phenomenon in Southeast Asia." *Fashion Theory* 17 (1): 77–111.

Peng, Matt. 2018. "How Forums Paved the Way for Streetwear." *Hypebeast*, January 8, 2018. https://hypebeast.com/2018/1/forums-nike-bape-supreme-internet-communities

Phạm, Minh-Ha T. 2015. *Asians Wear Clothes on the Internet: Race, Gender, and the Work of Personal Style Blogging*. Durham, NC: Duke University Press.

Rizzo, Mary. 2015. *Class Acts: Young Men and the Rise of Lifestyle*. Reno: University of Nevada Press.

Scott, Suzanne. 2019. *Fake Geek Girls: Fandom, Gender, and the Convergence Culture Industry*. New York: New York University Press.

Underline. 2016. "The Complete History of a Bathing Ape." *Medium*, November 4, 2016. https://medium.com/@contact.underline/the-complete-history-of-a-bathing-ape-59e07f4ab44b

Veblen, Thorstein. 2004. "Dress as an Expression of the Pecuniary Culture." In *The Rise of Fashion: A Reader*, edited by Daniel L. Purdy, 278–88. Minneapolis: University of Minnesota Press.

Wakabayashi, Daisuke. 2021. "The Fight for Sneakers." *New York Times*, October 15, 2021. https://www.nytimes.com/interactive/2021/10/15/style/sneaker-bots.html

Widjaja, Amelia, Samuel Afiat, and Desideria L. D. Leksmono. 2019. "The Phenomenon of 'Hypebeast' among Young People in Indonesia." Paper presented at the 15th International Conference on Language, Literature, Culture, and Education and the 5th International Conference on Mobile Education and Learning Technologies, Kuala Lumpur, September 14–15, 2019.

Williams, Rebecca. 2020. *Theme Park Fandom: Spatial Transmedia, Materiality and Participatory Cultures*. Amsterdam: Amsterdam University Press.

Wilson, Elizabeth. 1990. "All the Rage." In *Fabrications: Costume and the Female Body*, edited by Jane Gaines and Charlotte Herzog, 28–37. New York: Routledge.

Wilson, Elizabeth. 2008. "Exhibition Review: *Camouflage and Sailor Chic*." *Fashion Theory* 12 (2): 277–83.

10

This Is My (Floral) Design

Flower Crowns, Fannibals, and Fan/Producer Permeability

EJ Nielsen and Lori Morimoto

Belladonna for the heart, a chain of white oleander for the intestines, ragwort for the liver.
  —*Hannibal*, episode 2.06, "Futamono"

Think of all the activities that must be carried out *for any work of art to appear as it finally does.*
  —Howard S. Becker, *Art Worlds*

While flower crowns in various forms were used in many ancient cultures, the flower crown as meme first blossomed within the femalecentric fan culture of social media site Tumblr in 2013. Thought to have begun in the fandom of boy band One Direction, it reportedly drew from a 2011 tweet by Harry Styles in which he wrote, "I wish I was a punk rocker with flowers in my hair" (amanda b. 2013). In its original iteration, the meme involved *photoshopping* flower crowns onto images of the band. This genre of digital collage then spread laterally from One Direction fandom to Tumblr fandom writ large, resulting in myriad images of beflowered Doctor Whos, Sherlock Holmeses, and, in a particularly ironic iteration of the meme, characters from the NBC television series *Hannibal* (2013–15), a psychological horror show focusing on the exploits of cannibalistic serial killer Dr. Hannibal Lecter, a character best known for his appearance in *Silence of the Lambs* (dir. Jonathan Demme, 1991). For fans of *Hannibal* ("fannibals"), much of the appeal was the visual dissonance between the cheerful flower imagery of the meme and *Hannibal*'s dark narrative of a cannibalistic serial killer, ultimately resulting in fannibals' translating digitally altered images into material practice by wearing flower crowns at *Hannibal*-related events such as plays featuring an actor from the show. Since then, not only the wearing of flower crowns but their creation and idiosyncratic semiotics have become defining practices within and identifiers of *Hannibal* fandom. In this chapter, we explore the fannibal flower crown phenomenon through discussion of its iconographic signifi-cance and semiotics within the fandom, especially as it is used to physically create and denote fannibal spaces. Following this, we look at how fannibal flower crowns' boundary-blurring legitimization by the *Hannibal* production complicates the largely oppositional paradigm of fan studies scholarship on fan-producer relations, revealing dialectical and other potential models for considering the nature of fan-producer transactional exchange. By consid-ering new models outside of this oppositional framework, we can more fully understand contemporary fan-producer relationships.

FLOWER CROWNS AS FAN SEMIOTICS

Unlike some other traditional fan objects, flower crowns are objects designed to be ornamental for the wearer, attractive both in and of themselves and also as an enhancement when worn. In this, they can be seen as tying in with a larger movement of "feminized fandom," which includes collabora-tions between media producers and makeup companies, branded fashion lines from clothing companies targeted at female fans (like Her Universe and BlackMilk), and practices like closet cosplay and Disneybounding, all of which "[reflect] a desire to integrate fan practices into everyday life" (Affuso 2017, 184–85). Flower crowns, furthermore, are already culturally coded as femi-nine. They are additionally coded as celebratory or festive due to their con-temporary association with events such as weddings and festivals and their traditional association with victory, and in contemporary Anglo-American culture they have associations with ideas of counterculture, New Age, and Coachella. As crowns, they mark the wearer as special or set apart, though of course when worn as one crown among many, they mark the wearer foremost as a member of that group. Flower crowns function as a form of body adorn-ment that is wearable by and accessible to a wide range of body types, and that can be worn with any type of clothing or outfit. While not as "invisible" a fan practice as makeup, the crown may still be a form of fan performance that allows fans "to integrate the elements of costuming and interpretation into their lives in a manner that strips the codes of cosplay thus preventing them from ridicule or skepticism . . . by making this work distinct from the idea of costuming" (Affuso 2017, 188).

As fannish insignia, flower crowns stand out, therefore, because they neither are branded with nor exist within the media source material. Instead, they are an iconography generated entirely as visual imagery, first within the fannish communities of Tumblr and then as physical objects to be worn at fannibal events. Since they do not at any point appear in the source text of the TV series, flower crowns have no exact visual referent: there is no such thing as a mimetic or screen-accurate flower crown. If we consider flower crowns as a symbol of Hannibal fandom, then all flower crowns are created symbolically equal or, at least, symbolically *correct*, as they seek to evoke the fan's affective response to the text rather than re-creating anything from the text itself, especially as no crown would be more correct or accurate than any other crown.

While serving as *Hannibal* fandom referents, these crowns also refer back to the strong aesthetic stylings of the show itself. *Hannibal*'s dramatic visuals are reminiscent of a blending of Baroque artist Caravaggio, whose paintings "transgress the limits between aesthetic, illusionistic, and erotic pleasures" and "the boundary between pleasure and non pleasure" (Bal 1999, 20), and the unsettling imagery of twentieth-century painter Francis Bacon. Flowers feature frequently in the Baroque lushness of Lecter's elaborate tablescapes, whose combinations of exotic food items, natural objects, and meals made of people evoke the memento mori of traditional still life paintings. In perhaps the most memorable example of this memento mori aesthetic, which reminds the viewer that death is both inevitable and intimately entwined with life, Lecter grafts the body of one of his victims to a tree and fills the emptied chest cavity with poisonous flowers (episode 6.2, "Futamono"), thus literally uniting blooms and growth with death and decay.

FLOWER CROWNS AS FAN MERCHANDISE

In practical terms, the visual plasticity of the flower crown means that it is an incredibly accessible way of expressing fannish devotion in terms of both cost and location. The intellectual property (IP) holders of *Hannibal* make no money on "licensed" flower crowns, they need not be purchased from the same store used by the costume designer, and they don't need to be laboriously re-created using collected screenshots of the associated angles, as is often the case with cosplay and other fan craftworks. If a fan wishes to purchase one, they are readily available at chain stores or the fan could commission a custom crown to their exact specifications from a fannibal "fantrepreneur" (Scott 2019, 169). Similarly, if a fan wishes to create a crown, there are a wealth of materials and tutorials available to help them craft their own flower crown. The degree of personalization is entirely up to the individual. Because of the plasticity of the flower crown's iconography and the sheer variety of possibilities, flower crowns became a means of expressing a fan's membership as a fannibal and, simultaneously, their individual identity within that group.

The crown's colors, materials, flowers, and other details can be a way of expressing one's aesthetic, skill set, or even just favorite color while still identifying the wearer as a fannibal. At a fannibal event, the crown marks someone as being an attendee of that event. At a nonfannibal event, such as a play featuring one of the *Hannibal* actors or a more general fan convention, the flower crown marks (to those in the know) the wearer as a fan not just of that person but of that person's work in *Hannibal*. As actor Mads Mikkelsen (who played Hannibal Lecter) said upon seeing a group of fans wearing flower crowns in his autograph line at Wizard World New Orleans in 2019, "Ah, Fannibals!" The crown thus functions as a visible performance of *something* on the part of the wearer, though exactly what the performance is *of* may not be obvious to a nonfannish observer. Thus, the flower crown moves from a digital edit to a physical object, which then becomes a tool allowing a fan to participate in the act of being a fannibal in physical spaces (Woo 2014, 8.5); that is, the act of owning and wearing it "produces a common [experience] in the form of a community, a shared identity or even a short lived 'experience' that adds dimensions of use-value to the object" (Arvidsson 2005, 242). The physicality, of course, can become its own limitation for fans: if a fannibal is not observed by other fans, can they still participate?

FLOWER CROWNS AS AFFECTIVE CURRENCY

Flower crowns entered into producer culture during the Q and A portion of the 2013 *Hannibal* panel at San Diego Comic-Con, when a fan approached the microphone stand and was greeted by showrunner Bryan Fuller saying, in a singsong voice, "I love your crown." He then turned to the audience and continued, "And thank you all for wearing your flower crowns" (magicinthenumbers 2013), at which point the fan ran up to the stage and offered Fuller the crown, which he put on to great applause. As journalist Gavia Baker-Whitelaw (2013) observed, this exchange, in the context of frequently ambivalent and even antagonistic fan-producer relations, exceeded its apparent mundanity:

Putting on a flower crown during an audience Q&A may just seem like a cute nod to an incomprehensible Tumblr meme, but it's also symbolic of how well the Hannibal showrunners are treating their fandom. Comic Con is full of celebrity guests who are contractually obliged to attend, and who generally deal with the fan attention with a combination of PR stock phrases ("This is a really exciting project!") and outright bemusement. However, the Hannibal pannibal (yes, "pannibal") managed to engage with fandom without carrying the stigma of a "geek show" like Firefly or Orphan Black.

To this point, the *Hannibal* production had garnered no small amount of approbation among online fandoms for its respectful and attentive engagement with them. Fuller, producer Martha De Laurentiis, and other members of the production were singled out for their playful engagement with one another and fans during first-run broadcasts of the show, and in particular for Fuller's relentlessly enthusiastic bicoastal live-tweeting. The show's social media team, as well, was lauded for being almost uniquely attuned to the intricacies of online fan culture (Morimoto 2019). As Tumblr user StoryAlchemy (2015) wrote, "*Hannibal* has always been fan-aware. . . . But there's acknowledging fandom, there's encouraging fandom, and then there's *legitimizing* fandom." Thus, in accepting and wearing the crown, Fuller was engaging in precisely this kind of legitimization, implicitly rejecting all-too-common producer-side practices of "(re)segregat[ing] production and 'fandom' [and] symbolically distancing themselves" (Hills 2012, 37) from women's media fan culture. Nor was this legitimization of fans confined to social media paratexts; in episode 3.9, "And the Woman Clothed in the Sun," a character refers to Hannibal and Will as "murder husbands," a phrase originating within the fandom, thus converting fannibal metatext into show canon.

The crowns' origins and interfandom meanings notwithstanding, this intersection of fannibals' practice of wearing flower crowns and their adoption by *Hannibal* showrunner Bryan Fuller lends the crowns a certain transactional dimension. Historically, fans within transformative fan cultures and fan studies scholars have been primed to regard transactions in the fan-producer context as almost necessarily oppositional and absolutely unequal. This reflects an understanding of producer and fan cultures as neat binaries of agent and subject, in which the one parasitically capitalizes on the affective attachment of the other through aggressively strategized merchandising and marketing. Within this calculus, fan autonomy rests primarily in our ability to resist such a capitalist framework through alternative fan economies of, in particular, the gifting of creativity and labor within fan communities.

Yet, even assuming there was a time when fans and producers occupied such discrete subjectivities, today they and their cultures alike are characterized by nothing so much as the growing convergence of media cultures and practices, particularly as performed on porous social media platforms like Twitter and as embodied in what Suzanne Scott (2019, 150) has termed "liminal fan/producer identities." Understood in this way, this particular transaction reflects "a dialectic of value where both fans and producers can become self-reflexively engaged in circuits of exchange and use value" (Hills 2015, 191). Which is to say that everyone gets *something* out of the exchange, albeit to arguably different ends.

Fast-forward to the 2015 San Diego Comic-Con "pannibal," and what had begun as a generally spontaneous show of affection was now more codified: De Laurentiis arrived to the panel already adorned with a delicate ring of pastel flowers, while actor Hugh Dancy, looking out at the audience, observed, "There must be no more flower crowns left in the world!" For his part, Fuller enthusiastically bounded to the front of the stage and collected three proffered crowns from fans, plopping one each on his, Dancy's, and *Hannibal* newcomer Richard Armitage's heads. The actors settled them on their heads—Armitage even placed a small red dragon plushie (a reference to his *Hannibal* character Francis Dolarhyde, a.k.a. the "Great Red Dragon") in the center of his—but as a newcomer to both the show and the fandom, Armitage was frank in his unfamiliarity with the practice, responding to his first question from the panel moderator with, "I'll answer that question when someone tells me why am I wearing flowers on my head?" Dancy, seated next to him, guilelessly responded, "I actually don't know," and it remained to Fuller to explain, "Flower crowns represent the passion and floral beauty of the fandom, and our appreciation for their support" (GeekNation 2015). Nor was Armitage alone in his confusion; as one fannibal recalls, at the first Beyond the Red Dragon fan convention, in 2015, Mads Mikkelsen confessed that he didn't understand "the whole flower crown thing, and I [the fan] had to explain how the meme came about. And he was a bit shook that it came from the One Direction fandom" (pers. comm., 2019). Similarly, at television critic Matt Zoller Seitz's inaugural Split Screens Festival, in 2017, special guest Raúl Esparza was gifted a custom-made flower crown from a fan. He put the crown on his head, asking, "How did this get started?" A fan explained from the audience: "One Direction was photoshopping—the fandom—was photoshopping flower crowns onto the people in the band, and other internet communities started doing it, so we did, too. But Bryan saw it, and he didn't know about all the other internet communities. He just saw us doing it, so he was like, 'Oh, must be a fannibal thing.' And he put flower crowns on all the cast" (LadyJenevia 2017). If this fan suggests Fuller's active involvement in making flower crowns a "thing" on the production side of *Hannibal*, the fan who introduced Mikkelsen to them is more pointed, noting, "Depending [on] if Bryan is there and the amount of fannibals [present], some [cast] will wear it, but nearly as obligation" (pers. comm., 2019). In thus being adopted—or, arguably, appropriated—by Fuller as a visible signifier of both the *Hannibal* fandom and production-side acceptance and outreach, this practice of wearing crowns seems to edge toward the kind of manufactured engagement from which Baker-Whitelaw differentiated it in 2013.

Yet, this kind of differentiation between apparently discrete modes of engagement—what some pejoratively call "fan service," which panders to fans' presumed desires, versus "authentic" fan-producer interactions—risks "return[ing] us to the kind of fan studies account that fan studies emerged in opposition to" (Hills 2015, 190). That is, in suggesting that certain modes of fan-producer engagement constitute a kind of insidious manipulation to which fans are vulnerable, we are effectively returned to that same characterization of fans as cultural dupes that fan studies has argued against since its inception. The applause that greets Fuller, Dancy, and Armitage, not to mention that which welcomes Esparza's slightly less enthusiastic, "I never wear these, but I'll wear it for this for a few minutes" (LadyJenevia 2017), is sincere in its appreciation for members of the production crossing, however temporarily, the boundary of professional "propriety" into fandom. But as the above observations suggest, this doesn't preclude fans' awareness of the industrial context within which this exchange occurs. Indeed, fannibal practices of wearing flower crowns may equally, if differently, serve their own affective ends. Mikkelsen's recognition of and shout out to the crown-wearing fannibals at Wizard World New Orleans reflects the kind of reward fans may reap by understanding what their crowns signify in a transactional setting. In fact, fans are as likely to manufacture this kind of exchange as are producers; as the French fan who explained the crowns to Mikkelsen recounts, "When I was at Cannes . . . I purposely put my flower crown on (a small one, but still) so Mads would know that I was a fannibal, so maybe [I would] get priority on a picture. . . . [When] we arrived . . . he asked a bit hesitantly, 'Fannibals?' pointing at my flower crown, and I nodded. He added, 'Oh great, because everyone wears these here, and I don't know if it's fashion or . . .'" (pers. comm., 2019). The final proof of the flower crown's absorption by both the fan and the producer sides of *Hannibal* may be the licensed one-sixth scale figure of Hannibal Lecter produced by Threezero (figure 10.1). This figure, meant for collectors

Figure 10.1.
Threezero's Hannibal
Lecter figure with
accessories.

and not children, comes with accessories that include such canonical items as knives, a kill suit, and a wine glass . . . and a generic pink flower crown for Hannibal to wear, perhaps the closest that fannibals have come to having an official or licensed flower crown.

Indeed, as fannibals ourselves, we, too, have created our own flower crowns, which we wore at Beyond the Red Dragon 5 in London (figure 10.2). EJ's self-made crown uses red and black flowers as a backdrop for grayscale death's-head hawkmoths (*acherontia atropos*), which hover above the crown on thin wires. These moths are both a referent to the iconic death's-head hawkmoth imagery of the poster for the original *Silence of the Lambs* and a personal emblem of the author. EJ has a death's-head hawkmoth tattooed on their wrist, a permanent display of affect that is public in its position on the body but also private and personal in its multiple levels of meaning, some

Figure 10.2. The authors—Lori Morimoto (*left*) and EJ Nielsen—wearing their handmade flower crowns at Beyond the Red Dragon 5, February 2017. Photo by the authors.

of which are fannish (Jones 2014, 3.5). Due to the fragile nature of the hand-made moths and of the crown itself, EJ chose to wear their crown during their transatlantic journey rather than attempting to pack it. Their choice also led to other fannibals in these public spaces approaching and engaging with EJ, allowing them to meet other fans they might never have met while out in the world, other travelers in a strange land. As EJ's journey continued, additional sightings of other people wearing flower crowns served as visual markers of their increasing closeness to the convention site. When they reached the convention hotel lobby, filled with a small sea of flower crowns, their crown then became an in-group signifier of belonging.

Lori's paper crown, also made by her, was intended as a material expression of an essay on authorship and adaptation written for the anthology *Becoming: Genre, Queerness, and Transformation in NBC's Hannibal* (Mudan Finn and Nielsen 2019). The flowers were cut from pages in the Thomas Harris novel *Red Dragon* (1981), thus literally transforming the text in a way analogous to how *Hannibal* had transformed both Harris's novels and their film adaptations. Making it scratched an itch to engage in scholarly playfulness and creativity. At the same time, however, it was also entirely intended to attract attention from Fuller and Dancy, both of whom attended the convention; when it did, with Fuller peering at it across a table and asking, "Is that Red Dragon?" and Dancy gushing, "That's so cool!" (repeated the next day during a—paid—photo op), those exchanges became the highlight of Lori's experience of the convention. Put differently, the convention enabled us paid access to Fuller and Dancy, however fleeting, while the crowns allowed us to successfully turn the convention organizer's commercial interests to our own affective ends. The organizer, as well as Fuller and Dancy, walked away with more money than they'd had when the convention began, but as fans we willingly exchanged it for the affectively invaluable experience of being acknowledged by people we admired, fully facilitated by their understanding of the semiotics of the flower crown in *Hannibal* fandom and the delicacy of their roles in fan-producer transactions.

FLOWER CROWN ARRANGEMENT

While fan-producer transactions have frequently been framed in media studies as antagonistic or exploitative, we argue that a more productive framework would be to view these interactions not simply as transactional but with an understanding that the "transaction" in question occurs between the two informed parties of fan and producer and may be of benefit to both. Flower crowns, objects that were not generated by the original media but that were later embraced by the showrunner, are a clear example of why an antagonistic framing of these interactions is not simply demeaning to fans but also unhelpful as a lens for understanding them. Indeed, it could be said that the significance of flower crowns can only be understood through an always-evolving transactional framework, rather than one that is a priori antagonistic or exploitative.

It is also possible, and we would argue productive, to broaden our focus even further beyond interactions along the seeming polarities of fan and producer. What if instead of conceptualizing flower crowns as existing somewhere along this single axis, we consider flower crowns as existing within entire networks of connection and production that allow the creation of these semiotic and affective meanings as well as of the actual, physical materials being discussed and utilized? One way this can be done is through thinking of fan and media spaces as fields of cultural production, in which we cannot understand something without understanding the system in which it was created, and in which there is not a single hierarchy but instead shifting networks of power and cultural capital (Bourdieu 1993). Within this field, we can now consider how flower crowns were assigned meaning in broader Tumblr fandom prior to moving to physical fannish (but not at that point specifically fanniballish) signifiers, before being taken up by Bryan Fuller, whose great cultural capital within fannibal spaces allowed him to cocreate a semiotic meaning of the crowns with fannibals. This meaning is then reaffirmed by fans through ongoing usage within fan spaces, and by those associated with the production through a willingness to engage with these objects when engaging with fans. This construction of meaning takes place within virtual and physical spaces and is explicitly a *co*-construction around an object that possesses extant cultural meaning outside of any of these parties. Even if the impact or capital of each party is unequal, had any of these parties within this field of habitus not contributed to this new semiotic construction *it would not exist*—or, at least, it would not exist in the form it occupies presently.

Another, broader way of framing the flower crowns draws on Howard S. Becker's (1982, 5) concept of "art worlds," which encourages us to consider "all the activities that must be carried out *for any work of art to appear as it finally does.*" Viewed through this lens, flower crowns already exist within a web of meaning and production in which One Direction fans, Tumblr fans, fannibals, Bryan Fuller, and others all contribute to the development of their imagery and semiotics. This framing also takes into account the physical construction of the flower crowns, the makers of them (fannibal-affiliated and otherwise) and even the capitalist production models required to create, distribute, and resell the thousands of fake flowers and foliage frequently used in their making. Without these cheap and accessible supplies, for example, the building of flower crowns could never have spread as far as a fan practice.

CONCLUSION

In the context of sartorial fan objects, flower crowns reflect the increasingly muddied interplay of fan and producer prerogatives in contemporary media fandoms. Particularly where historically fan studies scholars have emphasized the "moral dualism" (Hills 2002, 6) of commercial versus amateur fan production ranging from fan fiction to fan wearables, flower crowns are noteworthy for their intrafandom origins and for the interplay between fans and producers that has in some sense "legitimized" them as *fannibal* objects rather than simply *Hannibal* objects. Flower crowns have also managed to achieve *autonomous* success with the fannibal community while avoiding external *heteronymous* success as sources of meaningful profit for the IP holders, the crown makers, or even the silk flower producers (Bourdieu 1993). Through production, purchase, and usage of these flower crowns fannibals have re-created extant objects as semiotic signifiers of their identity as *Hannibal* fans. Moreover, their development as signifiers provides us with examples of new ways to consider fan-producer interactions more broadly. By moving away from the assumption of an inherently antagonistic relationship, we can instead understand these interactions as transactional and collaborative, or as part of larger structures of production and signification beyond the original media site.

REFERENCES

Affuso, Elizabeth. 2017. "Feminized Fandom and Beauty Culture." In *The Routledge Companion to Media Fandom*, edited by Melissa Click and Suzanne Scott, 184–92. New York: Routledge.

amanda b. 2013. "Flower Crowns." Know Your Meme. Last updated July 10, 2013. https://knowyourmeme.com/memes/flower-crowns

Arvidsson, Adam. 2005. "Brands: A Critical Perspective." *Journal of Consumer Culture* 5 (2): 235–58.

Baker-Whitelaw, Gavia. 2013. "'Hannibal' Showrunners Cater to Fandom at Comic-Con." *Daily Dot*, July 22, 2013. https://www.dailydot.com/parsec/fandom/hannib al-comic-con-flower-crown-slash/

Bal, Mieke. 1999. *Quoting Caravaggio: Contemporary Art, Preposterous History*. Chicago: University of Chicago Press.

Becker, Howard S. 1982. *Art Worlds*. Berkeley: University of California Press.

Bourdieu, Pierre. 1993. *The Field of Cultural Production*. Edited and translated by Randal Johnson. New York: Columbia University Press.

GeekNation. 2015. "San Diego Comic-Con 2015 Hannibal Full Panel." Uploaded July 17, 2015. YouTube video, 41:15. https://www.youtube.com/watch?v=JlOF58zV6BE

Hills, Matt. 2002. *Fan Cultures*. London: Routledge.

Hills, Matt. 2012. "*Sherlock*'s Epistemological Economy and the Value of 'Fan' Knowledge: How Producer-Fans Play the (Great) Game of Fandom." In *Sherlock and Transmedia Fandom: Essays on the BBC Series*, edited by Louisa Ellen Stein and Kristina Busse, 27–40. Jefferson, NC: McFarland.

Hills, Matt. 2015. "Veronica Mars, Fandom, and the 'Affective Economics' of Crowd-funding Poachers." *New Media & Society* 17 (2): 183–97.

Jones, Bethan. 2014. "Written on the Body: Experiencing Affect and Identity in My Fannish Tattoos." *Transformative Works and Cultures* 16. https://doi.org/10.3983/twc.2014.0527

LadyJenevia. 2017. "'Hannibal' Raúl Esparza Panel (Split Screens Festival 2017)." Uploaded June 9, 2017. YouTube video, 21:46. https://www.youtube.com/watch?v=cT-atV4G26Q

magicinthenumbers. 2013. "Hannibal Panel SDCC 2013." Uploaded July 18, 2013. YouTube video, 47:28. https://www.youtube.com/watch?v=ixBpId84Ubg

Morimoto, Lori. 2019. "*Hannibal*: Adaptation and Authorship in the Age of Fan Production." In *Becoming: Genre, Queerness, and Transformation in NBC's Hannibal*, edited by Kavita Mudan Finn and EJ Nielsen, 258–82. Syracuse, NY: Syracuse University Press.

Mudan Finn, Kavita, and EJ Nielsen, eds. 2019. *Becoming: Genre, Queerness, and Transformation in NBC's Hannibal*. Syracuse, NY: Syracuse University Press.

Scott, Suzanne. 2019. *Fake Geek Girls: Fandom, Gender, and the Convergence Culture Industry*. New York: New York University Press.

StoryAlchemy. 2015. "#Hannibal Did This . . . and So Should Everyone Else." *Fan Meta Reader* (blog), January 8, 2015. https://thefanmetareader.org/2015/01/08/hannibal-did-this-and-so-should-everyone-else-by-storyalchemy/

Woo, Benjamin. 2014. "A Pragmatics of Things: Materiality and Constraint in Fan Practices." *Transformative Works and Cultures* 16. https://doi.org/10.3983/twc.2014.0495

11

From Muggle to Mrs.

The *Harry Potter* Bachelorette Party and "Crafting" Femininity on Etsy

Jacqueline E. Johnson

In 2018, the Knot, a popular wedding planning website, collected survey data on how much weddings and their ancillary events cost. From its 1,300 respondents, the Knot found that both wedding attendees and members of the wedding party were spending on average more than US$250 on wedding gifts and an average of US$98 on attire (not including accessories). Those who attended bachelor and bachelorette parties, in turn, reported spending over US$500 (Ross, n.d.). The wedding industry continues to expand as more and more brides and grooms seek to create one-of-a-kind events that can be curated, presented, and consumed on social media platforms. One way people have done so is through incorporating elements of their fandoms.

Though few scholars have looked at the intersection of fandom and weddings explicitly (but see Johnston 2015), several popular press outlets have cataloged the ways fans have incorporated elements from their fan object into their nuptials. A through line in many of these articles, which tend to either praise fans' themed weddings or curate ideas and list products for purchase, is that brides and grooms should integrate their fandom into their weddings in ways that are "tasteful" and "not cheesy" (Pippin 2016; Sullivan, n.d.; Torgerson, n.d.). Further, they often point to e-commerce platform Etsy as a way to find the materials one needs to pull this off successfully. While this advice is salient in articles speaking about wedding ceremonies and receptions, bachelor and bachelorette parties, widely known to be void of taste and filled with kitsch, provide an interesting site to explore fandoms' integration into weddings and the ways the norms of weddings and their ancillary events structure how fan identities are rendered in these types of celebrations. Bachelorette parties, like fandoms, are increasingly incorporating forms of sartorial expression, and the T-shirts and sashes the bride and her women friends wear during the festivities demonstrate important themes related to gender and normativity.

In this essay, I analyze products for bachelorette parties geared toward members of the *Harry Potter* fandom that are sold on Etsy. Bachelorette parties, as a gendered practice, demonstrate how gender affects fans' material practices and how platforms like Etsy structure fan engagement and participation. Building on scholarship about Etsy and creative labor in addition to research on gender and merchandising in fandom, I consider how *Harry Potter* bachelorette products, particularly screen-printed T-shirts and sashes, illustrate the ways in which highly gendered fan practices construct normative modes of femininity. *Harry Potter* bachelorette party products are a compelling test case for how Etsy acts as a crucial intermediary space where a rich and diverse source text can be adapted to successfully integrate fandom into the traditional Western wedding schema in ways that reinscribe the boundaries of traditional femininity.

ETSY, CREATIVE LABOR, AND FAN HANDICRAFTING

Founded by Robert Kalin, Chris Maguire, and Haim Schoppik, with an official launch in 2005, Etsy branded itself as a place where consumers could buy and sell vintage and handmade goods. Recent data from the e-commerce website boasts over fifty million items for sale and over US$3.25 billion in merchandise sales in 2017 (Etsy, n.d.). Setting itself apart from other e-commerce websites like eBay, Etsy brands itself as a "human" (and humane) alternative to traditional modes of consumption. The interactive "About" section of its website states, "In a time of increasing automation, it's our mission to keep human connection at the heart of commerce" (Etsy, n.d.). Etsy's construction of itself as a digital refuge against the alienating effects of capitalism is salient across its branding. This mirrors analysis from scholars like Susan Luckman who have theorized the return to the analog, emphasizing women's crafts and creative markets.

Through an analysis of the rise and popularity of spaces like Etsy, Luckman (2013, 265) examines the sale of women's crafts and assesses the radical potentialities of small-scale production models with women at the helm. Luckman (2013, 251) notes a seeming contradiction between the rise in visibility of handmade goods and an increasingly digital world, but she historicizes this irony, noting, "the renaissance in the handmade at a time of profound social, cultural, and economic change in the global West—the 'digital revolution'—has parallels with similar responses to the Industrial Revolution." In a similar vein to English consumers in the nineteenth century, Luckman argues, shoppers have turned to online marketplaces like Etsy as a response to the anomie produced by widespread technological upheavals and digitalization. In addition to locating Etsy in its appropriate sociohistorical moment, Luckman points to the ways Etsy exists as a place for users to evade capitalist exploitation, while simultaneously privileging white women of means. Etsy's conception of itself as a disruptive force belies who the platform is actually structured to serve. We can draw a distinct parallel to early fan studies scholarship that understood mostly middle-class, white women as resistant Others whose transformative fan practices had radical implications (Gray, Sandvoss, and Harrington 2017, 4). As my analysis of *Harry Potter* bachelorette products will illustrate, Etsy's potential for resistance is easily reformatted and adapted into normative frameworks.

Extending the work of Luckman, Anna Blackwell (2018, 28) analyzes the over three thousand items sold on Etsy that contain the popular phrase "though she be but little, she is fierce," from Shakespeare's *A Midsummer Night's Dream*, in order to situate them within the marketization of feminism. Blackwell notes that despite the line's initial context as an insult delivered from one women to another, the phrase has been reframed by sellers on Etsy, where it frequently appears on girls' clothing, as a "statement of female power." Blackwell (2018, 32) builds from Luckman to center how female creative labor operates under the self-governing logics of neoliberalism. Further, Blackwell notes the myriad ways that structural whiteness is evident on the platform. Detailing Etsy's location at the intersection of several tensions regarding gender and labor under late-stage capitalism, Blackwell, along with Luckman, provides the groundwork to think through how the bachelorette party as a site of highly gendered spectacle can illustrate or even exacerbate these fundamental tensions.

While Etsy sells vintage and handmade goods to cater to a variety of consumers, it has also become a destination for fans looking for material goods that reference their fandoms (Cherry 2016; Jones 2014). In this vein, Brigid Cherry argues that fans have a long history of handicrafting and that Etsy has provided a centralized location for fan-produced handmade goods to be bought and sold. Despite the proliferation of fan-oriented goods on Etsy, few fan studies scholars have focused on the e-commerce platform. In her book *Cult Media, Fandom, and Textiles: Handicrafting as Fan Art*, Brigid Cherry (2016, 5, 164) historicizes fan handicrafting and makes an important intervention in the theorization of transformative fan practices. Cherry argues that fan handicrafters are "avid transformers of the text" and pushes for their production to be considered in a similar vein as fan fiction. Though Cherry is mostly focused on Ravelry, she asserts that Etsy provides the space for entrepreneurial fans to "convert fan cultural capital into economic capital." While not disputing this point, I illustrate in this essay that the text of *Harry Potter* is also transformed and new meanings and associations are created through the production of themed items for wedding events. I bridge the scholarship on Etsy, creative labor, and fandom with work on gender and fan fashion to convey how *Harry Potter* bachelorette shirts and sashes demonstrate tensions between the subversive potential of subcultural spaces and practices and the ways in which they can also reinforce dominant structures of power.

FANDOM, GENDER, AND MERCHANDISING

As many scholars in fan studies have noted, the media industries have for years privileged adolescent male fans of "geeky" or "nerdy" media texts in their merchandising, especially in toys and clothing (Johnson 2014; Scott 2017). Due to being underserved, many female fans have had to produce their own material goods related to their fandom or make do with items designed for and marketed to boys and men. However, recent scholarship has examined the current rise in geek merchandise targeted at female consumers and has shown that media industries' attempts to court a female consumer base illustrate how essentialized notions of gender are transmitted through merchandising (Affuso 2017; Johnson 2014; Lamerichs 2018).

This scholarship illustrates that media companies have turned to fashion and everyday wear as well as beauty and makeup to attract female consumers. In her research on fandom, embodiment, and materiality through *The Hunger Games*, Nicolle Lamerichs (2018, 181) examines three sites where fans can display their fandom through sartorial practice: everyday wear, cosplay, and geek couture. Lamerichs notes that for the most part, both fan-produced products and official merchandise for *The Hunger Games* engaged with limited material from the source text, notably excising referents to the Capitol. My analysis extends Lamerichs's point that patterns emerge in what elements of a text are poached to put on everyday wear. Further, Lamerichs's research on fan fashion begins to address how the politics endemic to the source text need to be interrogated when repurposed for fans to wear. More critically engaged with the political, Elizabeth Affuso and Derek Johnson have both done important work in theorizing the ideological underpinnings of official merchandise made for female consumers.

In his analysis of licensed geek clothing brand Her Universe, Derek Johnson (2014, 896) asserts that despite Lucasfilm and Disney's "vernacular affirmation" of young, female fans like Katie Goldman (a first grader who went viral after being teased for liking *Star Wars*, supposedly a text for "boys"), scholars need to examine the ways that both industrial agents and popular discourses "work to affirm the identities of girl fans like Katie while simultaneously re-securing dominant ideals of femininity and heteronormativity." Additionally, through an analysis of brand Her Universe, which specializes in "fashion forward apparel for the female sci-fi fan," Johnson (2014, 902) illustrates how "the subjectivities constructed for female consumers also operate in limited, circumscribed, postfeminist ways." Similarly, Elizabeth Affuso's (2017, 185) analysis of fandom-oriented makeup lines illustrates how the branding imagines the products "as tools of feminine superpower indoctrinating readers into a postfeminist logic of consumer feminism where girl power is a commodity to be bought and sold." Affuso further articulates that analyses of commodity feminism and brand culture under neoliberalism are essential to understanding how media industries seek to hail female fans and also how they expect these fans to participate in fandom. Under the organizing logics of neoliberalism, female fans are expected to brand themselves as ideal postfeminist consumers. As fandom becomes more and more mainstream, it is crucial to interrogate how the media industries (and fans themselves) adapt media texts and fan practices in ways that reify, rather than resist, normative hierarchies and structures.

METHOD

As the go-to e-commerce platform for vintage and handmade goods, Etsy is available in multiple countries, languages, and currencies. For the purposes of this project, I based my search in the United States and used the US dollar. There are thousands of options for bachelorette party paraphernalia sold to US consumers through Etsy, and hundreds of products associated with the *Harry Potter* fandom. In November 2019, I input both "harry potter bachelorette party" and a more general "wizard bachelorette" into Etsy's search feature, and I organized the products that came up in this search by relevancy (customers can also sort results by price, customer reviews, and most recent). Though both of these searches yielded between ten and fifteen pages of products, I elected to use the first five pages of results for each search term in order to get a representative sample of items. Etsy does not make it clear to users how it assesses relevancy, but this is the default sorting mechanism to categorize products when users utilize the search function. I performed a textual analysis of the products my search generated, looking exclusively at products designed to be worn on the body, which here were almost exclusively T-shirts, sashes, veils, and some lingerie. In addition to examining the colors and styles of the products, I focused on the choice of words and phrases on the items to assess how fans use the text for wedding rituals and events. Further, I noted whether Etsy designated the products as "bestsellers" or "handmade" and how that fit into Etsy's brand identity.

9¾ WASTED: FANDOM FOR ADULTS

In her 2018 feature story about how the city of Nashville became a popular destination for bachelorette parties, *Buzzfeed* culture writer Anne Helen Petersen (2018) notes,

> The easiest way to identify a bachelorette party is by the matching T-shirts. . . . The attendees—bridesmaids, friends, moms, sister-in-law, anyone who's affiliated with the bride and willing to throw down for a weekend—wear identical tees in black or bright colors. The bride's, of course, is white. . . . Even without the matching clothing, you can spot a likely bachelorette party from 100 yards away: a group of (almost entirely) white women, wearing nice jeans, cute tops, fashionable boots. . . . They travel in packs, usually between 6 and 16. They always look mildly lost, yet resolutely determined. They tend to be spilling out of or piling into Lyfts or Ubers. And they *love* murals.

Petersen synthesizes how domestic tourism through bachelorette parties is restructuring urban space and economies as well as white femininities. I begin with Petersen's analysis here to think through the ways that *Harry Potter* bachelorette T-shirts and sashes do more than just communicate that the wearers are part of a larger fandom, they also illustrate how fans negotiate shifting age norms within fandom and which elements of the source texts are adapted for these types of products.

Similar to the ways that bachelorette parties in Nashville coordinate T-shirts with reductive puns and references like "BOOTS, BOOZE, and the

BRIDE" (Petersen 2018), *Harry Potter* bachelorette T-shirts and sashes have a few common themes: they remix repeated phrases and places, especially spells, to be about drinking alcohol or generally wreaking havoc, they reference the wizarding sport of Quidditch (which I will address in the following section), and in other cases they just use the font associated with *Harry Potter* to note positions such as bride, bridesmaid, and maid of honor. The shirt intended for the bride is almost always white, while shirts for her (assumed) female companions are frequently black, pink, or other bright colors. The seller ChipguStreet (figure 11.1), one Etsy vendor of such apparel, makes sure to communicate to potential customers that these shirts are versatile, work with a number of outfits, and make great gifts; however, the colors options and the product titles communicate important information about how the seller understands both the logics of Etsy and fans' desires in searching for these shirts. For example, the shirts come in either unisex or "ladies flowy tank," each with its own color options. The ladies flowy tank, which is similar to the type of shirt in figure 11.1, is available in neutral options like black, gray, and white, but the other colors skew feminine: berry, neon pink, red, teal, soft pink, and royal blue. Additionally, the title of the product is a collection of words and phrases: "Bachelorette Party Tank Tops, Bridesmaid Gift, House Bachelorette, Maid of Honor, Wizard Themed Bachelorette." While the references to *Harry Potter* on the actual shirts are obvious, it is telling that there is no explicit reference to the *Harry Potter* franchise in the title of the items. Presumably, the lack of "Harry Potter" in the title or on the shirts themselves shields both the platform and the seller from legal battles over copyright (for more on the relationship between licensed and unlicensed fan fashion, see Boumaroun in this collection). But, the title barely functions as one at all; rather, it is a collection of optimized, easily searchable terms, contributing to this product's placement on the first page of results. Ironically, despite Etsy's repeated characterization of itself as a human(e) alternative to commerce (and the platform's placing of a handmade label on this product), the titles of products illustrate the ways in which Etsy's model is predicated on *inhuman* algorithms.

The most striking element of these shirts is the actual text they are emblazoned with. Most resonant is the rephrasing of popular spells to be about alcohol consumption, a finding that connects to research about aging, life milestones, and fan practices. In their research on soap opera fans and (re)negotiations of fan identity over the life course, C. Lee Harrington and Denise D. Bielby (2010, 441) articulate that though fandom has become more mainstream in recent years, "there continue to be disparities in how fans

Figure 11.1. *Harry Potter* bachelorette party T-shirts sold on Etsy by ChipguStreet.

experience and express their fandom in public—and those disparities are shaped in part by age norms." *Harry Potter* is classified as children's literature. Because many fans who integrate the book series into their wedding events presumably read the books years prior to their bachelorette parties, fans have gravitated toward products that "update" material from the source text to mark adulthood. Further, because of the ways in which fans, especially fans of fantasy texts, have been pathologized and infantilized as obsessed loners who are unable to mature enough to succeed at appropriate heterosexual partnerships (Jenkins 1992; Stanfill 2011), these shirts offer an alternative conception of the fan as one whose fandom is completely compatible with age norms and heterosexual coupling. After sorting through hundreds of unique items for sale, I was immediately struck by the sheer repetition. Most T-shirts sold for *Harry Potter* bachelorette parties that referenced alcohol or partying relied on the same set of phrases, puns, and textual referents (e.g., "Avada some Vodka," figure 11.1). Seven books and eight films provide a wealth of material to adapt for T-shirts, yet just a small sliver of material is ever used.

Though these T-shirts and the celebration surrounding them can be read as nonnormative and interpreted as an attempt to speak back to the strictures of domestic femininity that become more circumscribed after marriage, in many ways these products and the celebrations they are for reinforce gender, racial, and class hierarchies. While some customers buy these shirts to be worn during a bachelorette party taking place in the home, dominant trends in these types of wedding events and even the framing of the shirts suggest that the majority of consumers purchasing these products are wearing them for a night of drinking and spectacle. Journalists and writers like Petersen have demonstrated that destination bachelorette parties have become increasingly more common, and this has large implications for the types of communities that large groups of women designate as their destination for a weekend of debauchery. Petersen (2018) argues, "Nashville—or whatever city they're visiting—becomes their playground. And in the case of the bachelorette parties, they get away with it (and have entire industries cater to them) in large part because they are white, and because they have money." In this way, the age norms and assumptions of both fandom and *Harry Potter* as a cultural text work doubly. While on the one hand, these bachelorette products allow female fans to update *Harry Potter* to mark an adult life transition, on the other hand, *Harry Potter*'s positioning as children's literature, and therefore its sense as playful or whimsical, protects the mostly white women who engage in public drunken celebrations. Having large groups of women engage in these activities emblazoned with *Harry Potter* textual references and iconography restructures the source text to give mostly white women space to utilize their privileged subject positioning in ways that can have detrimental effects for local residents. More specifically, large groups of loud women who stumble drunkenly down the sidewalk, some with props like blow-up penises, might not be disruptive in a city's downtown core; however, the move from using hotels for these types of events to relying on rideshare services and AirBnB rentals in residential neighborhoods for a more "local" experience has disrupted the daily lives of actual residents (Petersen 2018). In addition to leveraging their class status in making a locale "cater" to them, the whiteness of bachelorette party attendees shields them from many of the consequences of their public, drunken celebrations.

FROM MUGGLE TO MRS.: "CRAFTING" THE NORMATIVE FAN

In addition to alcohol puns remixed from phrases and spells in the *Harry Potter* book series, references to Quidditch are especially common. Through an examination of products that reference the wizarding sport of Quidditch and products containing the phrase "Muggle to Mrs.," I extend my argument that *Harry Potter* bachelorette parties repackage elements of the text to make them compatible with hegemonic modes of white femininity. Most sashes that reference Quidditch do so through the position of keeper, with phrases like "She Found Her Keeper" and images of the three goalposts. While the phrases that adorn these sashes and other products like them are obvious puns, they also take specific references from the sport and reframe them, so that men become the dominant actors. Quidditch, which is discussed at length across the *Harry Potter* novels, has players of all genders play any position. The only professional Quidditch team that is not mixed gender is the Holyhead Harpies, an all-women team whose name is a wry reclamation of a term used to degrade women as well as a magical creature in this universe. The phrase "She Found Her Keeper" operates at multiple levels. It functions as a cutesy play on words because the groom in this scenario is a "keeper" (he has been selected for long-term partnership), while also referring to a key position on the field.

By simultaneously activating the term *keeper* and including the goalposts, however, the phrasing positions the groom in the active position of the keeper (the one who guards the goal), while the bride is rendered passive, if not inanimate, by being positioned on the same plane as the goalposts. Even the slightly more common "She Found a Keeper," which appears on several shirts and sashes, contains the same underlying idea. In addition to the position of keeper, several shirts and sashes reference the Golden Snitch, a golden sphere with wings that when caught by the seeker is worth 150 points and ends the game. I found several shirts and sashes for bridesmaids that state "She's a Catch" (or "I'm a Catch," for the bride), with a picture of a Snitch. These shirts and sashes also rhetorically position the female bride as inanimate object while rendering the male groom an active participant in the sport: the seeker, whose job it is to find and catch the Snitch (in this case, the woman waiting to be caught). The references to Quidditch overwhelmingly make women passive, or even inanimate, which is a further illustration of the ways in which these products select parts of the text and reframe them to make them compatible with both hegemonic femininity and heteronormativity.

For my final example, I turn to the ubiquitous phrase that gives this essay its name: "Muggle to Mrs." Screen-printed on a variety of T-shirts, sashes, and veils, this phrase was continually deployed in the bachelorette products I surveyed for my analysis. In their examination of the themes of heteronormativity in children's G-rated films, Karin A. Martin and Emily Kazyak (2009, 323) argue that while heteronormativity is usually constructed as mundane, natural, and normal, children's films portray heteroromantic love as having "exceptional, magical, and transformative power." The phrase "Muggle to

Mrs." constructs heteroromantic love similarly: it makes marriage a transformative process, where women go from being mere Muggles and move into the category of Mrs. "Muggle," of course, refers to individuals in the *Harry Potter* universe who cannot do magic. In addition to marriage being transformative, in this instance it also holds an element of magical power; it has the ability to transform women from mundane Muggles into magical wives.

Mel Stanfill's (2011, 2.10) research on fandom, whiteness, and heteronormativity asserts that similar to how gender is enacted, whiteness is something that people *do*, and "fandom is one of the ways of doing whiteness incorrectly." Stanfill's framework can be applied to female fans of *Harry Potter* and the proliferation of *Harry Potter* wedding products. Most frequently, a fan identity is culturally constructed as a failure of white masculinity, although there is also a long history of white, female fans being maligned for their "obsessive" fan activities (Jenkins 1992). Stanfill argues that white fans, however, have the ability to reposition themselves in line with normativity. Looking at the narrative resolutions of *Fever Pitch* (dir. Bobby Farrelly and Peter Farrelly, 2005), *Fanboys* (dir. Kyle Newman, 2009), and *Trekkies 2* (dir. Roger Nygard, 2004), Stanfill (2011, 4.2) asserts that "although fandom doesn't have to be given up, it does have to be brought under control, and it is the alignment with the white norm that makes these fans eligible for redemption." Through bachelorette party paraphernalia, Etsy operates as an intermediary space that provides the tools for white female fans to renegotiate their relationship with their fan texts and thus be adopted into white heteronormativity. I do want to address a glaringly obvious possibility: queer women in relationships with women are purchasing these items on Etsy. Despite this very real and likely possibility, the products for *Harry Potter* bachelorette parties exist within heteronormative frames that reify existing hierarchies. While actual items for male partners appeared only a couple of times in my search, each "couples set" of shirts or sweatshirts was explicitly for a male and female partner, which at times was even designated by gendered colors.

Etsy sellers' problematic reframing of the *Harry Potter* franchise to fit the social scripts of white, normative femininity is further enhanced by *Harry Potter* author J. K. Rowling's transphobia. In December 2019 and June 2020, Rowling published a series of tweets and a blog post arguing that biological sex is "real" and has universal consequences for women globally, in response to an article that used inclusive language about menstruation (Gardner 2022). Rowling's tweets and her blog post re-essentialize gender by tying it to the sex assigned at birth and obscure the ways in which race and class affect how gender is articulated. For Rowling, gender and sex are essential, biological categories that have universal, material consequences. This line of thinking has been widely criticized for decades by a number of scholars and activists, from bell hooks to Jack Halberstam. While this essay is not the place to rehash some of the central debates of feminist studies or provide a literature review of transgender studies, I do want to make clear that Rowling's remarks are not new, were not made in good faith, and are not feminist. As I see it, Rowling's attack on trans people and communities is firmly in line with the bachelorette products I analyze here. Both seek to create an exclusionary category of woman that relies on a relatively singular experience of white femininity in the West. Bachelorette parties are seemingly nonnormative spaces—their traditions involve women consuming large amounts of alcohol, brazenly taking up public space, and making frequent sexual references—but the products I found in my research reinforce heteronormativity and in actuality create very little space for women to adopt counterhegemonic subject positionings.

ETSY: NEGOTIATING GENDER AND FANDOM

To close, I would like to think more actively about where both Etsy and fandom overlap in their relationship to gender and normativity. Etsy has positioned itself as a space that challenges the traditional construction of consumer capitalism and that prioritizes human connection and humane conditions. While Etsy is a place where many people, mostly women, create distinct handmade goods like jewelry or home decor, it also operates as a site where consumers can receive quickly made material goods that are much closer to the mass-produced fare available in traditional retailers than they are to products in line with the bucolic, analog aesthetic Etsy sells. Etsy is purportedly a place for women to monetize traditionally feminine skill sets and exert more control over their labor, and its branding traffics in progressive discourses of upending the alienation and male dominance of traditional capitalism. Despite selling itself as a disruptive force and a tool for women's economic empowerment, Etsy actually reinforces neoliberal economic and cultural doctrine, urges women to monetize their hobbies, further collapses the distance between work life and home life, and offers individualized market solutions for large-scale social and economic problems. While fan studies scholarship is reassessing early assertions about fans as maligned Others who resist the absolutist power of media industries, it is important for fan studies scholars to note how new media platforms can construct fan practices in ways that align fandom with white heteronormativity. Bachelorette parties, and their attendant sartorial expressions, are a productive site of analysis for fan studies scholars because of how they leverage both the subcultural and the (seemingly) subversive in ways that actually reinforce the very hegemonic structures many fandoms see themselves as pushing back against.

REFERENCES

Affuso, Elizabeth. 2017. "Feminized Fandom, Retail, and Beauty Culture." In *The Routledge Companion to Media Fandom*, edited by Melissa A. Click and Suzanne Scott, 184–92. London: Routledge.
Blackwell, Anne. 2018. "#DifferenceMakesUs: Selling Shakespeare Online (and the Commerce Platform Etsy)." *English Literature* 5:23–37. http://doi.org/10.30687/EL/2420-823X/2018/05/002
Cherry, Brigid. 2016. *Cult Media, Fandom, and Textiles: Handicrafting as Fan Art*. New York: Bloomsbury.
Etsy. n.d. "About." Accessed October 2019. https://www.etsy.com/about
Gardner, Abby. 2022. "A Complete Breakdown of the J.K. Rowling Transgender-Comments Controversy." *Glamour*, January 3, 2022. https://www.glamour.com/story/a-complete-breakdown-of-the-jk-rowling-transgender-comments-controversy
Gray, Jonathan, Cornel Sandvoss, and C. Lee Harrington, eds. 2017. *Fandom: Identities and Communities in a Mediated World*. 2nd ed. New York: New York University Press.
Harrington, C. Lee, and Denise D. Bielby. 2010. "A Life Course Perspective on Fandom." *International Journal of Cultural Studies* 13 (5): 429–50. https://doi.org/10.1177/1367877910372702
Jenkins, Henry. 1992. *Textual Poachers: Television Fans and Participatory Culture*. London: Routledge.
Johnson, Derek. 2014. "'May the Force Be with Katie': Pink Media Franchising and the Postfeminist Politics of HerUniverse." *Feminist Media Studies* 14 (6): 895–911.
Johnston, Jessica Elizabeth. 2015. "*Doctor Who*-Themed Weddings and the Performance of Fandom." *Transformative Works and Cultures* 18. https://doi.org/10.3983/twc.2015.0637
Jones, Bethan. 2014. "Fifty Shades of Exploitation: Fan Labor and *Fifty Shades of Grey*." *Transformative Works and Cultures* 15. https://doi.org/10.3983/twc.2014.0501
Lamerichs, Nicolle. 2018. "Fan Fashion: Re-Enacting *Hunger Games* through Clothing and Design." In *A Companion to Media Fandom and Fan Studies*, edited by Paul Booth, 175–88. Oxford: Wiley Blackwell.
Luckman, Susan. 2013. "The Aura of the Analogue in a Digital Age: Women's Crafts,

Creative Markets and Home-Based Labour after Etsy." *Cultural Studies Review* 19 (1): 249–70.

Martin, Karin A., and Emily Kazyak. 2009. "Hetero-Romantic Love and Heterosexiness in Children's G-Rated Films." *Gender & Society* 23 (3): 315–36.

Petersen, Anne Helen. 2018. "How Nashville Became One Big Bachelorette Party." *Buzzfeed*, March 29, 2018. https://www.buzzfeednews.com/article/annehelenpet ersen/how-nashville-became-one-big-bachelorette-party

Pippin, Chelsey. 2016. "27 Things You Need to Have a Classy AF Harry Potter Wedding." *Buzzfeed*, November 17, 2016. https://www.buzzfeed.com/chelseypippin/27-thin gs-you-need-to-have-a-classy-af-harry-potter-wedding

Ross, Sophie. n.d. "Here's How Much the Average Wedding Guest and Attendant Spend." Knot. Accessed October 2019. https://www.theknot.com/content/weddi ng-guest-cost-2018 (article replaced on site).

Scott, Suzanne. 2017. "#Wheresrey? Toys, Spoilers, and the Gender Politics of Franchise Paratexts." *Critical Studies in Media Communication* 34 (2): 138–47.

Stanfill, Mel. 2011. "Doing Fandom, (Mis)Doing Whiteness: Heteronormativity, Racialization, and the Discursive Construction of Fandom." *Transformative Works and Cultures* 8. https://doi.org/10.3983/twc.2011.0256

Sullivan, Claire. n.d. "A Moody-Magical 'Harry Potter'–Themed Wedding." *Martha Stewart Weddings*. Accessed October 2019. https://www.marthastewart.com/7874 812/harry-potter-themed-wedding-nirav-patel

Torgerson, Rachel. n.d. "Harry Potter Wedding Ideas That Are Totally Reception Worthy." Knot. Accessed October 2019. https://www.theknot.com/content/harry-pott er-wedding-ideas (article replaced on site).

12

Retcon

Revisiting Cosplay Studies

A. Luxx Mishou

When I learned that the Society for Cinema and Media Studies annual conference would be held adjacent to Emerald City Comic Con 2019, it was not a question of whether I should pack a cosplay, but rather a question of which one would fit in my luggage. As a stranger in a strange place, I wanted to bring a familiar comics cosplay, and as a volunteer usher for the Guardians of the Sexy burlesque show, I knew I had to be able to move easily among patrons seated in a small theater. I opted for an oft-worn favorite—the original Silk Spectre, from Dave Gibbons and Alan Moore's graphic novel *Watchmen* (1986). The character's retro aesthetic is similar to my own, and it was an easy choice that felt as comfortable as the dress I would wear to an academic panel. That I don't identify with the midcentury fame-seeking vigilante never keeps me from donning her fishnets.

The long-standing presumption of cosplay studies is that the act of cosplay is a purposeful performance of devoted fandom for a specific intellectual property (IP). Craig Norris and Jason Bainbridge (2009) write that cosplay "displays how heavily an audience member is invested in the ideals of the show or identifies with a particular character and shows others how 'serious' a fan they are," and Joel Gn (2011, 587) argues that cosplay "is primarily motivated by [the cosplayer's] intense attraction towards the character to which they were exposed." Barbara Brownie and Danny Graydon (2016, 109) say that "the costume communicates efficiently and specifically the subject of one's fandom, and their level of devotion to that particular cultural artifact," and Julia Round (2014, 147) suggests that "cosplay . . . signals the wearer's identity through their taste." These oft-cited researchers establish a truism that has come to define the field: cosplays purposefully and specifically communicate a cosplayer's fan identification. However, when asked in anonymous surveys to identify their motivations, cosplayers themselves articulate a fandom for cosplaying as a practice and social activity that is greater than simply a fandom for a particular manga or video game, and their responses call into question strictly observational practices in study of the fan phenomenon. This chapter uses these anonymous cosplayer narratives to argue for an understanding of the practice less as a fanatical performance of IP devotion, and more as a creative and social practice with numerous and varied motivations.

Foundational cosplay research distinguishes the specific practice of cosplay from the fan practice of donning officially branded merchandise. Researchers argue that in breaching social norms and donning costumes, cosplayers engage in an affective performance inspired by a more deeply felt sense of fandom than that of average consumers (Gn 2011; Birkedal 2019; Brownie and Graydon 2016). Thus, a person wearing a T-shirt with a familiar logo or character expresses interest in a subject, but purchasing and wearing the T-shirt demonstrates less dedication to the property than does crafting a replica "super suit" in which to wander the halls of a fan convention (Norris and Bainbridge 2009; Bainbridge and Norris 2013). According to this analysis, my embodiment of Silk Spectre would be reflective of personal identification with, and particular fandom for, the character of Silk Spectre. But for my anecdotal illustration, these presumptions are inaccurate. I do not identify as a fan on any level currently recognized in cosplay studies, and feel no investment or devotion to the artifact; like Nicolle Lamerichs (2011, 1.6), I adopt the character because it is "doable," and I'd rather cosplay than not. But though Lamerichs's research and personal cosplay narratives demonstrate a spectrum of fandom related to the embodied fan practice, readings of fandom in cosplay remain a central tenet of the field.

In this chapter I call the assumptions of fandom and cosplayer identity into question, and with them the ways in which cosplay is witnessed, researched, and analyzed. Existing cosplay research largely follows two methodological approaches: ethnographic observation and direct examination in the form of solicited interviews. Observational explorations into cosplay position the observer-researcher as the audience for the cosplay performance, and establish the role of the nonparticipant observer as one who consumes the cosplay as an analyzable text (Gunnels 2009; King 2016; Winge 2019). This approach is productive in the analysis of participant and nonparticipant interaction, trends in cosplay practices, and the impact cosplayers have on convention spaces (Scott 2015; Norris and Bainbridge 2009; Gn 2011; Kirkpatrick 2015; Anderson 2015; Truong 2013). However, strictly observational research is not well situated to speak to individual cosplayer identities or affective labor, as it is a reading of a performance on a public stage rather than a direct disclosure on the part of a cosplayer. Recognizing this limitation, researchers routinely utilize surveys and interviews to interrogate cosplayers on particular questions related to cosplay practice (Gittinger 2018; Rosenberg and Letamendi 2013; Dunn and Herrmann 2020; Leshner and De la Garza 2019). These studies approach cosplayers as "fanatic enthusiasts" who seek "a way of expressing their fandom and passion" (Rahman, Liu, and Cheung 2012, 320). They ask participants to self-identify as cosplayers, but not to self-identify as fans: fandom is a consistent assumption. Joel Gn (2011, 583) writes that the cosplayer "consciously desires and pretends to be an artificial, or fictional character," and he projects onto the cosplayer a fandom that relies on the connotations of a "fanatic"—an excessive attachment and dedication to particular media. Norris and Bainbridge (2009) similarly write that cosplay "is therefore not simply 'dressing up' but rather inhabiting the role of a character both physically and mentally," suggesting an attachment that extends beyond the observable convention performance.

While some cosplay researchers "other" cosplayers by casting them as super fans, many researchers demonstrate a more nuanced approach to reading identity in fan practice. Ellen Kirkpatrick (2015, 1.2) intervenes when she writes that "identity is . . . something dynamic and always subject to change," while "costuming is a visual means of transforming one's reading in identity, a way of being other, another way of being. It takes center stage in the performance of identity and has a broad repertoire, from the material to the digital." She further separates cosplayer from practice when she writes that her intention is not to elucidate the experiences of the players, but to "[identify] and then interrogat[e] the general understanding of the practices," recognizing the duality of the "source character and [the] cosplayer." As Paul Mountfort, Anne Peirson-Smith, and Adam Geczy (2019, 3) observe, "while cosplayers may be readily identifiable . . . cosplay is a deceptively complex practice that defies neat description and ready categorization," and Garry Crawford and David Hancock (2019, 5) agree, stating "it is much more complex and multi-faceted, and to some degree diverse, than any simple definition can ever hope to capture." Challenging research that does not stop to ask subjects *whether* they are fans, I argue that cosplay should be read not as a conclusive performance of fan identity, but as a nuanced site of creativity. Like Kirkpatrick (2015), I assert that cosplayers are a disparate object of study from their cosplays, and that the best means to gain an understanding of this complex and intersectional global community of fans, makers, and performers is to offer cosplayers the protection of anonymity in collecting survey data, and to closely read their individual narratives as unique texts.

Assertions of identity without the support of cosplayer narratives or data are potentially misleading, offering observational expectations as opposed to conclusions grounded in lived experiences—not just fandom, but also cosplayer gender identification or sexuality, for example. Reading cosplays as texts is a productive exercise, and allows for thoughtful interrogations of performance, maker culture, con culture, and fan labor (Crawford and Hancock 2019). But performativity is not a perfect articulation of self, and it is an unreliable lens for interrogating the complete experience of an individual.

This is demonstrably true when one seeks to understand the correlation between cosplay and fandom for a property being cosplayed, as demonstrated by Jen Gunnels's (2009) analysis of *Star Wars* cosplay at New York Comic Con. As a nonparticipant observer, Gunnels focuses on the observational surface, counting heads, witnessing photo ops, and speaking with selected cosplay participants. The joy of Gunnels's writing captures the positive social experience of participant and nonparticipant interaction. But what her research does not consider (or may not know to consider) is the unconscious learning of group participation—the social cues and expectations of participant performers, enacted for the entertainment of the nonparticipant observer. The fandom that Gunnels observes and records may be an act performed in response to her own enthusiasm.

In her analysis Gunnels (2009) specifically approaches *Star Wars* cosplayers to interview them on their practices and inspiration, asking productive questions of choice and community. The questions she asks are grounded in *Star Wars* fandom, directed at participants from a nonparticipant. Like researchers and con attendees are wont to do, Gunnels assumes that the *Star Wars* cosplayers she sees are devoted fans of the franchise, and that their costumed performances are a product of that fandom. However, what is not communicated is that this performance of fandom is part of the fantasy of cosplay. When approached by uncostumed con attendees who themselves express fandom for a property, as Gunnels does, cosplayers are likely to *perform* for the entertainment and inclusion of the other; it is a kind of unspoken social contract between the costumed and the uncostumed. This suspension of disbelief may extend to a performance of fandom where none may exist, so as to preserve the sense of positive community built at a con. Plainly, for a cosplayer to admit they are not a devoted fan of the IP they are representing kills the fantasy and joy of the costume, and may inadvertently other or insult the uncostumed observer. It destroys the moment, so cosplayers *pretend.*

This social contract is reflected in my anonymous surveys of cosplayers. In 2015 and 2019 I designed surveys to anonymously gather both demographic data and personal narratives from individual cosplayers. The surveys, which were approved by my institutional review board (IRB), focused on the personal experiences of cosplayers as unique individuals. Respondents were asked to provide demographic information, such as gender identification, preferred pronouns, and influential identity markers.[1] Multiple questions asked respondents to relate their cosplaying experiences, and additional questions were directed toward self-identified crossplayers, or cosplayers who dress as characters of gender identifications different from their own. The surveys included both multiple-choice and open-ended questions, as a primary goal was to gain a sense of cosplayer voices—what the individual thinks of their own experiences, and not just what an observer may discern at a cosplay event. To advertise the surveys I published links through my social media, as well as in private groups populated by cosplayers and variety performers. The posts were made public, and were subsequently shared by academic and performance colleagues alike. The surveys gathered a total of 168 unique responses in ninety days, from new cosplayers to veteran cosplayers. Most relevant to the present chapter are the four questions that asked respondents to indicate their inspiration for pursuing a particular cosplay, and to explain whether they've cosplayed characters or materials of which they are not fans.

Survey responses support my understanding that cosplayers willingly perform fandom and characters when approached at conventions: 65 percent of respondents affirm their preference for staying in character when approached at cons. As one cosplayer shared, "when I meet fans of the character, I love performing for them." While it is likely that many of Gunnels's (2009) interview subjects are true fans of *Star Wars*, it is also possible they were performing in the face of her excitement. Gunnels is not singular in the potential misconception of cosplayer motivation: Gn's (2011) research, cited extensively in cosplay studies, offers similar assumptions of fan investment in an IP rather than a consideration of the fandom of the practice as motivation. This misconception is now being addressed in part by research conducted by scholars who are themselves involved in the cosplay community.

As the field grows, an increasing number of cosplay scholars are framing their research through their own experiences as cosplayers (see Anderson 2015; Birkedal 2019; King 2016; Lamerichs 2018; Lome 2016; Scott 2015). This

---

1. The question about identity markers provided eight multiple-choice options (I am a cosplayer of color, I am a trans cosplayer, I am a disabled cosplayer, I am a chronically ill cosplayer, I am a fat cosplayer, I am a hijab-wearing cosplayer, I am a queer cosplayer, and I am a neurologically atypical cosplayer), as well as an option for respondents to include any additional markers I had failed to list.

shift toward autoethnographic research enriches the field, as scholars can better negotiate social contracts between cosplay creators and convention audiences. While Gunnels (2009) establishes a narrative of anthropologic distance from the cosplayers she observes and interviews, Kane Anderson (2015, 113) is able to recount his own unanticipated representation in cosplay research, when he finds that a photographer has, "without [his] knowledge or consent, posted pictures of [Anderson] dressed as Disney's Mr. Incredible specifically to lambaste [his] performance as a cosplayer." Anderson's research reflects both an academic understanding of research and analysis of costumed performance, and the affective load carried by his subjects: as people who perform, and who may find their performances harshly critiqued. Another self-identified cosplayer, Nicolle Lamerichs (2015, 104, 106) speaks from a place of experience when she introduces the concept that cosplay denotes not necessarily fandom of the material itself, but perhaps aesthetic appreciation or social conformity. Most informative is her observation that "a player might be ambivalent about a certain character's background story but might like his or her visual design." Lamerichs reports that "many of the cosplayers interviewed had in fact not played the game that they represent," but subsequent research has not yet fully accepted this common cosplay practice.

Cosplay is an embodied fan practice of incredible investment. Materially grounded, it is a performance art that relies on both mimicry and creativity, as participants use their own bodies as canvases and stages for performance. But as one survey respondent said, "Cosplayers are not the characters they're dressed as. . . . We're human beings." When asked directly, cosplayers demonstrate the diversity of identities and practices within the performance art. They illustrate a spectrum of fandom, from the deeply invested to the creatively intrigued, and an affront to definitive readings of gender, sexuality, and fandom. One cosplayer is particularly fond of her Beetlejuice (or Betelgeuse) cosplay, because she "had his voice down" and she "LOVE[S] the crowd interaction!" Another, who self-identifies as a heterosexual man, says that his joy in cosplaying the anime heroine Akemi Homura is aesthetically based: he "really like[s] wearing skirt/tights/heels." A fandom-motivated cosplayer most enjoys cosplaying Roger Taylor because "he's amazing and I very much love and appreciate him," while a more practically motivated cosplayer cosplays as Negan from *The Walking Dead* because "it was very easy to pull clothes from my closet." Each of these respondents chooses to cosplay, and each of them cosplays a character for reasons that may not be evident from their performance: love for the character, the fun of play, the ease of pulling a costume together, or the opportunity to dress in a favored fashion.

Cosplay is a hugely, and at times violently, policed site of performance and fandom, and cosplayers often weigh the potential consequences of their performances against fandoms and personal creative endeavors. Cosplayers routinely face gatekeeping—a form of harassment that works to regulate a social practice or social identity. The policing of creative boundaries reflects the critical social politics cosplayers face as people and creators. In his article "Playing with Race/Authenticating Alterity," John G. Russell (2012, 42) observes that "as a source of identity and component of selfhood, concepts of 'race' and their manipulation through stereotyped representation exert a powerful influence on constructions of Self and Other." For some cosplayers, this extends to the properties available that may be called "type"—that is, within a cosplayer's scope of natural mimicry in relation to characteristics such as height, body composition, race, and gender. As in Anderson's (2015) example, cosplayers may face derision and harassment when their cosplays do not conform to gatekeepers's expectations of race, gender identity, body type, or ability, and anxiety over harassment will influence cosplayers to make creative and practical choices for their cosplay and convention performances based on personal evaluations of risk. One well-articulated example of consequences faced by cosplayers from gatekeepers is that of Chaka Cumberbatch. Cumberbatch's 2013 article "I'm a Black Female Cosplayer and Some People Hate It" reflects the harassment she faces as a Black cosplayer. Cumberbatch is astonished by the "hell [that breaks] loose" following the publication of her Sailor Venus cosplay photograph; what begins as a joyous expression of fandom for a young woman dressed as her "favorite character from [her] favorite anime" becomes an exemplary critical discourse of identity, creativity, and politics in a subset of sci-fi and fantasy fandom. Social media users anonymously refer to Cumberbatch as "N——r Venus" and "Sailor Venus Williams," which the cosplayer laments keeps other cosplayers of color from attempting to portray characters to whom they are aesthetically other but personally invested. While expressing fandom through the wearing of branded merchandise is an accepted social practice, the act of representing an IP exposes cosplayers to unsolicited feedback and vitriolic "defense" of canon representation from bigoted or judgmental fans.

Recognizing the vitriol faced by some cosplayers—particularly cosplayers of color, fat cosplayers, and disabled cosplayers—I believe that anonymity is of great importance when researching cosplayers as people, rather than cosplay texts as performances. Honest and varied experiences are disclosed when cosplayers feel unburdened by the pressure to perform according to social expectations. This does not invalidate research that does not offer ano-

nymity, but con interactions and targeted interviews are themselves performances on the part of cosplayers as much as they are reflections of cosplay
practices and fandoms. Cosplayers are keenly aware of performativity by the
very nature of their endeavors, and they are cognizant of their representation
in interviews: they understand that their photographs and responses will be
published outside of the con, and thus there are personal risks involved in
disclosure. Offered anonymity, one LGBTQ+ cosplayer discloses that he has
"always felt male but also feel[s] forced to live as female by society/conserva-
tive family/career and cannot realistically entertain at this point attempting
to live as male, attempting to be as gender neutral as possible," expressing a
significant motivation for his cosplay practices as well as the concern that
would keep him from offering the same disclosure in a direct interview. These
interactions reflect social contracts as much as they do insight, and they are
valuable as a study of the social practices of cosplay and the relationships
between participants and nonparticipant fans. But anonymity releases performers from the anxiety of surveillance, and allows for more forthright and
even vulnerable disclosures without the threat of social consequences. These
can be consequences of fandom, credulity as a participant, or even the real
dangers associated with outing oneself (such as for the trans respondents
who are unable to publicly transition).

My surveys resulted in 168 unique responses across a spectrum of intersectional identities. Nine respondents identified as cosplayers of color, nine
identified as trans cosplayers, six identified as disabled cosplayers, thirteen
identified as chronically ill cosplayers, thirty-four identified as fat cosplayers,
forty-seven identified as queer cosplayers, and seventeen identified as neurologically atypical cosplayers. Two respondents utilized the "other" option
to identify as "old," and another divulged that they "have a history of anxiety,
depression, and body dysmorphic disorder; all of which have moderated and
have no/minimal impact for the past decade sans medication." Their cosplay
experiences ranged from novice (as few as one cosplay) to experienced (over
ten cosplays, competition veterans, etc.).

The 2019 survey asked respondents to indicate their motivation for creating a cosplay. They were allowed to select multiple motivations, and of the 133
respondents who answered this question, 117 did mark "fandom" as a motivation for cosplaying an IP. But fandom is not the only deciding factor in designing a cosplay: 87 respondents said that they are motivated by aesthetics, and
86 said that they are influenced by practical concerns. Eleven respondents
offered more personal motivations in open response: one is especially interested in couples cosplays, and another writes that "I do a lot of costuming for

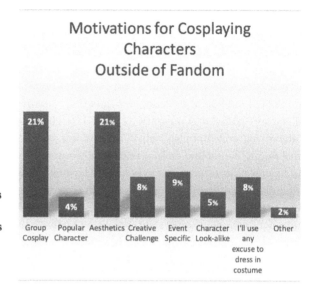

Figure 12.1. Responses to survey question 12, asking what motivates a cosplayer to present a character outside of personal fandom.

burlesque or other specific events that have themes, so that's often a jumping off point or something I need to find a character for." A physically active cosplayer uses cosplay as motivation to reach fitness goals, and a social cosplayer uses performances as "an easy way to identify myself to others with similar interests, and maybe make friends . . . ?" The breadth of responses adds nuance to the traditional assumption of dedicated fanaticism, and suggests that cosplay is less strictly dependent on the IP and more a broader opportunity for creative play and community-building. Through cosplay performers can express fandom, *and* they can indulge in extraordinary aesthetics, fulfill personal goals, and meet new people.

The 2019 survey further asked respondents, "Have you ever cosplayed a character or property of which you're NOT a fan?" The question as presented emphasizes a personal disassociation with a particular IP, in order to distinguish casual interest from cosplays adopted for strictly non-fandom-related purposes—like my own Silk Spectre cosplay. Over 25 percent of respondents indicated that they have cosplayed a character or property of which they are not a fan, directly challenging traditional assumptions of cosplay studies. In response to a follow-up question on their motivations for doing so (figure 12.1), respondents were given the opportunity to select more than one answer, allowing for a more complete picture of motivation rather than a personal ranking or justification. Twenty-seven percent of respondents related that they had cosplayed a character to meet the theme of a group cosplay rather than for their own fandom, and the same number of respondents cited aesthetics as a key motivator in cosplaying against fandom. These motivations are generally recognized in current cosplay research, as scholars acknowledge the significance of social dynamics in the success of cosplay, as well as the attraction to visual representations of cosplay characters. Beyond these findings, however, 12 percent of respondents cosplayed to meet the theme of an event, 10 percent indicated that they "use any excuse to dress in costume," and another 10 percent responded that they select cosplays for the creative challenges of building a costume rather than out of an attachment to the character or property itself, suggesting a kind of fandom or investment in maker culture rather than the IP. Two respondents selected "other," and one clarified that they have "subsequently fallen out of love with the fandom and its showrunner," revealing a process of fandom that considers developing discourse as opposed to static products. Another indicated that they were a fan of the *type* of character, if not the specific IP: "I was so excited to see a canon plus size woman who wasn't the butt of any jokes I wanted to cosplay her." These respondents, like the cosplayers who dress to fandom, articulate fandom for the practice itself, enjoying the play of their hobby. The spectrum of answers illustrates motivations related to the practice of cosplay as a site of creativity and social activity in addition to, or even contrary to, an investment in IP, and the multiple expressions of identity and enjoyment one can find even when cosplaying against fandom. To address the kinds of questions asked by nonparticipant observers of cosplayers, question 13 asked, "If you've cosplayed a character or property of which you're not a fan, how do you respond when your fandom is assumed? (i.e., Fans approaching at cosplay events)." Over 63 percent of cosplayers who admitted to performing as IPs of which they are not fans answered that they "play along" when their fandom is assumed, supporting my assertion that cosplayers are inclined to honor the social contract of fantasy and play rather than disrupt an audience's enjoyment of a cosplay.

The stories shared by anonymous cosplayers confirm the observation that cosplaying is an inherently social activity, which means that cosplayers enter public spaces occupied mutually by participants and nonparticipants and must navigate social interactions through the lens of their cosplay choices. This entails compliments, photo ops, and public appreciation for the maker's art, but it also means interrogation, being aggressively grilled in material minutia to defend a cosplay: "A *true fan* must display preference for an approved version of the costume, as agreed by his peers" (Brownie and Graydon 2016, 113, emphasis added). It may mean physical and sexual assault, a reality that gave rise to the movement Cosplay Is Not Consent. It means racism and sexism and ageism and ableism. When all a cosplayer wants to do is *play*, these truths bite hard, and they inevitably influence the creative process and subsequent performance. And these are the truths we learn from listening to cosplayers.

Cosplayer narratives demonstrate that the drive to cosplay cannot be distilled into performative fandom alone. Cosplayers express multiple reasons for character selection and execution, many even disclosing that they are not a fan of the properties they cosplay—performances that are nonetheless successful thanks to the depth of character information available through fan wikis. Rather than being fanatical for an IP, cosplayers who perform contrary to their media consumption pursue cosplay for creative challenges, social participation, or a fandom for cosplay itself. There is a great difference between reading a cosplay as a text produced—analyzing creative choice, performance, argument, and so on—at the site of performance, and reading the cosplayer and cosplayer's identity in a vacuum. Audiences experience cosplay in the narrative of the performative moment, influenced by their own history with the source material, the performative space, and their theoretical approach. To read the performance as such has strong academic precedent and is ethically sound, just as a scholar may read and analyze a comic, a play, a ballet, or the collection of a fashion designer. But to project fandom onto the *person* performing, especially in support of own's own conclusions, does not reflect the growing understanding of complex, intersectional identities. Cosplay *is* often inspired by fandom for the material represented. But it's not always. As cosplay studies moves forward and continues to grow and explore sites of fandom and making and identity, studies shouldn't confuse fandom for IPs and fandom for cosplay.

REFERENCES

Anderson, Kane. 2015. "Becoming Batman." In *Play, Performance, and Identity*, edited by Matt Omasta and Drew Chappell, 105–16. New York: Routledge.
Bainbridge, Jason, and Craig Norris. 2013. "Posthuman Drag: Understanding Cosplay as Social Networking in a Material Culture." *Intersections: Gender and Sexuality in Asia and the Pacific* 32. http://intersections.anu.edu.au/issue32/bainbridge_norr is.htm
Birkedal, Katarina H. S. 2019. "Closing Traps: Emotional Attachment, Intervention and Juxtaposition in Cosplay and International Relations." *Journal of International Political Theory* 15 (2): 188–209.

Brownie, Barbara, and Danny Graydon. 2016. *The Superhero Costume: Identity and Disguise in Fact and Fiction*. New York: Bloomsbury Academic.

Crawford, Garry, and David Hancock. 2019. *Cosplay and the Art of Play: Exploring Sub-Culture through Art*. London: Palgrave.

Cumberbatch, Chaka. 2013. "I'm a Black Female Cosplayer and Some People Hate It." *xoJane*, February 4, 2013. http://www.xojane.com/issues/mad-back-cosplayer-chaka-cumberbatch (site discontinued).

Dunn, Robert Andrew, and Andrew F. Herrmann. 2020. "Comic Con Communion: Gender, Cosplay, and Media Fandom." In *Multidisciplinary Perspectives on Media Fandom*, edited by Robert Andrew Dunn, 37–52. Hershey, PA: IGI Global.

Gittinger, Juli L. 2018. "Hijabi Cosplay: Performances of Culture, Religion, and Fandom." *Journal of Religion and Popular Culture* 30 (2): 87–105.

Gn, Joel. 2011. "Queer Simulation: The Practice, Performance and Pleasure of Cosplay." *Continuum: Journal of Media & Cultural Studies* 25 (4): 583–93.

Gunnels, Jen. 2009. "'A Jedi Like My Father before Me': Social Identity and the New York Comic Con." *Transformative Works and Cultures* 3. https://doi.org/10.3983/twc.2009.0161

King, Emerald L. 2016. "Tailored Translations—Translating and Transporting Cosplay Costumes." *Signata* 2:361–76.

Kirkpatrick, Ellen. 2015. "Toward New Horizons: Cosplay (Re)Imagined through the Superhero Genre, Authenticity, and Transformation." *Transformative Works and Cultures* 18. https://doi.org/10.3983/twc.2015.0613

Lamerichs, Nicolle. 2011. "Stranger Than Fiction: Fan Identity in Cosplay." *Transformative Works and Cultures* 7. https://doi.org/10.3983/twc.2011.0246

Lamerichs, Nicolle. 2015. "Express Yourself: An Affective Analysis of Game Cosplayers." In *Game Love: Essays on Play and Affection*, edited by Jessica Enevold and Esthet MacCallum-Stewart, 97–115. Jefferson, NC: McFarland.

Lamerichs, Nicolle. 2018. *Productive Fandom*. Amsterdam: Amsterdam University Press.

Leshner, Connor Emont, and Sarah Amira De la Garza. 2019. "Dress for Success: How Cosplay Plays a Role in Relationship Dynamics." *Journal of Interpersonal Relations, Intergroup Relations and Identity* 12:92–100.

Lome, Jordan Kass. 2016. "The Creative Empowerment of Body Positivity in the Cosplay Community." *Transformative Works and Cultures* 22. https://doi.org/10.3983/twc.2016.0712

Mountfort, Paul, Anne Peirson-Smith, and Adam Geczy. 2019. *Planet Cosplay: Costume Play, Identity and Global Fandom*. Bristol, UK: Intellect.

Norris, Craig, and Jason Bainbridge. 2009. "Selling *Otaku*? Mapping the Relationship between Industry and Fandom in the Australian Cosplay Scene." *Intersections: Gender and Sexuality in Asia and the Pacific* 20. http://intersections.anu.edu.au/issue20/norris_bainbridge.htm

Rahman, Osmud, Wing-Sun Liu, and Brittan Hei-man Cheung. 2012. "'Cosplay': Imaginative Self and Performing Identity." *Fashion Theory* 16 (3): 317–42.

Rosenberg, Robin S., and Andrea M. Letamendi. 2013. "Expressions of Fandom: Findings from a Psychological Survey of Cosplay and Costume Wear." *Intensities: The Journal of Cult Media* 5:9–18.

Round, Julia. 2014. *Gothic in Comics and Graphic Novels: A Critical Approach.* Jefferson, NC: McFarland.

Russell, John G. 2012. "Playing with Race/Authenticating Alterity: Authenticity, Mimesis, and Racial Performance in the Transcultural Diaspora." *CR: The New Centennial Review* 12 (1): 41–92.

Scott, Suzanne. 2015. "'Cosplay Is Serious Business': Gendering Material Fan Labor on Heroes of Cosplay." *Cinema Journal* 54 (3): 146–54.

Truong, Alexis Hieu. 2013. "Framing Cosplay: How 'Layers' Negotiate Body and Subjective Experience through Play." *Intersections: Gender and Sexuality in Asia and the Pacific* 32. http://intersections.anu.edu.au/issue32/truong.htm

Winge, Thérèsa M. 2019. *Costuming Cosplay: Dressing the Imagination.* London: Bloomsbury.

PART IV

Fashioning Fan Bodies

13

Disneybounding and Beyond

Fandom, Cosplay, and Embodiment
in Themed Spaces

Rebecca Williams

Fashion and costuming are integral to the contemporary theme park experience for many fans. Visiting sites such as Disneyland, Walt Disney World,
or Universal Parks in specific forms of dress enables fans to embody favorite characters, immerse themselves in fictional storyworlds, and "use their
park-going experience to explore selfhood, fandom, and style through creative styling" (Lantz 2020, 1335). However, while Universal Parks are relatively
accepting of this practice, Disney forbids overt cosplay within its parks for
guests over the age of fourteen (Walt Disney World, n.d.). In response, fans
have circumvented this prohibition through the practice of Disneybounding.
This has been characterized as an "interpretation" of cosplay, an "everyday
cosplay" in which participants "strive to dress like Disney characters in their
everyday lives" but also within the theme park spaces themselves (Brock 2017,
302, 313). Rather than explicit costuming, this involves the piecing together
of mass-market clothing items and accessories to reflect the style or color
palette of a specific Disney character, film, or theme park attraction.

Disney has now tacitly endorsed Disneybounding by producing official
dresses and accessories designed to be utilized as part of the practice and
partnering with its creator, Leslie Kay (2020). However, Disneybounding's
origins in acts of resistance to the company's official rules reveal the tensions
that can emerge when fannish costuming practices are enacted within theme
park spaces. In such privately owned corporate sites, there are both official
and ideological limitations on fan behaviors and the cultural contexts that
they operate in. Such issues highlight the importance of the spatial to the act
of cosplaying.

This chapter argues that the enactment of sartorial fandom within
theme parks has much to tell us about the relationship between fandom and

clothing, and between consumption culture and physical embodied experience. Garry Crawford and David Hancock (2019, 209) argue that cosplay functions as an act of reappropriation and resistance when undertaken in urban spaces (what they refer to as "urban poaching"). This may seem less possible in heavily controlled commodified locations such as theme parks, which charge an admission fee for entry and have regulations governing guest behavior. However, the battles over resistance for fans in themed spaces are complex and always in flux. For example, Victoria Pettersen Lantz (2020, 1348) notes that Dapper Day (an unofficial event where fans dress in formal, early twentieth-century attire to visit the parks) enables fans to "take ownership of fan desire within the strict structure of a Disney park" and "challenges the strictness of the parks or characters, including their adherence to binary gender." However, she explains, while there may be room for subversion of gender and sexual identities, these practices can also involve "problematically appropriating from other cultures and nationalities." Thus, despite their best intentions, the architectural spaces of theme parks (which are often influenced by "colonialism or Victorianism") mean that fans can never be truly resistant since they continue to be framed (and constrained) by the physical settings around them (Lantz 2020, 1336, 1350). As wider cosplay communities face pushback against the race-bending of characters (Kirkpatrick 2019), those engaged in Disneybounding often find that the spaces of the theme parks "marginalize . . . difference based in gender, race, ethnicity, and sexuality" (Lantz 2020, 1351).

Given these negotiations, the chapter also explores how fashion and the sartorial are now recognized by media companies as a crucial element of the themed branded experience. The complex tensions between the brand proximity generated by overt endorsement of one's fandom and the corporate cooption of fannish practices that are commercialized and sold back to fans (see Boumaroun in this collection) lead us to question whether this development exploits fan attachment or represents a desired validation of embodied fan practices. This chapter centers two opposing corporate responses to fannish practices—Disney's strictures for the *Star Wars*–themed Galaxy's Edge land and Universal Studios' more relaxed approach for the Wizarding World of Harry Potter—to argue that fans' embodied presence within commercially owned spaces remains bound by regulations and management of their practices.

Finally, the chapter turns to the practices of costuming and cosplay within Universal Studios Japan (USJ), in Osaka. It moves away from Disneybounding to examine fan practices outside of the "perceived Euro-American origin of theme parks" (Erb and Ong 2017, 145), acknowledging the role of national specificity, such as the Japanese culture of *kawaii* (or "cuteness"), in clothing and accessories among fans in themed spaces.

The analysis presented here developed from a broader project on theme park fandom and is rooted in participant observation carried out by the author during five trips to theme parks in Orlando, Florida, between 2011 and 2018, and a trip to Tokyo Disney Resort (Tokyo Disneyland and DisneySea) and USJ in 2018. Such physical presence allows for a "more emotional, experiential sense" (Brown 2018, 180) of the theme park space than is captured in many previous studies, since it "provides a different set of insights, immersed in the experiences of managing, working in, visiting and thinking about the theme park" (Bell 2007, ix). Thus, the analysis presented in this chapter draws on the methodological practices of "immersing in [the theme park] . . . for extended periods of time; observing the consumption of the park by tourists inside the park; listening to and engaging in conversations; . . . [and] developing a critical understanding of the issues and people" (Zhang 2007, 10). Alongside these physical visits, the research involved spending over eight years immersed online in the spaces of theme park fandom, including social media platforms such as Twitter, Instagram, and Facebook and official and unofficial fan-run blogs. It is from this grounded perspective, as well as my own position as a fan of Disney's and Universal's theme parks, that this chapter begins.

UNDERSTANDING THE THEME PARK FAN

The global theme park industry attracts large numbers of visitors, many of them loyal theme park fans. In 2019, there were nearly 156 million global visitors to Disney Parks, while Universal Studios drew over 50 million visitors across its sites in the same period (TEA/AECOM 2020, 11). Those who visit may be general tourists or fans of specific intellectual properties (IPs) that can be found within such sites (such as *Harry Potter* or Marvel). However, many have emotional attachments to the parks themselves and self-identify as theme park fans (Williams 2020). Despite the popularity of such sites, it is only recently that theme park visitors have been conceptualized as more than naive, culturally ignorant, or "passive consumers, neither actively engaged in the construction of their experience, nor particularly aware of the high degree of manipulation and influx of capital required to maintain the experience" (Borrie 1999, 74). In fact, theme park fans often engage in practices common across fan cultures, including seeking out information about the parks (Bart-kowiak 2012), meeting up with fellow fans online or on-site (Lutters and Ackerman 2003; Torres and Orlowski 2017), creating podcasts or vlogs (Kiriakou 2017), or indulging in themed experiences such as the consumption of food related to favorite story worlds (Williams 2020). Disney's parks have been the most widely analyzed, since its first park, Disneyland, embodied "the desire of fans of Disney's films to engage with their favourite fictional worlds" and offered "a utopian haven where mundane everyday reality could be forgotten and a multi-generational celebration of childhood and nostalgia" was offered (Koren-Kuik 2014, 146).

Such a "utopian haven" does not come cheap, however, and the very act of visiting involves a financial exchange to cross through the turnstiles and enter into the Magic Kingdom or Universal Studios. Theme park spaces are thus heavily contested sites of debate over commodification and commercialization. This makes clothing and other wearables (such as Disney's themed Mickey ears, or cosmetics produced by Disney in collaboration with MAC or ColourPop) a crucial avenue for exploring the intersections of fan fashion, place, and the often fraught relationship between theme park fans and those who own and operate the parks.

DISNEYBOUNDING, COSPLAY, AND CO-OPTION

Disney's parks have a complex relationship with fan clothing and seek to regulate what guests can wear during their visits. Costumes are banned for guests over the age of fourteen (except during special events such as Halloween and Christmas parties), primarily to avoid guest confusion over who the "real" characters are and to ensure child safety. Adult fans have had to adapt to express their fandom through the sartorial. As noted above, this resulted in Disneybounding, where fans dress to make subtle nods to favorite characters, films, or theme park attractions via the color palette and style of their outfits, accessories, hairstyles, and makeup. For example, to Disneybound as Minnie Mouse, one would wear a color scheme of red, black, and white, including white dots on a red background, yellow shoes, and accessories with red bows. Disneybounding is both *different from* and *subsumed under* cosplay (the practice of dressing as specific characters), which requires "a narrative, a set of clothing, a play or performance before spectators, and a subject or player" and "creates an intimate and complex relation between the fan and the character" (Lamerichs 2011, 1.2, 3.1).

Conventional Disney cosplaying can be seen at official conventions such as the D23 Expo, while Disneybounding can more easily be undertaken in everyday situations such as going to work. It functions as a form of "stealth cosplay" (Edidin 2014), allowing fans to "integrate fan practices into everyday life and speak[ing] to a marking of the body in intimate—and often less visible—terms" (Affuso 2018, 184). But Disneybounding is most associated with the theme parks themselves, where fans can use the environs as backdrops for photographing their creations and "framing the play experience in terms of the look, feel and *mise-en-scène* of the storyworld that the character inhabits" (Mountfort, Peirson-Smith, and Geczy 2019, 164). It is here that the relationship between favorite texts/characters, the physical embodied self, and related places can be played out (Williams 2020, 183), and where theme park fans can most clearly "move betwixt and between fictional, visual, and corporeal texts" (Lamerichs 2018, 176).

While Disneybounding began as a subversive fannish practice for guests to circumvent park rules, Disney has been quick to embrace it and produce a range of official products for fans. These include licensed dresses, some in conjunction with geek retail brands including Her Universe, Hot Topic, and Cakeworthy (see Santo in this collection), and some via the Disney Dress Shop label. Previous designs have been based on the iconography of park attractions such as the It's a Small World ride and the Haunted Mansion, or classic Disney films including *Dumbo* (dir. Ben Sharpsteen, 1941) and Pixar's *Monsters, Inc.* (dir. Pete Docter, 2001). These apparel items, alongside complementary accessories such as bags and jewelry, are marketed as deluxe fashion items, with the dresses typically priced at US$80 and upward. Disney has also partnered with other high-end fashion brands to produce items aimed at this price bracket, including Dooney & Burke and Loungefly for handbags, and Alex and Ani for jewelry. While some items are available online via the ShopDisney website, many are "park exclusive" and difficult to attain. Disney can thus appeal to those seeking to spend money on luxury items while also imbuing those who have been able to purchase exclusive items with levels of prestige, through limited-edition pieces. For these fans, modes of embodied performance represent their financial capital, geographic access to the parks, and sartorial ownership of desired products.

In embracing Disneybounding through its production of fan-inspired merchandise, however, Disney also undermines the unofficial and enthusiast Disneybounding industry that has sprung up on sites like Etsy, where fans sell their own self-made dresses, jewelry, and themed Mickey ears. We might view Disney's actions here as "vampiric" since they "reinforce . . . the economic dynamics between fans and media producers" and position fans as "canni-balistic consumers, buying products based on their own ideas yet kept out-side of the profit structure" (Kiriakou 2018). However, countless fans continue to post about their purchases of Disney's official fashion products on social media platforms such as Instagram, indicating that whatever resistance does exist, it is difficult to find among the glossy filtered images of Disney influenc-ers and fans in such online spaces.

FAN COSTUMING AND CONTESTED
CORPORATE/CORPOREAL CONTROL

Most studies of theme parks have focused on Disney. This is perhaps unsur-prising given its global presence (with six resorts across the United States, Europe, and Asia) and the overall cultural dominance that it exercises. How-ever, the Universal Studios brand is also a major player, and the two com-panies are often compared, with the perception that "Universal does not adhere to the squeaky-clean image characteristic of the Disney theme parks" (Lillestol, Timothy, and Goodman 2015, 233). For example, Universal offers the deliberately frightening Halloween Horror Nights event (which enables it to cater to a wide array of demographics and fandoms, including those of horror franchises), in contrast with Disney's family-friendly Mickey's Not So Scary Halloween Party.

When academic work has examined Universal Studios, it has focused on the *Harry Potter*–themed Wizarding World lands in California, Florida, and Osaka and the immersive potential these sites offer to fans of the franchise (Baker 2018; Waysdorf and Reijnders 2018). The use of cosplay and merchan-dise within the Wizarding World allows fans to "perform . . . [their fandom] publicly and connect . . . to others who felt the same way" (Waysdorf and Reijnders 2018, 184). This is especially visible given the emphasis on forming allegiances to one of the four Hogwarts houses: Gryffindor, Slytherin, Huf-flepuff, or Ravenclaw. Wearing house merchandise "announces a sense of membership in those Hogwarts Houses and associates fans with their attri-butes" (Godwin 2018). When on-site in the Wizarding World locations, Harry Potter fans can take this material identification further, choosing their own wands, which they can use to create "spells" at sites around the land via RFID technology. Fannish play is encouraged by such technology; the "interactive wands are not framed as games or competitions to score points or to com-plete quests, but instead as material parts of the story world," while clothing offers "playful engagement and immersion without forcing fans into predetermined narratives, framing devices, or roles" (Godwin 2018).

One point of contrast with the Wizarding World wands is the use of lightsabers in Disney's *Star Wars*–themed Galaxy's Edge lands, which opened in its California and Florida parks in 2019. Given Disney's restrictions on costumes for those aged over fourteen, there was initially confusion over how guests could dress when visiting Galaxy's Edge, with conflicting reports about whether the wearing of Jedi robes and the use of lightsabers was permitted (Whitten 2019). The immersive potential of the use of the lightsaber is built into the experience of being in Galaxy's Edge since guests are able to build their own at Savi's Workshop—for a fee of US$200. However, once this activity is completed, guests are often instructed by cast members to put away their "scrap metal" or reminded that "blades" are banned on the planet of Batuu (McCaffrey 2019). Even as costumes and accessories are sold in the land, these restrictions on usage limit the potential for immersion into the world.

This more restrictive attitude has been frequently contrasted with Universal's approach within the Wizarding World, where dressing even in clothing not purchased inside the parks, and engaging in play involving the RFID-enabled wands, is overtly endorsed (Whitten 2019). Universal's parks have thus been viewed as permitting fans the "freedom to 'geek out' and act like a fan in a way that transgresses society's normal proscriptions against such behaviour" (Waysdorf and Reijnders 2018, 184), in contrast with the Disney parks, which curtail practices such as cosplay and fan reenactment of moments from favorite texts. Both wand and lightsaber suggest the potential for immersion in themed spaces and imaginary worlds via the use of paratextual props, but in Disney's case, this promise of embodied experience is disrupted by the preexisting rules regarding costuming and discourses around the guest experience.

Ultimately, both Universal and Disney seek to profit from selling fan clothing and accessories to those who visit the parks, and we should be wary of positioning one as good and the other as bad in their fan engagement. Critiques of "object-oriented fans . . . [for being] inauthentic shills for the media industries" (Affuso and Santo 2018) remain common, even as fans "resist industry attempts to fix, limit, or define their experiences and actions, or to channel them solely or primarily into official consumption" (Godwin 2018). The contrast between the Wizarding World and Galaxy's Edge, however, highlights how themed sites may encourage or constrain different fan practices. It also demonstrates the tension between the "inherently private and personal nature" of fandom and the unavoidable "logic of capitalist exchange" (Sandvoss 2005, 116), which co-opts and commercializes fan practices to sell their favorite products and experiences back to them (Williams 2020, 248).

Another avenue for examining how fans of Universal Parks engage in forms of cosplay or costuming is to consider non-Western examples. For instance, the use of clothing and accessories in USJ in Osaka is quite different from displays within the US-based parks. In its published "Rules & Manners," USJ (n.d.) states that "the park welcomes guests who want to enjoy wearing various types of costumes and attire," making clear that both cosplay and bounding are permitted. Cosplay within the park is so common that guests must also avoid inconveniencing others through "photography or filming that may be disruptive to other guests, . . . changing costumes inside bathrooms, or blocking mirror spaces for makeup application." Signs in the bathrooms throughout the park also remind guests of these rules.

But, while guests within Osaka's Wizarding World behave in very similar ways to those within the US parks, those in other USJ lands often draw on the Japanese aesthetic of *kawaii* or cuteness (Dale 2016; May 2019) in their sartorial displays. The concept of "*kawaii* has various, somewhat contradictory meanings" (Nittono 2016, 81), and its "definition . . . is multiple and . . . diverse" (Monden 2014, 272). Issues with the concept of *kawaii* have also been raised in terms of its "racial caricature" (Bow 2009, 32) of East Asian people and cultures, and "a perceived difference in the power of the subject and object" (Ngai 2012, 87). Furthermore, it has been used differently in Japanese and Western contexts: "To the Japanese, expressions like '*kawaii* culture,' 'concept of *kawaii*,' etc. can appear weird. . . . It is us [Westerners] who speak of '*kawaii* concept' and '*kawaii* culture'" (Martorella and Pellitteri 2002, 268). It is, therefore, pertinent to be cautious when drawing on concepts such as *kawaii* to understand the fan practices of those in a different national and cultural context to that of the researcher.

Here, however, use of the term *kawaii* draws from its definition as having "a relatively agreed-upon range of meanings that go from 'cute' to 'sweet,' from 'tender' to 'childish,' from 'innocent' and 'gentle' to 'honest' and 'soft,' and from 'small' to 'lovely'" (Pellitteri 2018, 3), as with such entities as Pokémon and Hello Kitty (Allison 2004; Belson and Bremner 2004). At USJ in 2018, the most common form of costuming or cosplay was seen in guests dressing as, or inspired by, the characters of the Minions from Universal's *Despicable Me* movies and its *Minions* spin-offs. This ranged from people in complete Minion costumes (such as onesies or dungarees) to those using the color palette of blue and yellow with themed accessories such as scarves, umbrellas, jewelry, or bags.

Even more specifically, the most popular Minion character seen was Bob, whose design is the most typically "cute" of the Minion archetype; in the *Minions* movie Bob is positioned as the baby of the group, described as a "bald jaundiced child," and attached to his teddy bear, Tim. The character of Tim (who features on very little merchandise at Universal Studios Florida) was also a focus for guest costuming within USJ. A range of merchandise including teddy bear ears, bags, sweaters, jewelry, and scarves was hugely popular, and groups of young women dressed in coordinating outfits drawing on Tim's aesthetic were common within the park. This is perhaps because the design, of neutral brown and beige tartan or muted shades of red, brown, and cream, can be easily incorporated into existing outfits; many guests drawing on Tim's aesthetic were dressed in beige, brown, or cream-colored dresses or coats with brown boots or shoes. In this way, costuming worked as a form of fashion at USJ, allowing groups of guests/fans to use accessories based on Tim in different ways while maintaining group unity through the commonality of their accessories or color palette. The subset of Minions merchandise themed around Tim was entirely aimed toward women and girls, evoking this "cute" culture but also, more practically, creating issues around sizing and accessibility for those with larger-than-average body types and shapes (Winge 2019, 144–45). The link to the concept of *kawaii* is clear, given the design of the Minion or Tim accessories, which highlight "an emotional attachment to creatures such as chubby pups and roundish objects of small dimensions" and show how *kawaii* "is more often than not associated [with] a girl/girlish culture" (Pellitteri 2018, 3). Those employed within USJ also reinforce this link to *kawaii*; although I was not entirely in costume during my trip, my Minion-themed Christmas jumper and fluffy brown Tim ears attracted a frequent call of "*kawaii*" from staff as I moved around the park.

Much as USJ offers food specific to the Japanese market and attractions featuring Japanese actors and media, fans' costuming adheres to the notion of *kawaii* through its emphasis on cute figures such as the Minions, especially Bob and Tim. This glocalization of fan practices in USJ, which can also be seen in other Disney and Universal theme parks in Asia such as Tokyo Disneyland (Raz 1999; Van Maanen 1992) and Universal Studios Singapore (Chang and Pang 2017), highlights how fan behavior overlaps with, but also diverges from, practices such as Disneybounding and the use of costuming in the US-based Wizarding World locations. Costumes and fashion are important to fan guests in USJ, but they are filtered through the lens of a nationally specific mode or style. They demonstrate how "kawaii things, characters, and commodities—as a peculiarity of Japanese contemporary culture—move across mass media, impulse goods, [and] creative industries" (Pellitteri 2018, 5), and into themed and branded spaces such as Universal Studios Japan.

CONCLUSION

Of the many avenues where fandom and fashion or clothing may collide, the theme park space is perhaps one of the most inherently commercialized. While theme park guests are characterized as the perfect consumer in a space whose ultimate goal is "to naturalize consumption activities, so that visitors consume without being aware of it" (Yoshimoto 1994, 187), fans across different fan cultures struggle with established binary oppositions where "'good' fan identities are constructed against a further imagined Other: the 'bad' consumer" (Hills 2002, 27). However, there remains a "potentially curious co-existence within fan cultures of both *anti-commercial ideologies and commodity-completist practices*," as fans negotiate the tensions between resistance and incorporation that theme parks present (Hills 2002, 28). The commodified and branded sites of Galaxy's Edge and the Wizarding World offer fans the chance to inhabit previously unavailable narrative and imaginative spaces, but their embodied presence in such places remains subject to regulation and management. While the Wizarding World encourages fans to display their fannish allegiances and adorn their bodies with costumes and accessories, Galaxy's Edge threatens to limit the corporeality of the fan experience via its often irregular and confusing policing of the wearing of robes and the use of accessories such as lightsabers. You can buy, but you cannot participate. You can engage in the commercial exchange of money for goods, but your fannish practices remain subject to control within the corporate, branded world of the *Star Wars* franchise.

Universal's park experience appears to enable greater fan freedom when compared to Disney's restrictions on costumes. While Universal lacks a comparable fan practice to Disneybounding, experiences in USJ suggest that forms of costuming remain a common part of the guest experience as visitors wear clothing and accessories purchased in the parks. In this national context, it is the concept of cute or *kawaii* that appear to most clearly inform the sartorial choices made by the Asian visitors to the park, enabling them to engage in this style through use of items themed to Universal characters such as the Minions, or the company's licensing of figures such as Hello Kitty. More detailed study of guest behavior in the Japanese park is needed. However, bringing non-Western-centered perspectives on theme park fandom together with work on fan fashion across national contexts demonstrates how clothing and accessories are actuated in different ways. Such work can also help us better understand how corporate institutions work to restrict or encourage sartorial fan practices such as cosplay and costuming, according to modes of spatiality, branded context, and national specificity.

REFERENCES

Affuso, Elizabeth. 2018. "Everyday Costume: Feminized Fandom, Retail, and Beauty Culture." In *The Routledge Companion to Media Fandom*, edited by Melissa A. Click and Suzanne Scott, 184–92. London: Routledge.

Affuso, Elizabeth, and Avi Santo. 2018. "Mediated Merchandise, Merchandisable Media: An Introduction." *Film Criticism* 42 (2). https://doi.org/10.3998/fc.137612 32.0042.201

Allison, Anne. 2004. "Cuteness as Japan's Millennial Product." In *Pikachu's Global Adventure: The Rise and Fall of Pokémon*, edited by Joseph Tobin, 34–49. Durham, NC: Duke University Press.

Baker, Carissa Ann. 2018. "Universal's Wizarding World of Harry Potter: A Primer in Contemporary Media Concepts." In *Harry Potter and Convergence Culture: Essays on Fandom and the Expanding Potterverse*, edited by Amanda Firestone and Leisa A. Clark, 55–66. Jefferson, NC: McFarland.

Bartkowiak, Mathew J. 2012. "Behind the Behind the Scenes of Disney World: Meeting the Need for Insider Knowledge." *Journal of Popular Culture* 45 (5): 943–59.

Bell, David. 2007. "Preface: Thinking about Theme Parks." In *Culture and Ideology at an Invented Place*, by Zhang Pinggong, ix–xii. Cambridge: Cambridge Scholars.

Belson, Ken, and Brian Bremner. 2004. *Hello Kitty: The Remarkable Story of Sanrio and the Billion Dollar Feline Phenomenon*. Singapore: Wiley.

Borrie, William T. 1999. "Disneyland and Disney World: Designing and Prescribing the Recreational Experience." *Society and Leisure* 22:71–82.

Bow, Leslie. 2009. "Racist Cute: Caricature, Kawaii-Style, and the Asian Thing." *American Quarterly* 71 (1): 29–58.

Brock, Nettie A. 2017. "The Everyday Disney Side: Disneybounding and Casual Cosplay." *Journal of Fandom Studies* 5 (3): 301–15.

Brown, Stephen. 2018. "The Theme Park: Hey, Mickey, Whistle on This!" *Consumption Markets & Culture* 21 (2): 178–86.

Chang, T. C., and Juvy Pang. 2017. "Between Universal Spaces and Unique Places: Heritage in Universal Studios Singapore." *Tourism Geographies* 19 (2): 208–26.

Crawford, Garry, and David Hancock. 2019. *Cosplay and the Art of Play*. London: Bloomsbury.

Dale, Joshua Paul. 2016. "Cute Studies: An Emerging Field." *East Asian Journal of Popular Culture* 2 (1): 5–13.

Edidin, Rachel. 2014. "How to Get Away with Dressing like a Superhero at Work." *Wired*, January 27, 2014. https://www.wired.com/2014/01/stealth-cosplay/

Erb, Maribeth, and Chin-Ee Ong. 2017. "Theming Asia: Culture, Nature and Heritage in a Transforming Environment." *Tourism Geographies* 19 (2): 143–67.

Godwin, Victoria L. 2018. "Hogwarts House Merchandise, Liminal Play, and Fan Identities." *Film Criticism* 42 (2). https://doi.org/10.3998/fc.13761232.0042.206

Hills, Matt. 2002. *Fan Cultures*. London: Routledge.

Kay, Leslie. 2020. *DisneyBound: Dress Disney and Make It Fashion*. Los Angeles: Disney Editions.

Kiriakou, Olympia. 2017. "'Ricky, This Is Amazing!': Disney Nostalgia, New Media Users, and the Extreme Fans of the WDW Kingdomcast." *Journal of Fandom Studies* 5 (1): 99–112.

Kiriakou, Olympia. 2018. "Meet Me at the Purple Wall: The Disney 'Lifestyler' Influence on Disney Parks Merchandise." *In Media Res*, March 26, 2018. http://mediacommons.org/imr/2018/03/26/meet-me-purple-wall-disney-lifestyler-influence-disney-parks-merchandise

Kirkpatrick, Ellen. 2019. "On (Dis)Play: Outlier Resistance and the Matter of Race-bending Superhero Cosplay." *Transformative Works and Cultures* 29. https://doi.org/10.3983/twc.2019.1483

Koren-Kuik, Meyrav. 2014. "Desiring the Tangible: Disneyland, Fandom and Spatial Immersion." In *Fan CULTure: Essays on Participatory Fandom in the 21st Century*, edited by Kristin M. Barton and Jonathan Malcolm Lampley, 146–58. Jefferson, NC: McFarland.

Lamerichs, Nicolle. 2011. "Stranger Than Fiction: Fan Identity in Cosplay." *Transformative Works and Cultures* 7. https://doi.org/10.3983/twc.2011.0246

Lamerichs, Nicolle. 2018. "Fan Fashion: Re-Enacting *Hunger Games* through Clothing and Design." In *Wiley Companion to Media Fandom and Fan Studies*, edited by Paul Booth, 175–88. Oxford: Wiley.

Lantz, Victoria Pettersen. 2020. "Reimagineering Tourism: Tourist-Performer Style at Disney's Dapper Days." *Journal of Popular Culture* 52 (6): 1334–54.

Lillestol, Tayllor, Dallen J. Timothy, and Rebekka Goodman. 2015. "Competitive Strategies in the US Theme Park Industry: A Popular Media Perspective." *International Journal of Culture, Tourism and Hospitality Research* 9 (3): 225–40.

Lutters, Wayne G., and Mark S. Ackerman. 2003. "Joining the Backstage: Locality and Centrality in an Online Community." *Information Technology and People* 16 (2): 157–82.

Martorella, Cristiano, and Marco Pellitteri. 2002. "Kawaii." In *Anatomia di Pokémon: Cultura di massa ed estetica dell'effimero fra pedagogia e globalizzazione*, edited by Marco Pellitteri, 268. Rome: SEAM.

May, Simon. 2019. *The Power of Cute*. Princeton, NJ: Princeton University Press.

McCaffrey, Ryan. 2019. "Disneyland's Star Wars Galaxy's Edge Lets You Build a Custom $200 Lightsaber . . . but Won't Let You Play with It." *IGN*, September 17, 2019. https://www.ign.com/articles/2019/09/05/disneylands-star-wars-galaxys-edge -lets-you-build-a-custom-200-lightsabera-but-wont-let-you-play-with-it

Monden, Masafumi. 2014. "Being Alice in Japan: Performing a Cute, 'Girlish' Revolt." *Japan Forum* 26 (2): 265–85.

Mountfort, Paul, Anne Peirson-Smith, and Adam Geczy. 2019. *Planet Cosplay: Costume Play, Identity and Global Fandom*. Bristol, UK: Intellect.

Ngai, Sianne. 2012. *Our Aesthetic Categories: Zany, Cute, Interesting*. Cambridge, MA: Harvard University Press.

Nittono, Hiroshi. 2016. "The Two-Layer Model of 'Kawaii': A Behavioural Science Framework for Understanding Kawaii and Cuteness." *East Asian Journal of Popular Culture* 2 (1): 79–95.

Pellitteri, Marco. 2018. "Kawaii Aesthetics from Japan to Europe: Theory of the Japanese 'Cute' and Transcultural Adoption of Its Styles in Italian and French Comics Production and Commodified Culture Goods." *Arts* 7 (24). https://doi.org/10.33 90/arts7030024

Raz, Aviad E. 1999. *Riding the Black Ship: Japan and Tokyo Disneyland*. Cambridge, MA: Harvard University Press.

Sandvoss, Cornel. 2005. *Fans: The Mirror of Consumption*. Cambridge: Polity Press.

TEA/AECOM (Themed Entertainment Association/AECOM). 2020. *Theme Index / Museum Index 2019: Global Attractions Attendance Report*. https://www.teaconne ct.org/images/files/TEA_369_611616_200731.pdf

Torres, Edwin N., and Marissa Orlowski. 2017. "'Let's 'Meetup' at the Theme Park." *Journal of Vacation Marketing* 23 (2): 159–71.

USJ (Universal Studios Japan). n.d. "Rules and Manners." Accessed August 4, 2020. https://www.usj.co.jp/e/rules/

Van Maanen, John. 1992. "Displacing Disney: Some Notes on the Flow of Culture." *Qualitative Sociology* 15 (1): 5–35.

Walt Disney World. n.d. "Disney Theme Parks and Water Parks—Frequently Asked Questions: Q. What Is the Best Way to Dress for a Visit to the Parks?" Accessed July 1, 2022. https://disneyworld.disney.go.com/faq/parks/dress/

Waysdorf, Abby, and Stijn Reijnders. 2018. "Immersion, Authenticity and the Theme Park as Social Space: Experiencing the Wizarding World of Harry Potter." *International Journal of Cultural Studies* 21 (2): 173–88.

Whitten, Sarah. 2019. "You Can Buy Jedi Robes at Star Wars: Galaxy's Edge, You Just Can't Wear Them in the Park." *CNBC*, June 4, 2019. https://www.cnbc.com/2019/06 /04/you-can-buy-jedi-robes-at-star-wars-galaxys-edge-but-cant-wear-them.html

Williams. Rebecca. 2020. *Theme Park Fandom: Spatial Transmedia, Materiality and Participatory Cultures*. Amsterdam: Amsterdam University Press.

Winge, Theresa M. 2019. *Costuming Cosplay: Dressing the Imagination*. London: Bloomsbury.

Yoshimoto, Mitsuhiro. 1994. "Images of Empire: Disneyland and Japanese Cultural Imperialism." In *Disney Discourse: Producing the Magic Kingdom*, edited by Eric Smoodin, 181–99. London: Routledge.

Zhang Pinggong. 2007. *Culture and Ideology at an Invented Place*. Cambridge: Cambridge Scholars Press.

14

Wigs, Corsets, Cosmetics, and Instagram

The Prosthetics of Crossplay

Minka Stoyanova

Cosplay refers to the fan practice of costuming and (often) playacting characters from media. Cosplays can be derived from a spectrum of fan-oriented media franchises including comics, live-action television, cartoons, and more. Matthew Hale (2014, 6) argues that cosplay is less represented in fan studies because cosplay's embodied and performative nature did not seem to lend itself to the postmodern, intertextual readings that characterized early fan studies. However, as outlined by Paul Mountfort, Anne Peirson-Smith, and Adam Geczy (2018, 24), "Cosplay's particular form of détournement is a 'recontextualization' of sources which aligns it with other mixing and mashing practices, such as fanfiction." Still, a strictly textual analysis of cosplay can neglect cosplay's performative and embodied realization. Responding to this, previous research has read cosplay through the lenses of queer theory and play theory (Mountfort, Peirson-Smith, and Geczy 2018; Bainbridge and Norris 2013; Gn 2011).

While each of these analyses recognizes the embodiment inherent to the practice, they do not effectively address our current condition of embodied technosociality as key to cosplay's political potency. Alternately, by understanding the individual as an embodied techno-organic hybrid, cyborg theory offers an approach to the cosplayer that can both address cosplay's citationality and show how that citation is realized through prosthetically extended living bodies. This ethnographic study of cosplayers primarily in the New Orleans area applies cyborg theory to trace how the body becomes an originating site for layered hybridizations ("remediation," Bolter and Grusin 1999) of a virtual media object (the character) and a body through the practice of cosplay. Moreover, this analysis outlines how that hybridization intersects with contemporary politics of race, gender, and body representation.

METHODOLOGY

Over the last half century, discourse has moved away from essentialist notions of what it means to be human. While theorists like Marshall McLuhan (1964) suggested that media can be understood as prosthetic extensions of the individual, cybernetics and its descendant philosophies have shown how the integration of media and technology into ourselves results in new hybrid beings—transforming both the individual and the media/society/technology being integrated (Maturana 2002; Stiegler and Rogoff 2010). We are fundamentally *entangled* and *extended*, with fluid identities that are both informed by media and distributed across and through them. Donna Haraway's 1985 text "A Cyborg Manifesto" recognized this hybrid construction as "cyborg" and as fundamentally destabilizing to patriarchal binaries like nature/technology or female/male (Haraway 1998). But, as many contemporary media theorists recognize, the cyborg construct is not simply about deconstructing binaries; it is also about understanding the embodied self as a central locus in a distributed network of representations and techno-media interactions (Brians 2011; Tufekci 2013; Jurgenson 2011; Deleuze 1992). Personal representation (or fashion) is a powerful component of this construction. Malcolm Barnard (2020, 253) draws on Jacques Derrida's *Of Grammatology* to suggest that an individual's clothing functions as a "constitutive prosthetic," a prosthetic that is fundamental in the creation of the individual. Thus, cyborg theory, for the purposes of this discourse, refers to the cyborgian, mutually constructive (or constitutive) relationship that exists between individuals and their technological prostheses (including media).

Cyborg theory is particularly applicable to fan studies because it is able to capture the various modes of hybridity that fan activities encompass. Specific to cosplay, the act of interpreting a media object (character) through one's own body, as well as the documentary extensions of that inscription, can be understood as cyborg hybridizations. Here, I explore these hybrid identities by discussing the cosplayer's mediation of the fictional character through the body, through the photographic image, and finally through social media. At each stage, I consider how this new evolution of the character re-forms both the source material and the cosplayer.

This chapter is based on a series of informal interviews and participant observation conducted around the fandom convention MechaCon 2019. The convention was held in July 2019, and the interviews were all conducted between July and September of that year. I also bring to the analysis my experience as an intermittent attendee at New Orleans–area fan conventions for more than twenty years, an avid costumer outside of fan conventions, and an active member of Krewe Du Moon, a Sailor Moon dance troupe. MechaCon was an independently produced annual convention held in New Orleans between 2005 and 2021. From 2015 to 2021 (save for 2020, when it was canceled due to COVID-19), it regularly drew between fourteen thousand and sixteen thousand attendees from the surrounding area (MechaCon.com, n.d.). MechaCon was selected for this study not only because of its large annual draw, but also because of its inclusivity, and its influence in the regional cosplay community. For instance, MechaCon annually included a crossplay panel that included both crossgender and cross-body-type cosplayers as invited speakers. This general culture of inclusivity meant that most of my interviewees felt comfortable speaking candidly about their own crossplay experiences. All interview subjects are referred to by their cosplay brand name or Instagram handle as well as by their preferred pronouns. While some interviewees prefer gendered pronouns (he/him and she/her), others prefer gender-inclusive pronouns (ze/hir and they). There is, therefore, an inconsistent application of pronouns throughout the text in order to best respect individual interviewees' wishes.

THE BODY

Characters replicated through cosplay should be understood as media objects, or "virtual objects capable of shifting between systems of representation" (Gn 2011, 585). However, there is a key tension in cosplay between verisimilitude and interpretation. While valued, memetic reinterpretation of characters cannot stray too far from the source material as any interpretation must also be recognizable by the fan community. Thus, even though many characters are fantastical, animated, or alien (and exact verisimilitude between the source material and the cosplayer is functionally impossible), and even though a variety of actors might portray specific characters over the life cycle of a franchise, many cosplayers prioritize verisimilitude by selecting characters they already physically resemble (Lamerichs 2011; Gn 2011, 585). As A. Luxx Mishou observes elsewhere in this collection, "cosplayers may face derision and harassment when their cosplays do not conform to gatekeepers' expectations of race, gender identity, body type, or ability," and cosplayers therefore conduct "evaluations of risk" in their character selection process. In the American cosplay community this verisimilitude-focused practice is being challenged because it discounts the body as a site of *interpretation*, wherein individual cosplayers' unique identities are projected through the act of costuming and where cosplayers can explore alternative identities for themselves and for the characters they represent.

Clothing is not simply a functional prosthetic, protecting the wearer from elemental conditions. It is also a media form that both outwardly signals identity and/or social position while, as Barnard (2020, 253) argues, acting as a "constitutive prosthetic," a prosthetic that "makes the thing possible in the first place." In cosplay, Nicolle Lamerichs (2011,) relates this phenomenon to Stuart Hall's notions of identity as constructed and Judith Butler's analysis of drag as a transfiguration of the body that affects identity. Even so, past readings of cosplays in which the cosplayer's physical appearance does not match the character tend to oversimplify the relationship between the cosplayer's body, costume, and identity. For instance, Hale's (2014, 22–23) suggestion that most male-to-female crossplay is done explicitly for humorous effect while most female-to-male crossplay is done to avoid sexual harassment ignores nonbinary crossplayers that experience a more nuanced relationship to the practice. And, Jason Bainbridge and Craig Norris's (2013) argument that *all* cosplay can be read as drag performance ignores potentially differing incentives behind the practices. By choosing characters that don't match their physical bodies, cosplayers can not only project their unique identities through the character, but also reinscribe the character in their alternative bodies. As physical characteristics like gender, race, and body type are largely immutable characteristics that influence one's sense of personal identity within and outside of cosplay communities, this reinscription of the source characters can be a particularly political fan act.

While the term *crossplay* has traditionally been used to refer to crossgender cosplay specifically, each mode of reinscribing source material—crossgender, cross-race, and cross-body-type—can be understood as crossplay. This more expansive definition of crossplay allows us to better identify the relationship between the body and the virtual media object (the character) by showing how—in all cases—the persistence of the body in the prosthetic appropriation of a media character results in a nuanced rewriting of the source character in the cosplayer's own image. As many of my interviewees recognize, cosplaying characters with differing bodies than the cosplayer, like authoring fan fiction, both expands the source universe and increases the visibility of people who are traditionally Other. Key to this process is the hybridization that occurs between the body of the cosplayer and the character through the act of costuming.

Gender is, by far, the least contentious form of crossplay. It is regularly mentioned in academic discussions of cosplay, is common in most cosplay communities, and is widely accepted at conventions and in online forums internationally. Gender crossplay often occurs in one of two modes. Cosplayers can choose to play a character in the character's given gender (e.g., a female cosplayer might choose to dress as a male character and take on attributes of masculinity), or a cosplayer might "gender bend" a character, converting the character's canonical gender to the cosplayer's affirmed gender.

While all cosplay, as a sustained performance, can take a physical toll, the prosthetics used to transform the body for the first mode can be particularly physically taxing. For example, Star explained they follow the common practice of using binders to transform their "curvy" physique into something that cuts a more masculine visage. However, binders, corsets, tape, and other body shaping technologies can do long-term damage if used incorrectly. The *safe* use of these prosthetics is an annual topic in the MechaCon crossplay panel since, despite the discomfort, their continued use reflects that the transformations they afford are key to both achieving the desired verisimilitude and allowing a cosplayer to feel they have truly embodied a character with a different gender identity.

Often, these practices also intersect "real-life" fluid identities. For instance, Star, whose body presents challenges in and out of cosplay, "enjoy[s] crossplay because it allows [them] to present as masculine instead of being always feminine . . . [as a result of their natural physique.] . . . It's nice to feel comfortable." Star's assertion that crossplay is more comfortable reinforces that one's external presentation can stabilize an internal sense of identity. For Star, cosplay is not simply a chance to dress up as a character from a fictional world; it is a cyborgian process of using clothing, binders, and cosmetics to internalize an alternative identity.

Similarly, Ickabob was able to use hir original character, "the Mad Hatter's wife," to explore hir own gender fluidity. While Ickabob's character is technically an original character (the wife of the Mad Hatter), the character was conceived as a gender-bent incarnation of *Alice in Wonderland*'s Mad Hatter. By inventing this female realization, Ickabob was safely and playfully able to explore alternative gender identities without having to worry about verisimilitude. "Technically, there is not really a character, so I was able to work with what little I knew about makeup or hair. . . . I still had not come out as agender, so I was also having to fight against that anxiety in myself." The freedom for personal exploration Ickabob felt can be attributed in part to the Mad Hatter's position as a fluid media object, having already been interpreted in a variety of media. Notably, Ickabob's version draws heavily on the camp-forward realization of the character in Tim Burton's 2010 filmic adaptation.

While Ickabob's gender bend draws on an already fluid canon, NinjaYoYo's approach to gender bending reveals the practice as an overtly tactical reinscription of a source text. Instead of creating an original character or reinterpreting a character, NinjaYoYo cosplays male characters from within her female identity without making significant alterations to the canon costume. For NinjaYoYo, this gender bending of characters allows her to embody a media object while simultaneously suggesting an alternative (crossgender) canon for that character. This approach—and its inherent critique of fan material—can apply across gender and racial identity.

Racial crossplay, while increasing in visibility in the United States, is fraught in the global cosplay community particularly as it intersects with the impulse for verisimilitude, the lack of representation of Black and brown characters in the source material, and the minority position of Black and brown people in the global cosplay community. Addressing the lack of representation in the source material, many cosplayers I spoke to tactically reimagine canonically white or East Asian characters through their Black and brown bodies. NinjaYoYo cosplays the Japanese schoolgirl Sailor Neptune (from *Sailor Moon*) as "Sailor Neptune with an afro"—often dyeing her natural hair to match the iconic green of the source character. The hybridized result—like NinjaYoYo's gender bends—suggests an expansion of the source material.

While "race bending" a character through one's own raced body is a reinscription of the source character akin to gender bending, it is often less accepted by the cosplay community. Cosplayers of color like StardustMegu note that they are often identified not *just* as the character they are cosplaying but rather as the *Black* [insert character name] that they are playing or—more egregiously—as the as "n-word [insert character name]." Even outside of cosplay, the fan community has been slow to accept or even hostile to this type of expansion, as exemplified by the fan backlash against the sanctioned crossrace casting of Starfire from DC's *Titans* (Pulliam-Moore 2018), or Ariel from Disney's *The Little Mermaid* (Nesaf 2019).

In online communities, it is often suggested that darker-skinned cosplayers should only cosplay characters who match their natural skin tone. Due to the lack of representation in source material, this is a wholly unsatisfying and exclusionary suggestion. It also reveals that race (and racism) in the cosplay community is more related to colorism, or the specific darkness of a person's skin, than to their racial *identity*. While Sledgehammer noted that his Hawaiian heritage allowed him more flexibility in his cosplay because he was often misraced as Hispanic, StardustMegu noted that lighter-skinned cosplayers of color generally do not face the same biases as darker-skinned ones. This colorism results from the community's prioritization of verisimilitude over inclusion, regardless of actual identity (Kukkii-San 2019).

One example of this misplaced priority and the privilege it reveals is the use of blackface in the cosplay community. When cosplaying nonhuman characters with outlandish skin tones (such as green or blue), it is common practice to use body paint to recolor one's skin. Extending this logic, as most interviewees mentioned, light-skinned cosplayers have also used cosmetics (blackface) to portray darker-skinned human(oid) characters (Kukkii-San 2019). Understandably, this practice is offensive to cosplayers of color, who are reminded of the troubling history of blackface. As NinjaYoYo remarked, "there is a history there and it is still sensitive. Our parents lived through this." Beyond the offensive nature of blackface, the ability to (and therefore the expectation that one would) cosmetically change their skin tone to match a source character manifests another type of privilege granted to lighter-skinned cosplayers. Darker-skinned cosplayers often face difficulties effectively portraying nonnatural skin tones or replicating facial scarring in source characters.

Ultimately, as skin color intersects with racial identity, the prioritization of verisimilitude marginalizes darker-skinned players because it creates a community in which lighter-skinned cosplayers—regardless of racial identity—are more acceptable because of their ability to pass as a race other than their own. For lighter-skinned cosplayers of color, this colorism both undermines the political potency of remediating a character through a Black body and erases their racial *identity*. In response, the cosplay duo Wakanda Moon create new and hybrid characters that represent a uniquely *Black* identity. Paraphrasing the artist Marcus the Visual (Marcus Williams), Wakanda Moon noted, "Mainstream Hollywood is also trying to find any character to *turn* Black . . . and that's *diversity and inclusion* . . . like, no." Wakanda Moon are suggesting that Blackness is not simply about a specific skin color, but about an internalized racial identity; Blackness is a hybrid of *body* and *identity*. As such, representation cannot be achieved through simply hybridizing Black bodies with non-Black characters, or what Kristen J. Warner (2017) dubs "plastic representation." Instead, *characters* should evolve from their Black heritage and culture. Therefore, to imagine a more inclusive nerdverse, Wakanda Moon have created a mash-up brand that draws on the feminist parallels between the African warrior women the Dora Milaje (from *Black Panther*) and the Japanese schoolgirl warriors of Sailor Moon (figure 14.1).

Figure 14.1. Cosplay duo Wakanda Moon combine the aesthetics of the Dora Milaje from *Black Panther* with the classic "pretty sailor" suits from *Sailor Moon* to create a new, Black realization of the original "magical girls." Image courtesy of Wakanda Moon.

Wakanda Moon's original characters reimagine the Sailor Moon "pretty sailor soldiers" as Dora Milaje warriors by using traditional African prints, colors, and accessories to create Sailor Moon *fukus* (school uniform–inspired "pretty" battle gear). For the duo, this cosplay is powerful because it is "very authentically Black."

Similar to the second mode of gender crossplay, this mode of racial crossplay more directly engages the lack of representation in the source material. This is a fundamental aim for Wakanda Moon, who see themselves as supporting future generations by building a more diverse fandom. Responding to the positive feedback the duo received at Dragon Con 2019, one member noted, "I feel like it's not just them appreciating what we've done. Even more so, it's about their interests reflected back to them." When Wakanda Moon mirror others, they reinforce that the remediated character functions as a *new*, hybrid media object. In this case, Wakanda Moon's Black bodies become the locus in a network of (cyborg) hybridizations that facilitate a more inclusive mediaverse.

Body-type-related crossplay is, like racial crossplay, another highly contested form. As many interviewees noted, online commenters that are likely to accept an individual's gender crossplay will not hesitate to call out that same cosplayer for cosplaying across body type. This is particularly pernicious as body type often follows from biological sex or race, and, therefore, low body confidence often accompanies crossrace and crossgender cosplays. As StardustMegu observed, "It's harder for plus-sized and Black cosplayers to get recognition compared to thin and lighter-skinned cosplayers. . . . The only time a Black cosplayer will get praise is if they are lighter skinned or thin." Even veteran cosplayer Sledgehammer noted the slight hypocrisy in his own approach to body type and cosplay, stating that despite running positivity panels in which he tells cosplayers "not to let their cosplay dreams be dreams," he would "really like to cosplay some really cute anime character, but there's no way I'm going to look like them, so I don't even try." Thus, while Sledgehammer strongly supports people cosplaying whatever they want, his personal decision reflects the toxic undercurrent that accompanies imagining characters across body type. In many ways, though, as StardustMegu implies, it's those cosplayers who least resemble the characters they are cosplaying that have the greatest potential to change minds and expand the source material by stalwartly embodying any character they choose.

There are a number of technical ways that cross-body-type cosplayers attempt to balance the need for verisimilitude while embodying characters they don't naturally resemble. One such technique is to use the expected proportion between a character's props and their bodies to create the illusion of an appropriately sized body. Sledgehammer specializes in the creation of props and armor and notes that it's important to consider the size and bulk of the props being created in relation to the size of the cosplayer so that the proportional difference best matches the original media. For example, Sledgehammer relayed a story of a cosplayer who had not adjusted their props for their smaller stature: "I saw someone with a Buster Sword [from

Final Fantasy]. If you're a *six-foot-tall* person then the Buster Sword is supposed to be sixty-three inches long. . . . But this person, . . . a small person, had a sixty-three-inch sword. It just wasn't believable; it broke the whole illusion." Ky Hikari also noted that she often makes extremely large props to account for her over-six-foot height: "I'm doing Atalanta from *Fate/Apocrypha* and her bow is like a foot taller than her, so I'm making a seven-foot bow to walk around the con with." The illusion created by correct proportions between a prop and a cosplayer has the greatest effect in mediated contexts such as on stage or through photography—introducing another level of cyborg hybridization into the art of cosplay.

THE LENS

Photography (professional and amateur) is an important part of the cosplay experience as both a document and an extension of the cosplay into a wider media landscape. As Ella Brians (2011) observes, the distribution of images of ourselves across global communications networks constitutes an extension of the self—or, a distribution of the body through the network. Thus, an individual cosplayer's cyborg identity should be understood as being made up of a combination of professional and amateur images distributed through a variety of media. However, this section focuses primarily on professional photography as it best exemplifies the ways in which technics, the body, and the character are hybridized to create new cyborg entities.

As noted earlier, photography has the potential to smooth over inconsistencies between the cosplayer's body and the source character. It also has the ability to inject mood or atmosphere into the cosplay. Each of these functions results in the image becoming a new, qualitatively different, hybrid media object from the cosplayer in person. As one onlooker to my interview with Sledgehammer noted, "What you see in person is different from what you see in photos." These adjustments occur not only through the technical object (the camera) but also through the interpretive use of the camera and editing software by the photographer. Ky Hikari observed, "A really good costume will always photo well, but a really great photographer is what sets it over the edge."

If, following Brians (2011), we understand images to be cyborg distributions of the self, cosplay images as mediated through the photographer and lens are particularly interesting as they act both as extensions and as a validating practice. Ky Hikari and Star both noted that getting photographs back is exciting because it makes the cosplay *feel* more real to them. In other words, Star and Ky Hikari are only able to *see* their cosplay once it has been mediated through the photographer's gaze, thereby removing them from the embodied experience of *being* the cosplay. The validation that arises from this phenomenon of externality, of seeing yourself as others might see you, drives many cosplayers to see photographic documentation as a fundamental part of their cosplay practice. But, it's equally important that these images align with one's own self-image—particularly since they double as an extension of the self into virtual space. For instance, Sledgehammer feels a certain ambivalence toward the photographic image because he sometimes finds the mediation jarring. He recalled a story of two photo shoots that happened in the same location, back-to-back. In one case the photos aligned with his image, but in the other they didn't. Knowing that both sets of photographs would be shared online and would then become part of *Sledgehammer's* online identity, Sledgehammer was conflicted over his desire to support the individual creativity of photographers and his desire for control over his distributed identity. While Sledgehammer's popularity in the cosplay community makes it hard for him to fully control how he is seen online, many cosplayers try to avoid this situation by investing large amounts of time and money, as well as emotional and cognitive capital, into negotiating their relationships with photographers. Conversely, the photographers deploy a number of techniques to guarantee ideal outcomes.

Most often working in conjunction with cosplay events like conventions, photographers scope locations in or near the event venue for backdrops that match the fantastic worlds of the source material. In addition, photographers often use special lenses and lighting equipment to overcome the banal backdrops and harsh lighting conditions of most hotel venues. Many photographers prize lenses that allow maximum control through variable focal lengths and a wide range of aperture settings. Through these techniques, photographers can effectively draw attention to the cosplay and away from anachronistic or unflattering settings. Perhaps surprisingly, though, most interviewees suggested that their best cosplay photoshoots were ones in which the photographer used minimal technical devices, but had a personal connection to the source material or the practice of cosplay and had actively researched sites in advance of the shoot.

Postediting is another technique used by photographers to add their own style to the images. However, as photographs manifest an extended identity closely tied to one's physical body, photographers must tread a fine line between creating a magical-looking photograph and making a cosplayer look radically different from their "real-life" persona. Preferably, photographers should limit their bodily edits to removing stray hairs or visible undergarments and smoothing costume inconsistencies as most cosplayers want the final photographs to look and feel *authentic*. Ky Hikari said, "I like *some* special effects . . . to change the lighting to fit the mood. . . . [But,] none of them have ever tried to Photoshop *me*—like change my body shape—which I really appreciate because my brand is about being straightforward." Similar to Ky Hikari, StardustMegu noted that editing a cosplayer's body was "extreme," and she was glad to have never worked with someone who did that.

To avoid the need for extensive postediting, cosplayers often consider the photographic medium early in their costuming process. Some costumes are even designed to present better through photographic mediation than in person. For instance, in addition to the consideration of proportions, for Star, a self-described "trash" (budget) cosplayer, makeup is vital. "You can have a really good costume, great wig, but if you don't put on makeup, the pictures don't pop. . . . Alternatively, you can have a low-budget, crappy cosplay, but do *all* the effects and crazy stuff on your face and like, that's it. That's your costume." This consideration of the photographic lens early in the cosplay process constitutes another level of hybridity. By designing and executing costumes with the lens in mind, cosplayers are integrating the technology of the camera as well as the distribution of images into their cosplay from its inception. Agnès Rocamora (2020, 729) discusses similar trends in fashion broadly, where now "[fashion] shows are full of 'made-for-Instagram' moments" and designers "have discussed how their collection was conceived considering social media."

Also reflecting trends in the fashion industry (Rocamora 2020, 732–33), the preconsideration of the lens in the construction of a cosplay applies to nonprofessional, spontaneous photography as well as professional photography; cosplayers should be *naturally* "camera ready" to be seen as *authentic*. StardustMegu and I discussed how improving her makeup skills freed her from using mobile applications to heavily edit her spontaneous photos, which lent greater authenticity to her online brand. And, while many other interviewees also confessed to using filtering applications, they also all warned against noticeable filtering because it detracts from the authenticity of their identity. This identity maintenance entails negotiating a delicate balance between portraying an authentic version of oneself and curating that self for both the platform and the community (Davis 2014; Nkulu 2017). This negotiation constitutes the third, and final, hybridization discussed in this chapter—the hybridization of the cosplayer and the platform.

THE PLATFORM

Social media, particularly Instagram, is foundational for the cosplay community because it allows cosplayers to distribute their identities across global communications infrastructures and to build (or maintain) communities beyond their immediate geographic surroundings. For some cosplayers, presence on online platforms is even a primary or secondary mode of income, and the work of maintaining their online persona is often a full-time job. In our interview, Star noted the intense levels of work that go into the process. "I saw my friend had a spreadsheet that was like, the photo they posted, the time of day, and the engagement. . . . I don't think I could handle the pressure." Instagram, as an image-based platform, lends itself well to the interconnected visual practices of cosplay and cosplay photography and is, therefore, the primary social platform for cosplayers at this time. Not all cosplayers monetize their practice, but platforms like Instagram provide professional-level tools for profile management based on the type of account and the account's followership and engagement. Thus, even cosplayers that don't intend to make a living or "get famous" from their accounts can be motivated by the platform to treat their cosplay identity as a professional brand. Therefore, like Rocamora (2020, 734) observes in contemporary fashion, "understanding practices of contemporary [cosplay] also means understanding practices of digital media."

Instagram's mobile-first design premise was intended to encourage spontaneous (real-time) image sharing. However, the increasing presence of corporate and curated accounts has elevated users' expectations. For some, the finished images prove more viral than more "authentic" content like works in progress (WIPs), while for others (like Sledgehammer) who are well known for their technical skills, the WIPs can outperform the finished images. Ky Hikari and StardustMegu try to control this disconnect by creatively leveraging the structure of Instagram, using the "stories" portion of the profile to share less finished content and only sharing polished pictures in their feeds. Other cosplayers diversify their brand presence and use specific platforms for different aspects of their brand identity. While NinjaYoYo has profiles on all major social media sites specifically to maintain control of the brand, StardustMegu uses Twitter as a platform to speak frankly about diversity, but uses Instagram to share her cosplay photos.

The integration of social media into one's distributed self is not only about the technical or algorithmic components of the platform; it is also about responding to the user community both on and off the platform. Accep-

tance on these platforms is based on large and small forms of social validation, including increased followership, likes, and positive comments. Online
responses influence the modes and tactics used by crossplayers to diversify
the landscape, but can also be harrowing. According to Wakanda Moon, "it's
super weird because it's *basically inviting commentary*. You put your face,
your body, out there for the world to digest and comment on." And, as A. Luxx
Mishou notes elsewhere in this volume: "cosplay is a hugely, and at times violently, policed site of performance and fandom." Moreover, as StardustMegu
and Sledgehammer noted, the more distributed one's identity becomes, the
more difficult it becomes to manage. Once other people (such as photographers) start sharing a cosplayer's image, the cosplayer becomes more vulnerable to people outside of their immediate cosplay circle. They must rely
on the accounts sharing their image to manage negative speech and protect
their online identity. StardustMegu hopes that by sharing images from non-
traditional cosplayers, calling out trolls, and calling out those accounts that
allow negativity, open-minded cosplayers can reverse the social forces currently making it more difficult for crossplayers and that these diversifying
practices can become normalized.

This analysis, across three levels of hybridization—the body, the photograph, and social media—reveals how an individual cosplayer uses prosthetics and other techniques to merge their physical body with a media character, how that merger is further hybridized with the technical apparatus of
the camera and the creative identity of a photographer, and how the resulting images, shared through (and influenced by) online platforms, create a
distributed brand identity. At each stage cosplay is revealed as a practice
wherein individuals can use their marginalized bodies as a central locus in an
extended and distributed (cyborg) network that citationally expands the fan
canon, increases representation in fan communities, and tactically addresses
intolerance within and outside of fandom.

REFERENCS

Bainbridge, Jason, and Craig Norris. 2013. "Posthuman Drag: Understanding Cosplay
    as Social Networking in a Material Culture." *Intersections: Gender and Sexuality in
    Asia and the Pacific* 32. http://intersections.anu.edu.au/issue32/bainbridge_norr
    is.htm
Barnard, Malcolm. 2020. "Fashion as Communication Revisited." In *Fashion Theory: A
    Reader*, edited Malcom Barnard, 2nd ed., 237–58. New York: Routledge.

Bolter, Jay David, and Richard Grusin. 1999. *Remediation: Understanding New Media.* Cambridge: MIT Press.

Brians, Ella. 2011. "The 'Virtual' Body and the Strange Persistence of the Flesh: Deleuze, Cyberspace and the Posthuman." In *Deleuze and the Body*, edited by Laura Guillaume and Joe Hughes, 117–43. Edinburgh: Edinburgh University Press.

Davis, Jenny. 2014. "Triangulating the Self: Identity Processes in a Connected Era." *Symbolic Interaction* 37 (4): 500–523.

Deleuze, Gilles. 1992. "Postscript on the Societies of Control." *October* 59: 3–7.

Gn, Joel. 2011. "Queer Simulation: The Practice, Performance and Pleasure of Cosplay." *Continuum* 25 (4): 583–93.

Hale, Matthew. 2014. "Cosplay: Intertextuality, Public Texts, and the Body Fantastic." *Western Folklore* 73 (1): 5–37.

Haraway, Donna. 1998. "A Cyborg Manifesto: Science, Technology, and Socialist-Feminism in the Late Twentieth Century" (1985). In *Simians, Cyborgs, and Women: The Reinvention of Nature*, by Donna Haraway, 149–81. London: Free Association.

Jurgenson, Nathan. 2011. "Digital Dualism versus Augmented Reality." *Cyborgology* (blog), February 24, 2011. https://thesocietypages.org/cyborgology/2011/02/24/digital-dualism-versus-augmented-reality/

Kukkii-San. 2019. "All Black and White? Racism and Blackface in Cosplay." *Wigs 101* (blog), October 20, 2019. https://wigs101.com/all-black-and-white-racism-and-blackface-in-cosplay

Lamerichs, Nicolle. 2011. "Stranger Than Fiction: Fan Identity in Cosplay." *Transformative Works and Cultures* 7. https://doi.org/10.3983/twc.2011.0246

Maturana, Humberto. 2002. "Autopoiesis, Structural Coupling and Cognition: A History of These and Other Notions in the Biology of Cognition." *Cybernetics & Human Knowing* 9 (3–4): 5–34.

MechaCon.com. n.d. Accessed Aug 3, 2022. http://www.mechacon.com/news/

McLuhan, Marshall. 1964. *Understanding Media: The Extensions of Man.* New York: McGraw Hill.

Mountfort, Paul, Anne Peirson-Smith, and Adam Geczy. 2018. *Planet Cosplay: Costume Play, Identity and Global Fandom.* Bristol, UK: Intellect.

Nesaf, Li. 2019. "18 Responses People Had to the New Black Ariel." *Bored Panda*, July 2019. https://www.boredpanda.com/people-reactions-disneys-black-ariel/

Nkulu, Rina. 2017. "Immaterial Girls." *Real Life*, September 5, 2017. http://reallifemag.com/immaterial-girls/

Pulliam-Moore, Charles. 2018. "Sorry Racist Nerds, but Starfire Is a Black Woman." *Gizmodo*, July 25, 2018. https://gizmodo.com/sorry-racist-nerds-but-starfire-is-a-black-woman-1827865298

Rocamora, Agnès. 2020. "Mediatization and Digital Media in the Field of Fashion." In *Fashion Theory: A Reader*, edited Malcom Barnard, 2nd ed., 725–37. New York: Routledge.

Stiegler, Bernard, and Irit Rogoff. 2010. "Transindividuation." *e-flux* 14. https://www.e-f lux.com/journal/14/61314/transindividuation/

Tufekci, Zeynep. 2013. "We Were Always Human." In *Human No More: Digital Subjectivities, Unhuman Subjects, and the End of Anthropology*, edited by Neil L. Whitehead and Michael Wesch, 33–47. Boulder: University Press of Colorado.

Warner, Kristen J. 2017. "In the Time of Plastic Representation." *Film Quarterly* 71 (2). https://filmquarterly.org/2017/12/04/in-the-time-of-plastic-representation/

15

"Model Tries Crazy IU KPop Diet"

Embodied K-Pop Fandoms and Fashionable Diets on YouTube

Tony Tran

With the growing circulation of South Korean popular culture across the globe—often referred to as the Korean Wave or Hallyu—idols (musical artists) within the South Korean popular music industry (K-pop) have become major influencers in global fashion trends (Sayej 2020). It is common for items worn by idols to quickly sell out from brands such as Nike, Calvin Klein, and Fendi. However, in order to continue being leaders in global fashion, K-pop artists must also maintain certain figures to wear the clothes as fashion inherently calls attention to the physicality of the body. Due to these pressures, many idols employ strict diets, which have been increasingly revealed to fans through official press releases. Similar to fan responses to fashion items, these promotions have produced fashionable diets among global fans of K-pop, which have manifested as YouTube "diet challenges" where fans document their bodies as they follow these trendy regimens.

This chapter explores embodied performances of these K-pop diet challenges to examine how understandings of Hallyu's fashionable bodies are negotiated and conceptualized at the intersections of fashion, dieting, and fandoms on YouTube. As this is a growing subgenre, I draw my analysis from a wide range of videos, but I focus particularly on three videos from fashion and lifestyle YouTubers that document the "IU Diet," as well as the responses from these videos' viewers. This diet is named for South Korean superstar IU (Lee Ji-eun), who is one of the best-selling solo K-pop artists of the last decade, as well as an actor in several globally popular Korean television programs. Throughout her rise in global fame, the twenty-nine-year-old celebrity (as of 2022) has often been described as a "fashion icon" by K-pop fansites and has several endorsement deals with designer clothing brands; currently, IU is an ambassador and a *Vogue*-declared "muse" for Gucci (Okwodu 2020). In a 2013

235

interview, IU revealed that her "secret" to maintaining her slim figure before photo shoots was a weeklong diet consisting of an apple for breakfast, a sweet potato for lunch, and a protein drink for dinner—roughly three hundred calories a day—all accompanied by daily cardio exercise. With the release of a new album in 2017, the IU Diet began recirculating within global K-pop fansites and became part of the vlogging trend of K-pop diet challenges.

Through a textual analysis of these videos and comments within the context of YouTube culture and Hallyu's industries and fandoms, I explore how the physical reenactment of the IU Diet creates spaces for fans to expose K-Pop's industrial mechanisms that fabricate stylish bodies. While these videos can materially showcase and celebrate the dedicated labor of K-pop stars, they also create an ambivalent sense of embodied involvement in promoting unhealthy body standards and dietary trends. As a result, the discourses surrounding K-pop diets have the potential to push for ethical practices in the interwoven Hallyu entertainment and luxury fashion industries. Nevertheless, this potential is largely obscured by YouTube's media environment of self-branding, which encourages vloggers to generate views rather than producing prolonged critiques of Hallyu and its control over idols' bodies. Ultimately, these diet challenges are confined to the contours of Hallyu's definitions of the fashionable, which position idols' slender bodies and the intense labor to sustain these figures as positively desirable and worthy of public praise.

THE MULTIDIMENSIONALITY OF FASHION AND HALLYU FAN CULTURE

For idols and fans, K-pop extends beyond music. In May 2019, Soompi, a popular website devoted to South Korean pop culture, published "7 Fashion Labels K-Pop Idols Are in Love with." The article is filled with images of idols wearing their favorite fashion brands—including Gucci, Chanel, Supreme, Moschino, and Nerdy—and opens by asking the fan/reader whether they have "ever been watching a broadcast or just strolling through pictures of your favorite group at the airport and suddenly you feel the need to own their complete outfit? Well, you're not alone" (Malis 2019). There are even entire social media accounts dedicated to documenting the clothing of individual superstars. The Instagram accounts @leejieunstyle and @iufashionstyle, for example, follow IU, offering daily updates and links for fans to purchase the same outfits.

These practices of desiring and obtaining the fashion of one's favorite idols highlight the multiple ways fashion helps make fandom embodied and tangible for global consumers. As several scholars argue, fashion is inherently linked to material bodies: "attention to dress is inseparable from attention to the body" (Hanson 1990, 113) because it is bodies that are continually acted on and culturally (re)fashioned (Venkatesh et al. 2010; Entwistle 2000; Kaiser 2012; Wissinger 2015). Thus, when Soompi notes the desires of fans to wear the clothes of K-pop celebrities, it implicitly calls for fans to look at idols' bodies and envision occupying the space underneath the clothes with their own bodies.

For many fans, this process of celebrity emulation through fashion "has created new and different ideals of dress and self-presentation—and particularly of body shape" (Gibson 2012, 19). In general, rather than being a rarified object, fashionable beauty is seen today as an everyday aspiration, where the "model ideal" is attainable by the general public and exists alongside recommendations of diet and exercise (Wissinger 2015, 146). This entanglement of fashion, celebrity, and embodied fandom, however, is not uniform; as part of the global economy, fashion is a fluid social process where bodies are situated within specific contexts (Cavallaro and Warwick 1998). The bodies that constitute Hallyu and its fandoms have always been ideologically contested within overlapping yet unique constellations of industries, histories, and cultures.

Several scholars—as well as Hallyu fandoms—have documented how these particular contexts play out in K-pop. Youna Kim (2013, 8–9) describes the Korean star system as extremely rigid, where idols' public images are heavily manufactured by private South Korean management agencies and music labels. Most idols are recruited at a young age, go through "Spartan training," and "exemplify a sort of pop perfectionism—catchy tunes, good singing, attractive bodies, cool clothes, mesmerizing movements, and other attractive attributes." Ultimately, Suk-Young Kim (2018, 7) argues, little is left to chance in the world of K-pop, where "what could come across as spontaneous improvisation on stage is a result of years and years of hard, formulaic practice." As this suggests, central to these carefully curated careers is a focus by talent agencies on "perfecting their idols' physical features" (Jung 2013, 107); for women idols, there is intense pressure to match South Korean definitions of gendered beauty, which favor slim figures and low weight (Soyoung Kim 2018; Baek and Choo 2018).

The regulation of these bodies, however, does not solely remain within South Korea, as the "Korean cultural industry has been developed as a national project competing within globalization, not against it" (Y. Kim 2013, 4). With the growing popularity of Hallyu and its devoted fandoms demonstrating significant purchasing power, global fashion companies—particularly luxury brands—have begun developing relationships with K-pop artists over the last decade. Besides becoming official brand ambassadors and securing endorsement deals with luxury fashion houses such as Yves Saint Laurent, Christian Dior, and Prada, K-pop stars have become prominent fixtures in the front rows of Fashion Week shows and fashion publications across the world (Sayej 2020). This crossover is not surprising, considering that similar to Hallyu, institutions of global fashion have also historically defined fashionable bodies as thin (Kaiser 2012; Wissinger 2015). In addition to regulating models' bodies and presenting constrictive media representations, these discourses of thinness manifest through material clothing, with many global luxury brands—including many associated with K-Pop stars—lacking inclusive sizing (McCall 2018). Resultantly, within the fashion world and popular culture, the "aesthetic labor" of crafting fashion models' bodies to have the ability to wear fashionable clothing is frequently linked to eating disorders, extreme dieting, and other health issues (Venkatesh et al. 2010).

Yet while these links are partially a result of models' unattainable bodies being "mistaken as natural" in some contexts (Entwistle 2000, 141), what is critical in the evolving relationships between K-pop, fashion, and consumer fandom is that the aesthetic labor behind maintaining idols' bodies is purposely visible, celebrated, and heavily linked to their stardom in the Korean cultural industries. This is partly a by-product of the growing integration of food and diet within Hallyu's global branding, which "expanded the scope of Hallyu from the exports of popular culture to tourism, Korean food, and fashion" (Jin 2016, 7). For idols, this means that the fashionable diets that maintain their slim bodies are increasingly being detailed for fans through official media releases, creating multilayered star texts for fans to literally consume. Given Hallyu's multidimensionality—and the strength of its fandom, with "K-pop fans [being] arguably one of the most enthusiastic fan bases"—it is understandable that knowledge and ownership of the fashions, foods, and diets of idols have become intertwined in the performance of K-pop fandom (S.-Y. Kim 2018, 8). Emerging from fan attention to the fashionable bodies and diets of K-Pop idols is the IU Diet challenge.

EMBODYING FASHIONABLE K-POP DIETS
AND AMBIVALENT FANDOM

In her analysis of fans of Hallyu, Anna Lee Swan (2018, 550) emphasizes that due to language differences, embodiment plays a significant role in K-pop fan reaction videos, making material bodies central to the production of fan knowledge, identity performance, and avenues of communication in the contemporary digital community. Here, I would like to focus on a specific form of reaction videos, the IU Diet challenge, to explore how the embodiment of K-pop diets by Hallyu fans helps shape their understandings of idols' fashionable bodies. As a global subgenre, the IU Diet challenge has more than fifty-five thousand videos on YouTube. These videos vary in terms of production, ranging from posts by young K-pop fans with minimum editing to polished vlogs by fitness influencers with little history with Hallyu.

To illuminate this particular intersection of fashion, celebrity diets, and K-pop fandoms, I center on three women YouTubers: Lisa Ring, Ally Gong, and Ritta Kelly. Lisa Ring, who is based in Germany and describes her channel as having an interest in "beauty, fashion, and lifestyle," uploaded "I TRIED THE IU DIET (아이유다이어트) FOR A WEEK! vlog + results" in November 2018 and received over 54,000 views. Ally Gong, who is based in the United States, uploaded "model tries IU diet" in June 2018 and received over 205,000 views. Ritta Kelly, who is also based in the United States, uploaded "MODEL TRIES CRAZY IU KPOP DIET" in September 2017 and received over 288,000 views. In addition to having relatively large view counts for their videos, all three YouTubers focus on content directly related to fashion, including outfit try-ons and style advice. Furthermore, all directly identify as Hallyu fans and have produced additional content related to Hallyu culture beyond the IU Diet.

While the production contexts of IU Diet challenge videos vary greatly, the overall narrative structure is fairly standardized. These vlogs normally open with a direct address that explains the IU Diet and the purpose of the video. A common way to situate the diet challenge is to describe it as an "experiment" to illustrate what happens to the body in following IU's diet; as Ritta Kelly elaborates, the video should showcase "why you shouldn't really take on these crazy diets, because it's not going to make you feel good." In a similar fashion, Lisa Ring's goal for the video is to "spread awareness" of the diet's unhealthy nature. Resultantly, the majority of diet challenge videos have some form of textual disclaimer that discourages viewers from trying the diet, which again reaffirms the challenge as an "experiment" and not dietary advice. As part of the genre, before-and-after shots and measurements are integral elements. In the three videos discussed here, all vloggers recorded weighing themselves in workout attire, with the camera panning up and down their bodies to document their figures. Lisa Ring is the most intense; she also provided the viewer with measurements of her waist, hips, and thighs (figure 15.1).

The videos then transition to repetitive segments of YouTubers eating the same three foods—an apple (or a similar fruit), a sweet potato, and a protein

Waist: 70cm   Hips: 102cm   Leg: 60cm

Figure 15.1. Lisa Ring's "before" measurements.

shake—over the course of five to seven days. Since IU provided little elabo-
ration on her exercises, most YouTubers employed a generic exercise schedule along with their regular daily activities. As these vlogs progress, viewers
can see the deterioration of these YouTubers' conditions. By the fourth day,
Lisa Ring states she "felt miserable" and "super moody," resulting in a "spi-
raling depression and hunger pains"; at the end of the diet, she simply states
"my whole body hurts." Ally Gong became highly confused when her body
began to accept less food, stating, "whenever I eat something, I don't get that
full." On the verge of a breakdown, Gong frustratingly confesses to the camera in a close-up shot that "I'm like four days in, and my body is depleted of
energy," and she adds the text "#ded" on the screen to further demonstrate
her malnourished state. The vlogs then conclude with a debriefing session
that reflects on the results. Despite the intense displeasure caused by the diet,
it does not seem to result in significant weight loss, which is often expressed
as disappointment. For Ritta Kelly, the diet caused her to feel constantly
"exhausted," "anemic, and starved" and was not overall effective. Likewise,
while Lisa Ring did lose weight and a few centimeters, she concludes the
experience was not worth it.

    While the diet is normally not marked as successful, what it does pro-
duce is a complicated media text that allows Hallyu fans to temporarily

embody K-pop stars and to experience, on some level, the processes of creating fashionable bodies. In visualizing these diets and the discomfort that is a by-product of maintaining idols' bodies, these documentations of fashionable diets raise questions around the ethics of consuming K-pop and produce ambiguous fandoms. This ambiguity follows Alladi Venkatesh and colleagues' (2010, 467) observations of how women "look to fashion models as incorporating aesthetic values while at the same time they are troubled by the unattainable goals projected by the models." Despite being undertaken by fans of IU and Hallyu, these diet challenges produce negative reactions from vloggers and viewers to the working environment within the K-pop industry.

This is not surprising, considering the mental and physical deterioration that is showcased in these vlogs, along with most vloggers filming in private spaces (homes, bedrooms, etc.) and employing direct address to create an intimate connection with viewers to communicate their discomfort from the diet. For example, Ritta Kelly, in an exasperated manner on the last day, states, "I don't understand how [IU] does it so often. I don't understand how K-pop idols do these crazy diets in general. . . . I . . . I wouldn't be able to perform a whole concert doing this type of crap!" Several YouTube commenters concurred, saying, for example, "It's crazy how IU goes through this. I feel so bad." Overall, these comments suggest some guilt and a momentary recognition of the problematic construction of idols' bodies, reactions that produce space for the possibility of imagining better treatment of fashioned bodies, where the labor behind producing the fashionable should not be ignored or accepted uncritically.

These demonstrations of the strenuous working conditions faced by many K-pop idols are further enhanced by the way that some of the YouTubers position themselves as "aspiring models." In stressing their "model" status in their titles—as well as providing footage of modeling gigs in their other content— Ally Gong and Ritta Kelly symbolically connect their bodies to dominant discourses of models, which, as explored above, invoke underlying aesthetic labor related to thinness, eating disorders, and extreme diets. For instance, several commenters compliment these vloggers' skinny figures. However, it is precisely their failure in the diet challenge that underscores K-pop's problematic system of bodily control; even at an amateur level, if "thin" models of the fashion world are struggling with the IU Diet, then Hallyu's cultural industries are revealed to viewers to be seemingly worse than the notoriously harsh body standards enforced by the modeling and fashion industries. While the boundaries of fashion model and K-pop idol are blurred for stars like IU, the global circulation of the IU Diet allows for comparisons to be made between

South Korea's Hallyu and other global cultural industries, which can possibly highlight dangerous practices.

Curiously, the IU Diet has trended even though it is known among many K-pop fans that IU herself has faced health problems resulting from this diet. In 2014, IU publicly shared her battles with eating disorders, and this was further documented on English-language sites like Soompi and other international fan forums (Pao 2014). Likewise, growing research has illuminated the complex connections between increased body dissatisfaction and eating disorders among South Korean women faced with Hallyu's presentations of thin bodies (Chae 2014; Soyoung Kim 2018; Baek and Choo 2018). These elements are implicitly acknowledged by several YouTubers through broad mentions of eating disorders, particularly in their introductions and disclaimers. Furthermore, although with less frequency, some viewers have also criticized the concept of diet challenges with comments such as "IU has said before that she suffered from an eating disorder" and (originally shouted in all caps) "IU was diagnosed with bulimia stop making her diet a trend." Overall, these vlogs and comments' evocation of eating disorders and visual documentation of malnutrition recall and illustrate the material impact of Hallyu's promotion of the fashionable under unrealistic beauty standards.

THE LIMITS OF EMBODIED FANDOMS

While these videos have the potential to shed light on the harmful yet influential embodied practices resulting from the circulation of Hallyu's celebrity culture, it is crucial to remember that the multiplicity of Hallyu, fashion, and ambivalent fandom are also imbued with conflicting desires and appreciation of celebrity/model bodies. Resultantly, these media objects also discursively reinforce Hallyu's and the fashion industries' notion that maintaining thinness is fashionable. Discourses of thinness and weight loss are abundant on diet challenge vlogs, with many comments offering alternative weight-loss advice or highlighting the nonnecessity of a diet by remarking that the aspiring models/YouTubers' bodies are already beautiful because of how "skinny" or "thin" they appear in the before shot. Although these comments can be read as striving for healthier views of bodies and fitness, they also implicitly reward weight loss and frame thinness as ideal and attractive, which does not disrupt K-pop's construction of gendered bodies.

This reinforcement of the K-pop industry's standards is also achieved through the YouTubers' praise of IU's mental and physical strength in completing the diet, which reads as celebratory veneration for K-pop idols and validates the precarious labor used to maintain these slim figures. In the middle of the challenge, Lisa Ring notes the importance of the mental side of the diet, remarking, "I don't know if it's just a mental thing that you can push through if you really want it, but I couldn't do it." While this comment marks her own failures in the challenge, it implicitly compliments IU's mental fortitude and desire to be successful in the world of K-pop. More directly, Ritta Kelly reminds viewers multiple times that "IU still works out and does all her dance practices . . . and all that good stuff while she's on this diet," consistently giving IU credit for her labor. At the end of her vlog, Ally Gong concludes she has "lots of respect to people who have to do this for their career and maintain it," as it was an impossible challenge for her.

While these comments create potentially critical comparisons between Hallyu and the fashion world, they also locate IU's self-control, willpower, and dedication to her craft as well above that of her fans. Consequently, these YouTubers' admiration of IU's star text allows for fans to (re)interpret IU's bodily labor as inspirational and honorable; rather than producing guilt, this reading of IU's labor is rendered for fans into more pleasurable forms of consuming celebrity culture. This provides outlets that justify IU as a fashion icon worthy of imitation and downplay the dangers of her diet, resulting in comments such as "huge applause for your effort and also to IU" or the light-hearted note of "It's easy to do for 1–3 days which is what she would do since she only did this to prepare for a photo shoot lol." These presentations and readings of IU's embodied labor as coveted also follow dominant discourses of weight loss in South Korean and global media, where thin bodies are associated with righteous "hard work" while overweight bodies, larger clothing sizes, and fatness signify laziness and failure to control one's individual impulses (Baek and Choo 2018; Zimdars 2019). With IU's body and star text remaining unchallenged—and even fortified—standards of the fashionable held by Hallyu and the fashion industries that position thin bodies as attractive emerge largely unscathed.

We must also contextualize these videos within YouTube's media environment. Sarah Banet-Weiser's (2011, 283) work on girls' online self-branding practices has illustrated how YouTubers are "encouraged to be a product within a neoliberal context," which presents itself as empowerment through consumerism, but where gendered bodies are subject to disciplining. Likewise, Sun Jung and Doobo Shim (2014) argue that although YouTube does provide Hallyu fans with various forms of empowerment, we still need to pay attention to YouTube's position as a corporate-controlled global media conglomerate. Here, we need to consider how YouTubers and their bodies operate through self-branding and how the platform encourages specific media content to circulate. Through this lens, different logics emerge as to why these videos were created. Although many IU Diet challenge videos are positioned as "experiments" to showcase the detrimental effects of the diet, it is also an experiment that is unneeded; beyond IU's resulting struggles due to this diet, most would comprehend the unsustainability of a three-hundred-calorie diet and all three YouTubers already acknowledge the unsurprising end results with disclaimers in their introductions.

Rather, we can see these diet challenges as "visibility labour" of digital influencers as they seek to gain viewers in YouTube's attention economy (Abidin 2016). It is common for K-pop diet challenge vloggers to mention how their inspiration came from seeing other people in their YouTube feed doing the same challenge. For example, despite wanting to "spread awareness" of the diet's dangers, Lisa Ring also states she is doing the diet "because it is the most popular one on YouTube." In addition to demonstrating the limited effectiveness of diet challenges as experiments intended to discourage crash diets, these points of inspiration showcase these vloggers' recognition of the IU Diet's ability to attract viewers and their desire to reproduce its popularity. On this front, it is a successful tactic. In a follow-up Q and A video, Ritta Kelly stated that she believes her use of "IU" and "KPop" in her title caused You-Tube's recommendation algorithm to circulate her video beyond her usual audience and attract viewers from overlapping online communities including health/fitness, fashion, and K-pop fandoms. Subsequently, the IU Diet videos are ranked as among the most popular videos for all three YouTube channels; for instance, as of September 2021, Ritta Kelly's channel had 585,000 total views, with over 288,000 of these coming from her IU Diet challenge vlog. Thus, while all three YouTubers lamented the distress caused by the IU Diet, both Lisa Ring and Ritta Kelly asked viewers to propose other extreme K-pop diets, which further indicates the importance of a video's viewing numbers over a focus on health concerns.

Similarly, for users, although recommendations are personalized, consumption of these videos is often accompanied by other IU and K-pop diet challenges on YouTube's interface, promoting continued viewing and even production of these fashionable diet videos despite knowledge of the end result. For instance, one comment on Ally Gong's vlog states enthusiasm in replicating the diet challenge ("I love your video you make me want to try this diet!!"), while others promote their own results and YouTube channels, such as with (the originally shouted) "Sis I tried it too and it destroyed my metabolism." Rather than dissuading viewers, YouTube's digital ecosystem (re)produces more engagement with the IU Diet and IU's body. Despite the vloggers' constant disclaimers, these tactics and comments suggest a larger desire to follow trends in producing content that grows an individual YouTuber's brand rather than generating long-term critiques of the dangers of the IU Diet and Hallyu's standards of fashionable bodies in general.

CONCLUSION

As this chapter illustrates, elements of these vlogs have the potential to highlight Hallyu's problematic mechanisms of control on K-pop idols. By creating critiques and facilitating viewer comments that seek to locate and embody these mechanisms, these vlogs open possible sites of resistance and fan agency. Along with expressed feelings of repulsion, however, are complicated sites of desire shaped by the multiplicity and ambivalence of K-pop fandom and celebrity bodies. Despite these vloggers' claims to illustrate Hallyu's detrimental practices, these widely produced and circulated diet challenge vlogs also reproduce the harmful methods they seek to undermine by generating visibility and profit for K-pop industries, idols' bodies, and vloggers' own branding through YouTube's digital culture of neoliberal self-promotion.

Focused more on the popular circulation of the vloggers' dieting and quantified bodies, these videos are limited in terms of their direct structural critique of Hallyu and lack concrete suggestions from YouTubers to address these potentially harmful body politics. Instead, they help reinscribe dominant notions of weight loss and bodily maintenance in the contexts of Hallyu and fashion. Working alongside K-pop fan accounts, endorsement deals, and major fashion publications like *Vogue*, these vlogs (in their celebratory positioning of IU's diet and thin body) continue to articulate fashionable bodies through frameworks governed by Hallyu's corporate cultural industries and its partners in global fashion. With IU's continued popularity in Hallyu culture and the fashion world—as well as the growing convergence of Hallyu celebrities and luxury fashion—Hallyu's global circulation and fan practices produce environments that confine gendered bodies to narrow definitions of what is fashionable and limit the range of body sizes and diets that are deemed acceptable.

Despite their limitations, these fan practices exemplify how the fashionable stimulates "not only your wardrobe according to fashion but also your body" (Wissinger 2015, 274). With fashion being materialized through bodies and the labor placed on them, "bodies are pivotal to production, distribution, consumption, and other processes" within circuits of fashion culture, and it is only through bodies that the process of fashion *becoming* can occur (Kaiser 2012, 192). The intersections of fashion, celebrity, and fandom as social and cultural practices are never isolated from the body, and we must continue to engage with fashioned bodies and the global currents that carry them as both link to larger sites of ideological negotiation and bodily maintenance.

REFERENCES

Abidin, Crystal. 2016. "Visibility Labour: Engaging with Influencers' Fashion Brands and #OOTD Advertorial Campaigns on Instagram." *Media International Australia* 161 (1): 86–100.

Baek, Eunsoo, and Ho Jung Choo. 2018. "Everybody Loves Beauty? The Moderated Effect of Body Attractiveness among Young Koreans." *Fashion and Textile* 5 (16). https://doi.org/10.1186/s40691-018-0130-8

Banet-Weiser, Sarah. 2011. "Branding the Post-Feminist Self: Girls' Video Production and YouTube." In *Mediated Girlhoods: New Explorations of Girls' Media Culture*, edited by Mary Celeste Kearney, 277–94. New York: Peter Lang.

Cavallaro, Dani, and Alexandra Warwick. 1998. *Fashioning the Frame: Boundaries, Dress and the Body*. New York: Berg.

Chae, Jiyoung. 2014. "Interest in Celebrities' Post-Baby Bodies and Korean Women's Body Image Disturbance after Childbirth." *Sex Roles* 71 (11–12): 419–35.

Entwistle, Joanne. 2000. *The Fashioned Body: Fashion, Dress and Modern Social Theory*. Cambridge: Polity Press.

Gibson, Pamela Church. 2012. *Fashion and Celebrity Culture*. New York: Berg.

Gong, Ally. 2018. "Model Tries IU Diet." Uploaded by Allyinspires, June 2, 2018. YouTube video, 10:52. https://www.youtube.com/watch?v=lCGGVOvquyY

Hanson, Karen. 1990. "Dressing Down Dressing Up—The Philosophic Fear of Fashion." *Hypatia* 5 (2): 107–21.

Jin, Dal Yong. 2016. *New Korean Wave: Transnational Cultural Power in the Age of Social Media*. Urbana: University of Illinois Press.

Jung, Eun-Young. 2013. "K-Pop Female Idols in the West: Racial Imaginations and Erotic Fantasies." In *The Korean Wave: Korean Media Go Global*, edited by Youna Kim, 106–19. New York: Routledge.

Jung, Sun, and Doobo Shim. 2014. "Social Distribution: K-Pop Fan Practices in Indonesia and the 'Gangnam Style' Phenomenon." *International Journal of Cultural Studies* 17 (5): 485–501.

Kaiser, Susan B. 2012. *Fashion and Cultural Studies*. New York: Berg.

Kelly, Ritta. 2017. "Model Tries Crazy IU KPop Diet." Uploaded September 28, 2017. You-Tube video, 14:54. https://www.youtube.com/watch?v=_0JLWEqZVmQ

Kim, Soyoung. 2018. "Eating Disorders, Body Dissatisfaction, and Self-Esteem among South Korean Women." *Social Behavior and Personality* 46 (9): 1537–46.

Kim, Suk-Young. 2018. *K-Pop Live: Fans, Idols, and Multimedia Performance*. Stanford, CA: Stanford University Press.

Kim, Youna, ed. 2013. *The Korean Wave: Korean Media Go Global*. New York: Routledge.

Malis, Carolina. 2019. "7 Fashion Labels K-Pop Idols Are in Love with." Soompi. May 15, 2019. https://www.soompi.com/article/1321267wpp/7-fashion-labels-k-pop-ido ls-are-in-love-with

McCall, Tyler. 2018. "Luxury Fashion Has a Plus Size Problem." *Fashionista*, May 7, 2018. https://fashionista.com/2018/05/luxury-designer-plus-size-clothing-problem

Okwodu, Janelle. 2020. "K-Pop Star IU Stole the Show in Gucci's Front Row." *Vogue*, February 19, 2020. https://www.vogue.com/article/iu-south-korean-singer-gucci -fall-2020-front-row

Pao. 2014. "IU Reveals She Received Treatment for Bulimia on 'Healing Camp.'" Soompi. July 14, 2014. https://www.soompi.com/article/628777wpp/iu-reveals -she-received-treatment-for-bulimia-on-healing-camp

Ring, Lisa. 2018. "I Tried the IU Diet (아이유다이어트) for a Week! Vlog + Results." Uploaded November 20, 2018. YouTube video, 21:58. https://www.youtube.com /watch?v=eBnw7qjGr7c (video now private).

Sayej, Nadia. 2020. "How the K-Pop Craze Is Taking Over Fashion Week." *Forbes*, February 21, 2020. https://www.forbes.com/sites/nadjasayej/2020/02/21/how-the-k-p op-craze-is-taking-over-fashion-week/

Swan, Anna Lee. 2018. "Transnational Identities and Feeling in Fandom: Place and Embodiment in K-Pop Fan Reaction Videos." *Communication, Culture & Critique* 11 (4): 548–65.

Venkatesh, Alladi, Annamma Joy, John F. Sherry Jr., and Jonathan Deschenes. 2010. "The Aesthetics of Luxury Fashion, Body and Identity Formation." *Journal of Consumer Psychology* 20 (4): 459–70.

Wissinger, Elizabeth A. 2015. *This Year's Model: Fashion, Media, and the Making of Glamour*. New York: New York University Press.

Zimdars, Melissa. 2019. *Watching Our Weights: The Contradictions of Televising Fatness in the "Obesity Epidemic."* New Brunswick, NJ: Rutgers University Press.

16

Underwear That's Fun to Wear

Theorizing Fan Lingerie

Suzanne Scott

The expo hall at San Diego Comic-Con is the primary retail space for fan fashion and merchandise at the convention. At either end of this football field–length space, looming over everything, is a series of massive T-shirt towers. For those who attend Comic-Con annually, they are comforting in their consistency: they stand watch over the con, year in, year out. In 2015, I was browsing one of these towers and was startled to come across an array of superhero-themed lingerie, nestled in among the standard T-shirts that cover every square inch of the tower like barnacles. This was not the first time I had seen fan lingerie. On the contrary, I was well aware of both the long history and the contemporary boom in fannish intimates. By 2015, licensed underwear emblazoned with the iconography of mainstream fan franchises, from *Wonder Woman* to *Star Wars*, could be easily procured by fans of all ages at big-box retailers like Target. Underoos, the superhero fan underwear sensation that I will return to in more detail later in this chapter, had relaunched a year prior, in 2014, now nostalgically targeting the adult demographic that had originally been fans of the brand as children in the late 1970s and early 1980s.

This also wasn't the first indication of gendered fan retail markets, either at the fan convention or in geek culture more generally, as has been discussed in foundational work by scholars such as Derek Johnson (2014) and Elizabeth Affuso (2018). Additionally, I have argued elsewhere (Scott 2019, 184–219) that fan fashion and beauty culture is one of the primary arenas in which women are recognized and hailed as fans. And Hollywood's relationship to fan fashion and lingerie is much longer, with media representations historically playing a large role in setting trends for intimates and undergarments. One particularly iconic example is the intimate apparel company Warner's releasing its Merry Widow corset to capitalize on the 1952 Lana Turner film of the same name (dir. Curtis Bernhardt). From an industrial perspective, we can also examine early business relationships between movie studios and bras-siere manufacturers, such as the 1935 deal between Paramount Pictures and the Hollywood-Maxwell Brassiere Company (Fields 2007, 101). These partner-ships and their marketing campaigns, such as the 1937 "Worn by the Stars" slogan deployed by Renee of Hollywood bras, courted female fans through their perceived desire to emulate their favorite movie stars (see Fortmueller in this collection), promising a sense of intimacy with a celebrity fan object through shared intimate apparel.

What was jarring about being visually confronted with this array of nerdy negligees, pop culture panties, and other forms of fannish lingerie at San Diego Comic-Con in 2015 was the cognitive dissonance created by my decade-long understanding of the T-shirt tower as a historically unisex, and staunchly sexless, fan fashion retail space. The chiffon, spandex, and bedaz-zled ornamentation of these fan intimates stood in stark contrast to the stiff heavy cotton, three-for-thirty-five-dollar, mass-produced fan fashion objects typically housed in these T-shirt towers. What struck me immediately is that these fan intimates were given literal space, something that is at a premium in these overcrowded retail towers. They were given bodies, svelte yet curvy headless mannequins, also unprecedented. This very public, looming display of fan lingerie thus provoked a nagging question: namely, which fans were these items ultimately designed for, the wearer or an assumed cisgender, het-erosexual male fan audience? Even if we presume the former, that those who purchase and wear this fan lingerie do so for their own personal pleasure, or as a self-expression of their own fan identity, the paltry sizing options and modelesque mannequins suggested a literal one-size-fits-all vision of accept-able and desirable fan bodies. This, again, stood in stark contrast with the rest of the T-shirt tower's approach to fan fashion, which stressed abundance in terms of designs but also far more inclusive sizing options.

I open with this anecdote in order to emphasize our lack of attention to fan intimates and lingerie in our consideration of sartorial fan expression. This chapter marks a first step toward theorizing fan lingerie and intimates, but before delving into a narrow subset of fan undergarments for the purpose of this analysis, I want to stress the flexibility of lingerie and intimates as a mode of fan expression. Jill Fields (2007, 5) suggests in her book *An Intimate Affair: Women, Lingerie, and Sexuality* that the history of undergarments must be placed in conversation with social and economic shifts, as these contexts in turn prompt "transformations in the shaping, conceptualization, and rep-resentation of female bodies." Fan undergarments might similarly reflect the shifting and highly contextual understanding of the fan body in our cultural consciousness as fan culture is mainstreamed and fan demographics become more industrially desirable.

When we talk about fans, and particularly when we discuss fan merchandise and fashion, we tend to do so through the language of affective expression or even fan performance and self-branding. And it is true that we could easily locate fan intimates and lingerie as a mere offshoot of broader fan fashion trends, or as further affirmation of Avi Santo's (2018, 329) claim that fandom has been reconstituted "as a lifestyle category rather than a communal experience." Unlike other forms of fan fashion such as T-shirts, which still might provoke a limited "communal experience" in the form of an impromptu conversation with or a nod of acknowledgment from a fellow fan of the referenced media object, fannish intimates are by design even further removed from this possibility. In other words, if sartorial fan expressions might be considered examples of conspicuous consumption (though perhaps more a display of excessive fan affect rather than wealth), fannish intimates, underwear, and lingerie constitute a form of inconspicuous consumption. These more private or personal modes of sartorial fandom may be more difficult to study, but an analysis of fannish intimates and fans' relationship to them might help us better theorize the intimacies of fan experience and identity, as well as our frequently intimate relationships with fan objects.

INCONSPICUOUS CONSUMPTION: FAN LINGERIE IN CONTEXT

Within fashion and consumer research, "inconspicuous consumption" tends to refer to those sartorial brand choices that eschew labels or brand identifiers in favor of "the use of subtle signals that are only observable to people with the requisite knowledge to decode their meaning" (Berger and Ward 2010, 556). While some have linked inconspicuous consumption to comparatively inconspicuous fashion items like underwear (Vigolo and Ugolini 2016), I would suggest a slightly modified understanding of the term. Not only are fan lingerie and intimates inconspicuous in the sense that they tend to remain hidden from view under other clothing, they also offer a comparatively inconspicuous expression of fan identity. This is especially the case because, as prior research on underwear documents, these "inconspicuous" items still reveal a great deal about the consumer's self-concept and are purchased to affirm the wearer's "ideal congruity" or the "individuals' needs to increase their positive feelings of self-regard by behaving in ways that approach their ideal self-image" (Vigolo and Ugolini 2016, 420). Fan intimates in particular might allow the wearer to perform a true or "ideal" fan identity in spaces where that might be socially less acceptable.

If fan undergarments are, by and large, the sartorial fandom equivalent of lurking (Bury 2018; Kushner 2016), then perhaps the various cultural framings of intimates and lingerie might provide an illustrative starting point to help us account for and analyze forms of sartorial fan expression that are more difficult to study because they are hidden from view. Consider, for example, the Victorian framing of undergarments as "unmentionables" in England or, even more evocatively, "inexpressibles" in France (Fields 2007, 11). For some fans, and I imagine aging fans in particular, for whom public bodily displays of fandom might be less normalized or less easily incorporated into work wear, fannish underwear or intimates might function as a comparatively inconspicuous but nonetheless potent everyday expression of fan affect.

Scholarly work on undergarments as a form of inconspicuous consumption affirms that despite being a less visible mode of sartorial expression, "choosing the 'right' underwear, can be seen as a tool in constructing female identity" (Tsaousi 2016, 468). For a fan, the "right" underwear might be the item that resonates with or allows them to more covertly convey their fan identity or affect for a fan object. Alternately, given the persistent infantilization of fans, these instances of inconspicuous consumption might afford a space to be playful or whimsical. In other words, if "underwear is part of a woman's embodied cultural capital according to the requirements of the field she is situated in" (Tsaousi 2016, 472), fannish intimates might be a space of pleasurable dissonance or slippage between identities, or might allow the wearer to situate themselves in a fannish field as they go about their daily lives. While much of the literature focuses on women's relationship to intimate apparel, surveying fans across the gender spectrum would be vital to this work.

Jill Fields (2007, 3) notes that intimate apparel "places the body in ambiguity. Adorned in undergarments, the body is clothed but not dressed. And, as the first layer of clothing, they are also the last barrier to full disclosure of the body." In addition to the sorts of pleasurable tensions articulated above, many designs of fan underwear or intimates explicitly position themselves as threshold items between the fan self and the fan object. The remainder of this chapter considers fan intimates and lingerie that explicitly draw links between fan affect and the fannish desire to embody favorite characters through intimate apparel. Though themes of fantasy and play run throughout all these examples, the target demographics (e.g., children vs. adult women) as well as the design, cut, and presumed audience for these examples of sartorial fan expression all shape their capacity to communicate something broader about fan identity.

UNDERWEAR THAT'S FUN TO WEAR: UNDEROOS AND FAN EMBODIMENT

The remainder of this chapter focuses on fan lingerie and intimates that aesthetically evoke character costumes and cosplay as a fan practice, beginning with the emergence of Underoos in 1977. The matching underwear and tank top/undershirt sets were initially drawn from four major comics and cartoon licenses (Marvel Comics, DC Comics, Archie Comics, and Hanna-Barbera) and promised kids the ability to become their favorite superheroes and cartoon characters. Underwear was an inspired merchandising choice, aesthetically evoking the abundance of briefs over tights in early superhero costume design, which was in turn sartorially inspired by circus strongmen. As the advertising slogan promised, Underoos were "underwear that's fun to wear," transforming the most mundane of daily undergarments into a space of fantasy and functioning as a precursor to the "everyday cosplay" fan merchandise that has proliferated in recent years. Underoos commercials featured children striking superhero poses, much as a cosplayer at a fan convention might in order to evoke a particular character, and in some cases literally transforming.

An Underoos commercial from 1978, for example, features a white, brunette girl performing the iconic Wonder Woman spin, popularized by Lynda Carter on ABC's *Wonder Woman* television series (1975–79), to transform her boring white underwear set into *Wonder Woman* Underoos. A later commercial, from 1986, explicitly opens with the promise "When you change into . . . Underoos underwear, you can pretend to change into a hero!" This ad copy, which drops the "pretend to" when the closing line repeats, is accompanied by images of boys transforming into their favorite 1980s cartoon characters, like Optimus Prime from *The Transformers* (1984–87). For example, a white boy with a blond, bowl haircut is shown putting on a tan *He-Man and the Masters of the Universe* (1983–85) Underoos T-shirt that visually evokes the titular hero's armor and breastplate. As the boy punches his arms through each sleeve, we see his arms literally transform into He-Man's muscled cartoon biceps. As the boy pulls his head through the neck hole, the blond cartoon head of He-Man similarly emerges. There is a white flash on the screen, and the transformation is complete. This moment in the commercial is jarring in its shift from live action to animation, as well as in the replacement of a child's physicality with that of a muscular grown man, but it also potently articulates the promise of embodiment that Underoos sold to a generation of fans.

Elsewhere, I've explored the significance of fan fashion, and dresses specifically, with similar trompe l'oeil designs (Scott 2019, 198–208). Jean Baudrillard (1988, 158) described trompe l'oeil as an "enchanted simulation," and a large part of Underoos' appeal derives from their playful verisimilitude. Indeed, the creator of Underoos, Lawrence D. Weiss, initially worried that Underoos might be *too* fun to wear. In a 2002 letter responding to a minister who asked whether Weiss had ever faced moral or ethical challenges in his career, Weiss recounted that he had hesitated when launching the Underoos brand after seeing the massive appeal the product had with both children and parents. Specifically, Weiss was "afraid the product was too good," and specifically that "a child might hurt themselves thinking they had superhuman powers." Weiss brought these concerns to his pastor at the time at the fundamentalist Assembly of God church. Reportedly, the pastor looked over the superhero samples and packaging, and, according to Weiss (2002), "His face lit up in smiles and he said, 'How wonderful. Children will love them. Maybe you can do one showing the empty tomb?'" Perhaps unsurprisingly, superhero Jesus never made it onto children's underwear, and Weiss shortly thereafter sold the product concept to Union Underwear, makers of Fruit of the Loom.

As this anecdote and the advertising campaigns suggest, what made Underoos fun to wear was their promise of embodiment, of identification and transformation. Indeed, Underoos are doubly powerful in that they conceptually draw on the transformational properties of superheroes as well as the long tradition of lingerie promising a sense of personal or bodily transformation. As Christian Jantzen, Per Østergaard, and Carla M. Sucena Vieira's (2006, 179) work on consuming lingerie suggests, "working on identity by purchasing and wearing lingerie may fulfil or generate longings, thus potentially leading to intensified experiences, feelings and sensations of 'who I really am.'" Simultaneously selling this sensation of becoming who we really are and the nostalgic promise of revisiting who we once were, the Underoos brand was sublicensed to Bioworld, rebooted in 2014, and distributed through subcultural chain retailers like Hot Topic (see Santo in this collection). Now demographically pitched at adult fans, complete with nostalgic packaging that mimics the original pouches and art style of the 1970s and 1980s, Underoos thus offered a dual promise of embodiment: to imagine our

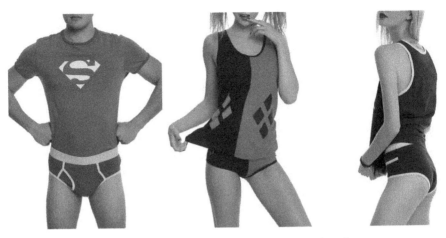

Figure 16.1. Promotional images from the rebooted Underoos brand in 2014.

current selves as superheroes, and to reconnect with the feelings and sensations of our childhood.

This appeal was confirmed in a 2017 interview in the *Hollywood Reporter*
with Frank Bottaro, vice president of underwear and sleepwear for Bioworld.
Bottaro emphasized, "a lot of the first customers of Underoos in the '70s and
'80s are now parents and are now able to embrace their inner superheroes as
a family. We get a lot of nostalgic pictures of side-by-sides of our fans wearing
their Underoos when they were a kid and today" (J. Weiss 2017). The claim
that these adult fan consumers "are now able" to embrace their inner superhero speaks to the mainstreaming of geek culture and fan fashion, but also
powerfully reinforces Denise Bielby and C. Lee Harrington's (2010, 434–35)
repeated calls for the value of life-course approaches to fan studies. Indeed,
the promotional discourse and fan response to the 2014 Underoos relaunch
sit neatly at the intersection of four age-based issues centered in Bielby and
Harrington's work: fandom and life milestones, changes in the fan (self) over
time, age norms within fandom, and changes in the fan object over time.

In addition to this consideration of age and fan identity, it is worth noting that the marketing campaign for the Underoos reboot overwhelmingly
featured white, able-bodied, cisgender, fit, and slender models, all of whom
appeared at least a decade too young to have worn the brand the first time
around or have any preexisting fan connection to it. The superhero action
poses of the original ad campaign persisted to promote Underoos for men,
whereas the Underoos for women tended to be marketed through coquett-

ish poses, with models frequently tugging on their tank tops to evoke either the bodily awkwardness of adolescence or the potential for undress (figure 16.1). The Underoos lines aimed at women also notably were the only ones to include images of the undergarments that emphasized the models' posterior, simultaneously drawing on and serving as a bodily counterpoint to the hypersexualized "broken back" poses of impossibly buxom superheroines (Cocca 2014). While the Underoos reboot marketing playfully evokes the (pre-)adolescent fan body, other forms of fan lingerie that similarly sell embodiment take a different approach.

SLITHER'N TO YOUR DMS: LINGERIE AND THE SEXUALIZED FAN BODY

Jill Fields (2007, 11) notes that "the strong association of lingerie, corsetry, and other forms of underwear with eroticism imbues these articles of dress with a sexual life and history of their own, detached from the female bodies they are meant to adorn." It is crucial to consider which bodies fan lingerie does tend to adorn, as these tell us a great deal about either assumed or aspirational fan demographics and bodies. Alternately, these products can reveal just how powerfully entrenched conventional body types are to fashion marketing, even within a moment when inclusivity and body positivity are touted in both fan and fashion cultures. It will likely surprise no one to learn that just as with fashion and beauty culture more generally, the bulk of fannish lingerie is marketed through white, young, able-bodied, cisgender models that adhere to the narrowly defined standards of Western beauty culture. Taking a cue from Roland Barthes's (1983, 3) semiotic approach in *The Fashion System*, in which he considers fashion magazine copy as "written garments" in addition to the "image-clothing" being photographed and presented, we can also see how website descriptions of more explicitly conventional fan lingerie conceptually detach the products from the female fan bodies they are meant to adorn. By extension, we must interrogate to what degree this detaches these intimate items from a presumed fan identity for the wearer as well.

We might categorize this subcategory of fan underwear, sold through retailers like Yandy (founded in 2007), as falling more broadly into the category of "trashy" lingerie, in terms of its low price point and use of synthetic materials, as well as the presumption it will be used only on occasion, for role-playing during a sexual encounter or for wearing on Halloween or at a costume party. For example, figure 16.2 shows two "costume lingerie" offerings from Yandy. While the item titles appear strategically designed to avoid copyright infringement claims against these (likely) unlicensed goods, a caption like "Slither'n to your DMs" (a reference to Slytherin House in *Harry Potter*, whose mascot is a snake) also importantly positions the lingerie as a fetish object for the bearer of the look rather than the wearer. Similarly, for the Snow White costume, the apple referenced here quickly becomes unmoored from its narrative context to evoke biblical themes of temptation or sexual awakening, as well as euphemisms like "apple pie" to describe female genitalia. The "written garments," in these cases, tend to position the authentic fan as the visual consumer of the apparel rather than as the (presumed) fan body inhabiting it. Alternately, the imagined wearer and/or consumer of these costume lingerie items might not be considered a fan of the referenced media properties at all. In that reading, these items offer sexualized stereotypes more generally, with an iconic fan twist: the naughty (wizarding) schoolgirl, the (Disney) princess in need of rescue, and so on.

These hypersexualized stereotypes are compounded by the fact that this subtype of fan lingerie is commonly and explicitly marketed as costumes or cosplay, not only constructing an implied audience for these garments but connecting them to the broader racist, misogynist, sizeist, and ableist facets of many cosplay communities. Indeed, Paul Mountfort, Anne Peirson-Smith, and Adam Geczy (2018, 257) devote an entire chapter of their book *Planet Cosplay: Costume Play, Identity and Global Fandom* to "cosporn" and the "structural and affective qualities that pornography shares with cosplay," suggesting that both place a premium on "contrivance" and are focused on the body's "objectification" and "extraction" from the real world. These costume lingerie examples similarly extract the fan affect from the act of donning this form of fan lingerie. This is not to suggest that a fan of *Harry Potter*, or a fan who identified as Slytherin within that fictional world, would not purchase this lingerie or take pleasure in wearing it; rather, I mean that these intimates lack the iconography that would make them immediately legible as a sartorial form of fan expression. Whether the item in question is a lace teddy that offers a sexualized spin on a character costume, or a simple black cotton brief with text across the crotch in the iconic yellow *Star Wars* font reading "Execute Order 69" (a play on "Order 66," which somewhat confoundingly seems to be an exercise in eroticizing a fictional Jedi genocide), the promise of sexual availability or accessibility does seem to be the core component of branding feminized fan identities through certain examples of intimate apparel.

$29.95

Poisoned Apple Princess
Lingerie Costume

$38.95

Slither'n To Your DMs
Lingerie Costume

Figure 16.2. Two
examples of "costume
lingerie" from online
retailer Yandy, evoking
Snow White (*left*)
and *Harry Potter*'s
Slytherin House.

BEYOND BASICS: HIGH-END FAN LINGERIE

The bulk of fan underwear and lingerie discussed thus far generally falls in
the category of relatively cheap or mass-produced, licensed fan merchandise.
As a result, fannish intimates are frequently housed in the juniors' section of
mainstream retailers like Target, liminally positioned between childhood and
adulthood. Likewise, the cuts of these undergarments tend toward briefs and
boy short styles, whether as an aesthetic nod to their juvenile antecedents
like Underoos or as a way of aligning with broader underwear trends. There
is, however, a middle ground between these boyish brand elaborations on the
Underoos business model and the hypersexualized lingerie costumes, which
arguably have minimal claim to embodiment and only tenuous connections
to fan affect and identity for the wearer.

As the market for fan lingerie continues to grow, we have seen new consumer tiers emerge that offer some of the promise of character embodiment
or cosplay elements of the aforementioned categories while simultaneously
delivering high(er)-end fan intimates that could reasonable "pass" as high-
quality lingerie. Take, for example, the Japanese fashion brand SuperGroupies,
which has over the years featured several intimate apparel lines connected to

beloved anime and video game properties. This includes a 2015 *Neon Genesis Evangelion* (1995–96) line, which presented lace bra-and-panty sets around particular character costume color palates with feminine detailing (lace dots, small bows, and ribbons), as well as the 2018 *Street Fighter* collection evoking the popular fan cosplay video game character Chun-Li through blue satin with gold piping and details (figure 16.3). While there are clear parallels to both Underoos and costume lingerie in terms of referencing specific character costume attributes, these examples neither draw on infantilized notions of playing dress-up nor function as explicit fannish fetish objects. Rather, these items seem to be pitched at fans of these franchises who *also* are fans of quality lingerie. While the price point for these items, which starts at around 8,800 yen (US$80) for a set, is in no way comparable to that of other high-end lingerie brands like La Perla, where a bra alone might cost several hundred US dollars, it is nonetheless higher than for most novelty fan underwear or lingerie. Accordingly, though these items might function as a form of fan expression, they also are likely to express the wearer's commitment to higher-end intimate apparel. As the images within this chapter suggest, even within the realm of cosplay-oriented fan lingerie, there is incredible diversity in terms of aesthetic approaches, cuts, styles, and degrees of iconic referentiality. Where there is limited diversity, particularly in these higher-end fan lingerie offerings, is sizing: for example, the largest hip measurement that SuperGroupies accommodates their *Street Fighter* Chun-Li lingerie set is ninety-six centimeters (roughly thirty-eight inches), or a US size 8.

CONCLUSION AND CALL FOR FUTURE RESEARCH

As I hope the above analysis of advertising images and copy makes clear, a more nuanced understanding of what makes fan underwear fun to wear certainly demands that we remain mindful of who is invited to play with embodiment and who is conceptually excluded. For example, in both the 1970s/1980s and 2010s iterations of Underoos, superhero embodiment (and fan identity by extension) is, with some exceptions, overwhelmingly pictured as the domain of white bodies. The lingerie costumes and high-end lingerie featured above also present a highly limited and normative understanding of the fan body: slender, overwhelmingly white, and able bodied. There are encouraging emergent trends toward gender-affirming undergarments from brands like TomboyX, which offer more gender-neutral, as well as size-inclusive, styles in fannish prints such as the *Wonder Woman* logo. Likewise, chain retailers

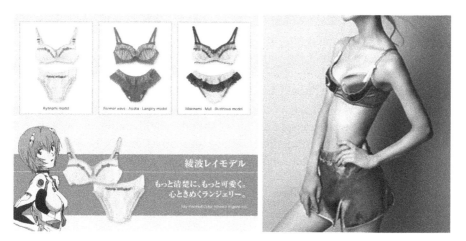

Figure 16.3. High-end fan lingerie for *Neon Genesis Evangelion* in 2015 (*left*), and *Street Fighter* in 2018, both from the Japanese fashion brand SuperGroupies.

like Torrid offer similar fan intimates, focus on plus sizing, and commonly feature Black, Indigenous, and people of color (BIPOC) models. Thus, even as we acknowledge the hegemonic or heterosexist ways in which the bulk of fan lingerie and intimates are designed, packaged, and sold, we must also account for the wide array of uses and gratifications that fan lingerie might provide to actual fans.

While more sustained ethnographic work is needed to begin addressing fans' affective experiences with fan-oriented lingerie, it is precisely the intimate nature of both the garments and fans' relationship to them that demands we approach this work carefully and ethically, first building trust with our research participants. Fannish intimates and lingerie also open up a unique opportunity to deploy a sensory ethnography approach (Pink 2015), which might move beyond the visual work that dominates ethnographies to better address the tactile and embodied experiences of fan identity and affect. Differences in the cut, fabric, and fit of fan intimates will invariably shape the fan's sensory experience. Likewise, understanding how fan intimates that evoke a specific character or costume may operate differently from those that merely replicate a media property's logo or iconography is a core component of this work. Fan intimates that present as conventional lingerie and bear no discernable mark to the fan object aside from the label, as with the case of celebrity-driven fan lingerie lines (such as Rihanna's Savage X Fenty or Dita Von Teese's lingerie brand), might function for the wearer differently still.

To conclude, then, I would like to pose a research question that might serve as a starting point for further qualitative or ethnographic research on the relationship between fan bodies and intimate apparel. Simply put, do fannish foundation garments reveal anything foundational about fan identity? "Foundation garments" are defined by the US Patent and Trademark Office (n.d.) as "devices which are specifically designed to fit the human body [and] to protect, compress, support, restrain or alter the configuration of the body." Ethnographically accounting for the range of motivations for beginning to build an ensemble with fannish underwear (whether emerging from a desire to restrain, protect, or alter one's relationship to a fan object), then, is essential to this work.

REFERENCES

Affuso, Elizabeth. 2018. "Everyday Costume: Feminized Fandom, Retail, and Beauty Culture." In *The Routledge Companion to Media Fandom*, edited by Melissa A. Click and Suzanne Scott, 184–92. New York: Routledge.

Barthes, Roland. 1983. *The Fashion System*. Translated by Matthew Ward and Richard Howard. Berkeley: University of California Press.

Baudrillard, Jean. 1988. *Selected Writings*. Edited by Mark Poster. Stanford, CA: Stanford University Press.

Berger, Jonah, and Morgan Ward. 2010. "Subtle Signals of Inconspicuous Consumption." *Journal of Consumer Research* 37 (4): 555–69.

Bielby, Denise, and C. Lee Harrington. 2010. "A Life Course Perspective on Fandom." *International Journal of Cultural Studies* 13 (5): 429–50.

Bury, Rhiannon. 2018. "'We're Not There': Fans, Fan Studies, and the Participatory Continuum." In *The Routledge Companion to Media Fandom*, edited by Melissa A. Click and Suzanne Scott, 123–31. New York: Routledge.

Cocca, Carolyn. 2014. "The 'Broke Back Test': A Quantitative and Qualitative Analysis of Portrayals of Women in Mainstream Superhero Comics, 1993–2013." *Journal of Graphic Novels and Comics* 5 (4): 411–28.

Fields, Jill. 2007. *An Intimate Affair: Women, Lingerie, and Sexuality*. Berkeley: University of California Press.

Jantzen, Christian, Per Østergaard, and Carla M. Sucena Vieira. 2006. "Becoming a 'Woman to the Backbone': Lingerie Consumption and the Experience of Feminine Identity." *Journal of Consumer Culture* 6 (2): 177–202.

Johnson, Derek. 2014. "'May the Force Be with Katie': Pink Media Franchising and the Postfeminist Politics of HerUniverse." *Feminist Media Studies* 14 (6): 895–911.

Kushner, Scott. 2016. "Read Only: The Persistence of Lurking in Web 2.0." *First Monday*, May 28, 2016. https://firstmonday.org/article/view/6789/5519

Mountfort, Paul, Anne Peirson-Smith, and Adam Geczy. 2018. *Planet Cosplay: Costume Play, Identity and Global Fandom*. Chicago: Intellect.

Pink, Sarah. 2015. *Doing Sensory Ethnography*. 2nd ed. Los Angeles: Sage.

Santo, Avi. 2018. "Fans and Merchandise." In *The Routledge Companion to Media Fandom*, edited by Melissa A. Click and Suzanne Scott, 329–36. New York: Routledge.

Scott, Suzanne. 2019. *Fake Geek Girls: Fandom, Gender, and the Convergence Culture Industry*. New York: New York University Press.

Tsaousi, Christiana. 2016. "'What Underwear Do I Like?': Taste and (Embodied) Cultural Capital in the Consumption of Women's Underwear." *Journal of Consumer Culture* 16 (2): 467–92.

US Patent and Trademark Office. n.d. "Classification Resources." Accessed July 1, 2022. https://www.uspto.gov/web/patents/classification/uspc002/defs002.htm

Vigolo, Vania, and Marta Maria Ugolini. 2016. "Does This Fit My Style? The Role of Self-Congruity in Young Women's Repurchase Intention for Intimate Apparel." *Journal of Fashion Marketing and Management* 20 (4): 417–34.

Weiss, Josh. 2017. "Underoos: How an Underwear Craze Got Its Origin Story." *Hollywood Reporter*, June 2, 2017. https://www.hollywoodreporter.com/movies/movie-news/captain-underpants-how-underoos-got-origin-story-1008804/

Weiss, Lawrence D. 2002. Letter to "Craig" on moral and ethical conflict in business. Gort.net. December 24, 2002. https://www.gort.net/Sermonsandstudies/Ethicsconflictletter.htm

Contributors

Elizabeth Affuso is academic director of Intercollegiate Media Studies at the Claremont Colleges, where she teaches media studies at Pitzer College. She is coeditor with Avi Santo of "Films and Merchandise," a special issue of *Film Criticism*. Her work on beauty, fashion, fandom, and consumer culture has been published in *Jump Cut*, *The Routledge Companion to Media Fandom*, *Point of Sale: Analyzing Media Retail*, and *Documenting Fashion*.

Suzanne Scott is associate professor in the Department of Radio-Television-Film at the University of Texas at Austin. She is the author of *Fake Geek Girls: Fandom, Gender, and the Convergence Culture Industry* and the coeditor of *The Routledge Companion to Media Fandom*. Her work on fandom, convergence culture, and transmedia storytelling has been published in *New Media & Society*, *Cinema Journal*, *Critical Studies in Media Communication*, *Feminist Media Histories*, *Transformative Works and Cultures*, and *Participations*, as well as in numerous anthologies.

Lauren Boumaroun is a PhD candidate in cinema and media studies at the University of California, Los Angeles, writing her dissertation on media-inspired clothing and geek fashion. Her main research interests are costume and costume designers, fan fashion cultures, and cinema therapy. Her publications include "Becoming Annie: When Film Costume and Fashion Converge" in *Fashion Theory*, "Costume Designers/Everything: Hybridized Identities in Animation Production" in *Framework*, and "I'm the Villain in My Own Story: Representations of Depression and the Spectatorial Experience" in *Perspectives on Crazy Ex-Girlfriend: Nuanced Post-Network Television*.

Samantha Close earned her PhD in communication at the University of Southern California. Her research interests include digital media, theory-practice, fan studies, gender, race, and Japanese media. She focuses particularly on labor and the creative industries. Her documentary *I Am Handmade: Crafting in the Age of Computers*, based on her most recent research project, is hosted online by Vice Media's Motherboard channel. Her writing appears in edited volumes and academic journals including *Feminist Media Studies*, *Transformative Works and Cultures*, and *Anthropology Now*.

Kate Fortmueller is assistant professor in the Department of Entertainment and Media Studies at the University of Georgia. She researches historical and contemporary film, television, and digital production labor. Her work has appeared in *Film History*, the *Historical Journal of Film, Radio and Television*, *Journal of Film and Video*, *Media Industries*, and *Television & New Media*. Dr. Fortmueller is the author of *Below the Stars: How the Labor of Working Actors and Extras Shapes Media Production* and *Hollywood Shutdown: Production, Distribution, and Exhibition in the Time of COVID*.

Paxton C. Haven is a doctoral student in the Department of Radio-Television-Film at the University of Texas at Austin, with a BA in political science from the George Washington University. His current research interests include digital networks of contemporary music scenes, brand and consumer culture, and the cross-platform negotiations of the creative industries' media production and labor. His published scholarly work can be found in *Flow*, *Velvet Light Trap*, and *New Media & Society*.

Jacqueline E. Johnson is a PhD candidate in the Division of Cinema and Media Studies at the University of Southern California. She received her MA in media studies from the University of Texas at Austin, where she studied Black audience reception and contemporary television. Currently, she researches race, gender, "new" media, television, and genre. Her dissertation project examines Black women as both the producers and subjects of romance narratives in television, podcasts, and novels in the United States and the United Kingdom.

Nicolle Lamerichs is senior lecturer and team lead in the Creative Business program at HU University of Applied Sciences, Utrecht. She holds a PhD in media studies from Maastricht University. In her book *Productive Fandom*, she explores intermediality, affect, costuming, and creativity in fan cultures. She has published extensively about cosplay, participatory fan cultures, and play.

A. Luxx Mishou (she/her) is a Victorianist and gender studies scholar researching cosplay, comics, fashion, and the gothic. She holds a doctorate in Victorian literature and gender studies from Old Dominion University, where her dissertation was titled "Holy Stitches Batman: Performative Villainy in

Gothic/am." She has contributed chapters to *Intersectional Feminist Readings of Comics* and *Fashion and Material Culture in Victorian Popular Fiction and Periodicals*. Dr. Mishou has presented her research at the annual conferences of the Modern Language Association (MLA), the Society for Cinema and Media Studies, the Northeast MLA, and the Comics and Popular Arts Conference. Her first scholarly monograph is *Cosplayers: Gender and Identity*. She currently works as an independent scholar.

Lori Morimoto is assistant professor (general faculty) in the Department of Media Studies at the University of Virginia. Her research focuses on East Asian regional media coproduction, distribution, and consumption, as well as transcultural fandom. Her work has been published in the journals *East Asian Journal of Popular Culture*, *Transformative Works and Cultures*, *Participations*, *Asian Cinema*, and *Mechademia: Second Arc*, and in such anthologies as *Fandom: Identities and Communities in a Mediated World*, 2nd ed., *The Routledge Companion to Media Fandom*, and *A Companion to Media Fandom and Fan Studies*.

EJ Nielsen is a doctoral candidate in communication at the University of Massachusetts Amherst, where their research focuses on fan studies, monstrosity, hauntology, gender/sexuality, and the complex ways in which these intersect. Sections from their doctoral thesis, "Framing Fanart," appeared in *A Fan Studies Primer*. In addition to contributing book chapters on gender and monstrosity in *Supernatural*, queerness in *James Bond*, and queerbaiting in the BBC's *Sherlock*, they have published in the *Journal of Fandom Studies*, *Transformative Works and Cultures*, *Quarterly Review of Film and Video*, *InMedia*, and *Somatechnics*, as well as in multiple edited collections. They also coedited the collection *Becoming: Genre, Queerness, and Transformation in NBC's Hannibal*.

Elodie A. Roy is a media and material culture theorist based in Newcastle, United Kingdom. She is the author of *Media, Materiality and Memory: Grounding the Groove* and the coeditor with Eva Moreda Rodríguez of *Phonographic Encounters: Mapping Transnational Cultures of Sound, 1890–1945*. Her research interests include the social and material history of sound recording, alternative and DIY publishing (notably fanzines), popular music and sound across media, theories and practices of material culture, and archival and heritage practices in physical and digital environments. She has held research and teaching positions at the Glasgow School of Art, the University of Glasgow,

Humboldt University of Berlin, and Newcastle University, and currently works as a research fellow at Northumbria University (Newcastle).

Avi Santo is full professor and chair of the Department of Communication at the University of North Carolina at Chapel Hill. He is the author of *Configuring the Field of Character and Entertainment Licensing: The Licensing Expo and Other Sites of IP Management* and *Selling the Silver Bullet: The Lone Ranger and Transmedia Brand Licensing*, and coeditor with Derek Johnson and Derek Kompare of *Making Media Work: Cultures of Management in the Entertainment Industries*. His research focuses on the intersections of media, merchandise, and retail environments and strategies, including the reimagining of fandom as a lifestyle category.

Minka Stoyanova is an Assistant Teaching Professor in the Becker School of Design and Technology, Clark University. Minka's artistic and academic research is focused on cyborg-based approaches to contemporary art and culture, and results in writing and creative works that investigate the real and speculative effects of technology in society. In addition to being an alum of the US Fulbright Scholars Program and a former National Science Foundation, Computing Innovation Fellow, Minka's written work has been published in Leonardo, Digital Culture and Society, Visual Communications Quarterly, and the International Journal of Performance Arts and Digital Media.

Tony Tran is assistant professor at Boston College in the Communication Department. His work explores the intersections of Asian diasporic identities, digital media, and popular culture. His latest research focuses on the relationships between digital food cultures and the circulation of global tastes within Asian diasporas. He has published in *Popular Communication, Communication, Culture & Critique*, and *The Moving Image: The Journal of the Association of Moving Image Archivists*.

Alyxandra Vesey is assistant professor in journalism and creative media at the University of Alabama. Her research focuses on gender, music culture, and media labor. Her first book, *Extending Play: The Feminization of Collaborative Music Merchandise in the Early Twenty-First Century*, is forthcoming. Her work has also appeared in the *Journal of Cinema and Media Studies, Feminist Media Studies, Television & New Media, Journal of Popular Music Studies, Camera Obscura, Velvet Light Trap*, and *Emergent Feminisms: Complicating a Postfeminist Media Culture*.

Rebecca Williams is associate professor in media audiences and participatory cultures at the University of South Wales. Her work on fandom and audiences has appeared in journals including *Popular Communication, Continuum, Transformative Works and Cultures, Participations,* and *Television & New Media.* She is the author of *Theme Park Fandom: Spatial Transmedia, Materiality and Participatory Cultures* and *Post-Object Fandom: Television, Identity and Self-Narrative,* editor of *Torchwood Declassified Investigating Mainstream Cult Television* and *Everybody Hurts: Transitions, Endings, and Resurrections in Fan Cultures,* and coeditor of *A Fan Studies Primer: Method, Research, Ethics.*

Index

Note: Illustrations are set in italics.

.